Joe Paterno:
"Football My Way"

JOE PATERNO:

"Football My Way"

Mervin D. Hyman and Gordon S. White, Jr.

Collier Books

A Division of Macmillan Publishing Co., Inc.

NEW YORK

Collier Macmillan Publishers

LONDON

Macmillan Publishing Co., Inc.
866 Third Avenue, New York, N.Y. 10022
Collier Macmillan Canada, Ltd.

Library of Congress Cataloging in Publication Data

Hyman, Mervin D.
    Joe Paterno: "football my way."

    1. Paterno, Joe, 1926-   2. Football coaches—
United States—Biography.   I. White, Gordon S., joint
author.
GV939.P37H9 1978   796.33′2′0924 [B]   78-12927
ISBN 0-02-029000-4

First Printing 1978

Printed in the United States of America

For our wives
Ruth and Jane
Who uncomplainingly
endured so many lonely hours

Contents

Acknowledgments

In writing this book, it was apparent early on that we would need the assistance of many people who at one time or another were involved in the life and career of our subject. Dozens of people contributed their reminiscences and appraisals of Joe Paterno and it is impossible to list them all, but our appreciation for their aid is no less sincere. However, there are some whose help must be acknowledged here.

First, of course, there was Joe Paterno himself, who patiently gave up untold hours of his precious time to talk frankly into a tape recorder under our sometimes not-so-gentle probing. Then there was Sue Paterno, a gem among wives who, in her own inimitable and honest fashion, provided us with a rare insight into the personality, character and ambitions of her husband as well as the trials, tribulations and occasional escapades of a coach's mate. No less helpful was George Paterno's recollection of events and discoveries when he and his brother were growing up in Brooklyn and later pursuing their respective athletic and coaching careers.

We are also greatly indebted to Jim Tarman, Penn State's very knowledgeable Associate to the Athletic Director and former Director of Athletic Public Relations, a veritable font of information whose wise counsel and general expertise on the subject of Joe Paterno was invaluable; to his wife, Louise, who contributed a distaff point of view; and to Charles A. "Rip" Engle, the man who was responsible for launching and nurturing the coaching career that has had such an impact on college football.

There were others, too, who gave willingly of their time and opinions, like the members of the Penn State athletic family— Dean Robert J. Scannell, Athletic Director Ed Czekaj, Assistant Athletic Director Sever "Tor" Toretti, Assistant Athletic Director Richie Lucas, former Basketball Coach Johnny Bach, Sports Information Director John Morris—former president Eric A. Walker, retired Dean and Athletic Director Ernest McCoy, Dixon Johnson, the university's Director of Public Information, past and present members of the Penn State coaching staff—Jim O'Hora (and his wife, Bets), Earl Bruce, Frank Patrick, J. T. White, George Welsh, Dan Radakovich, Bob Phillips, Jim Weaver, Jerry Sandusky and John Chuckran—and former players Dennis Onkotz and Mike Reid.

Also, Coaches Darrell Royal of Texas, Tom Cahill of Army, Carmen Cozza of Yale, Frank Navarro of Columbia, John Bateman of Rutgers and Vic Fusia of Massachusetts, among many others in the college football coaching fraternity; George Olsen, the esteemed executive director of the Gater Bowl; Carroll H. "Beano" Cook, the irrepressible and onetime college football press director for ABC Sports, now with CBS; Ridge Riley, Mickey Bergstein, Skip Rowland and Steve Garban, longtime Paternophiles; Sarah Pileggi, who struggled so valiantly (and capably) to transcribe the many tapes which were made during countless interviews; and Mrs. Margaret White and Mrs. Frankie McArdle, who put our hieroglyphics and last-minute second-thought editorial changes into readable manuscript form.

We are especially grateful, too, to Dick Brown of the *Centre Daily Times*, Bob Beese of Penn State, Penn State Photo Shop, Pennsylvania State University Still Photography Studios and Pat Cahill of UPI, whose generous cooperation made it possible to reproduce many of the photographs which appear in these pages.

To all of them, we express our sincere thanks.

MERVIN D. HYMAN
GORDON S. WHITE, JR.

Preface

FOOTBALL IS A GREAT GAME. It demands a young man's total commitment—emotionally, mentally and physically. It challenges our young people to do their very best, to discipline themselves to develop mental, as well as physical, toughness. At its best it is a wonderful and worthwhile experience, which will have immense future character benefits for its players. But it must be at its best to continue to be meaningful for our young people of today. Its intrinsic essence of hard work and honest competition should not be polluted by hypocritical actions of its leaders and coaches. Its character benefits should not be diluted by dishonest and misleading recruiting procedures. We should not at any time let any of its participants be exploited for the personal ambition of any man or institution. For these reasons I agreed to this book by Merv Hyman and Gordon White. I have spoken frankly, with high hopes that perhaps this effort will help call attention to some of the malpractices which should be eliminated from the game I love—intercollegiate football.

JOE PATERNO

1: Mr. Paterno Goes to Washington

Two LONG BLACK LIMOUSINES turned off Connecticut Avenue and dipped down the steep service road to the Washington Hilton Hotel in order to pick up a group of men waiting to travel to the White House for a command performance one January afternoon in 1970. The men who piled into the cars were famous in their field—college football coaching. But they were more nervous at that moment when the limousines arrived for them than they ever were before sending a team onto a gridiron.

One of them, Joseph Vincent Paterno of Pennsylvania State University, was the most apprehensive of the lot about to visit and talk with President Richard M. Nixon, whose claim to football fame was that he was a mere substitute at Whittier College in California some years before. Paterno stepped into the second of the two automobiles and just could not settle back comfortably for the few minutes of travel to the home on Pennsylvania Avenue. After all, he was going to meet President Nixon only a few weeks after he let it be known exactly what Mr. Nixon could do with a plaque the President wished to present to Joe and his great undefeated football team of 1969.

Paterno had gained the distinction of being the only sports figure in history to tell a President of the United States to take an award and throw it into the Potomac or some other appropriate location.

Joe hadn't told Mr. Nixon directly and the fast approaching confrontation was to be Paterno's first face-to-face meeting with Citizen No. 1. But the President had received the indirect message loud and clear and now the Penn State coach, a forty-three-year-old genius of the game, was to meet Mr. Nixon. He could only wonder what was in store for him, though not once since the incident of the plaque or on that ride to the White House did Paterno feel he would ever have done differently.

These football coaches going to the White House constituted the board of trustees of the American Football Coaches Association, which was holding its annual convention in Washington at the time Paterno stepped into pickup limousine No. 2. In the group with Paterno were Paul Dietzel of South Carolina, the president of the American Football Coaches Association; Frank Broyles of Arkansas; Duffy Daugherty of Michigan State; Earl Edwards of North Carolina State; Ben Schwartzwalder of Syracuse; Paul S. "Bear" Bryant of Alabama; Bob Blackman of Dartmouth and Bill Murray, former Duke coach and the executive director of the AFCA. They were going to the White House to present Mr. Nixon with an award of their own, as such groups are wont to do in order to get some extra attention that always spills from a Presidential audience. It was the Tuss McLaughry Award, given each year to the man who has done the most for college football.

During those few minutes Joe Paterno and his fellow coaches rode from the hotel to the White House, the coach of Penn State had ample time to remember all the steps that led to his apprehensive feeling on that winter day. After all, doesn't a man's whole life go before him when he walks the last mile? And Paterno had to review only a few weeks of his life on the drive, during which, he admits, "I was plenty nervous."

It all began a couple of months earlier when someone decided it would be a good idea for President Nixon to present either the University of Texas or the University of Arkansas football team with a trophy as the No. 1 college team in the nation. The presentation of this unique No. 1 trophy was to be made immediately after Texas and Arkansas played their 1969 game at Fayetteville, Arkansas, on December 6. The game would be nationally televised and the whole of sportsdom could witness Mr. Nixon bestowing "No. 1" on the victorious team.

Ohio State University, which was rated No. 1 through most of the 1969 season, had come a cropper against Michigan on November 22. This left only Texas and Arkansas, in the minds of many, as the teams able to be No. 1 at season's end. The Longhorns from Texas and the Razorbacks from Arkansas had to meet, so the problems could easily be settled in their season finale—so some said.

Texas and Arkansas had gone undefeated until their game. Those who advised the President held to the old theory that any undefeated team playing in the company kept by Texas and Arkansas must be great. So it was decided a few days before the Texas-Arkansas game that Mr. Nixon would make a grand appearance at Razorback Stadium that Saturday afternoon while the Americn Broadcasting Company caught the whole action of football and President. What could be better for a TV rating, anyway?

Bud Wilkinson, one of the sportscasters on those televised college games, was also a special advisor to Mr. Nixon. The former Oklahoma coach has been accused of instigating "Operation No. 1."

The only problem was that sitting not so quietly, nestled in a valley in central Pennsylvania, was Pennsylvania State University, where Joe Paterno had developed a team of unusual qualities— a team that then owned a twenty-one-game winning streak and had not lost in twenty-nine straight games. This Penn State team had one of the strongest defenses in the history of college football, then just one hundred years old.

Actually, Penn State nestled quietly in the valley until it was known that Mr. Nixon, or some deep thinker, decided Texas and Arkansas were the only teams eligible for Presidential blessings as the best college team in the land in the sport's centennial year.

Students, alumni, faculty, players and coaches suddenly became diametrically opposed to all of Mr. Nixon's policies, if they hadn't been so before that time. Even Governor Raymond Shafer of Pennsylvania nearly turned from Republican to Democrat. Although the Pennsylvania chief executive didn't take that drastic step, he did take on the President, objecting loudly to the fact that Penn State was completely overlooked in the Presidential No. 1 sweepstakes.

But the high-level decision was made and announced before anyone thought out the Penn State complications and Mr. Nixon became the first President to crown a college football team "No. 1," even if that team was really not deserving of "No. 1."

When the noise came from Pennsylvania there were those second thoughts common when Presidents make boo-boos. The quick thinkers, who dreamed up the Presidential trip to Fayette-ville in the first place, went through the motions of political escape.

The solution was that Mr. Nixon would, at the appropriate time, present Joe Paterno and his Penn State team with a trophy "for the longest winning streak in college football."

"Who needs it?" So thought Paterno when he first heard about that idea.

All of these things went through Paterno's mind on that ride to the White House.

As things moved along that week of the Texas-Arkansas game they led Paterno to the eventual position of telling off Mr. Nixon quite firmly.

Penn State finished its regular season on November 29 by trouncing North Carolina State University, 33-8. The Nittany Lions were going to the Orange Bowl for a January 1 date with the University of Missouri, also a strong candidate for the No. 1 spot although a one-time loser during the regular season. Paterno hadn't yet begun to work on the Orange Bowl game with his coaches or team when President Nixon blessed Texas as "No. 1." It was Texas, since the Longhorns, in an exciting affair, whipped Arkansas, 15-14, and earned the added benefit of going to the Cotton Bowl game.

Mr. Nixon, in a hot and noisy dressing room, gave the "No. 1" plaque to Darrell Royal, coach of Texas, before millions watching on TV. One of those millions was Joe Paterno, sitting home at

Penn State and viewing, with some degree of disgust, the post-game program from that Texas locker room.

At the end of the loud presentation on TV, Mr. Nixon reminded everyone that he was going to give Penn State an award for its long unbeaten streak, the longest of its nature on the 100th anniversary of football. This was just too much for Paterno.

He went to the telephone and called Jim Tarman, then the Penn State Sports Information Director. He insisted that Tarman write a statement for immediate release pointing out that Penn State wanted nothing to do with such a "streak plaque." Tarman, never before in a position of taking on a President, said, "Now, just a minute, Joe. Hold everything. Just hold it."

Tarman suggested, after Joe insisted, that Paterno inform Dixon Johnson, the university's overall director of publicity, and ask his advice. O.K. It was done, and Johnson, after thinking it over, gave his unofficial blessing. The result was that both Tarman and Paterno wrote a statement and, within a couple of hours, they combined and rewrote the release which was the polite but unmistakable way of telling the President to throw that plaque somewhere.

The statement read:

"First I wish to congratulate Coach Royal, not only on a great victory, but for having the courage to go for two points. This will stand him in good stead in the Cotton Bowl. It appears that Texas and Arkansas read the script from our Orange Bowl game last year and from our win over Syracuse this year [both 15-14 Penn State victories resulting from late 2-point plays such as Texas executed against Arkansas].

"In response to numerous telephone calls I received today regarding President Nixon's television remarks concerning a plaque to Penn State for having the nation's longest unbeaten streak, I have heard nothing official about any such plaque.

"Before accepting such a plaque, I would have to confer with my squad. I'm sure they would be disappointed at this time, as would the Missouri squad, to receive anything other than a plaque for the No. 1 team. And the No. 1 team following the bowl games could be Penn State or Missouri.

"To accept any other plaque prior to the bowl games, which

are supposedly to determine the final No. 1 team, would be a disservice to our squad, to Pennsylvania and to the East, which we represent, and perhaps more important, to Missouri, which might just be the best team in the country.

"Due to the fact that I had to baby-sit with our four children while trying to watch today's game I did not get to hear all of President Nixon's remarks. But it would seem a waste of his very valuable time to present Penn State with a plaque for something we already have undisputed possession of—the nation's longest winning and unbeaten streaks."

Paterno continued to remember that this statement had gotten him in "hot water" as many persons wrote to him saying, "How dare you say this to the President! How dare you!"

This was going over and over in his mind as the Penn State coach rode in limousine No. 2. It was ironic since Penn State finished No. 2 in the football polls and obviously in Mr. Nixon's mind.

Riding with Paterno was Duffy Daugherty, the Michigan State University coach and a man used to battling for No. 1 in the nation. Daugherty is a round-faced Irishman with the Irish charm of a pixy.

As the limousine pulled up to the White House with worried Paterno and smiling, cheerful Daugherty and the other coaches, one of the White House guards leaned toward the car and said, "Is Coach Paterno in there?" Duffy began to roar with loud laughter, knowing how Paterno was feeling at the moment.

The Michigan State mentor, practically rolling on the carpeted floor of the automobile, said, "Paterno, you've gone and done it again. See, they're goin' to send you back to Sicily. You're so smart. You had to take on the President of the United States."

Paterno spoke up nervously, "Yes, I'm Coach Paterno."

"Wait here a minute, please, the sergeant wants to see you."

The sergeant went over to the No. 2 limousine, looked at Paterno and said, "Hey, Joe, glad to see you. I just want you to know that we think the boss is all wet. He wouldn't know a No. 1 team if he fell over it. We're all from Pennsylvania around here."

Ah, the relief Paterno felt.

Within minutes Paterno and the eight other coaches were meeting the President. Bud Wilkinson was making the introductions and when he got to Paterno, he said, "Mr. President, this is Joe Paterno."

Mr. Nixon, shaking hands with his critic, said, "Oh, I know *him*. I know *him*."

Mr. Nixon added, "You know, I don't know exactly why I got into this thing between Penn State and Texas because I always had been a Penn State fan. You know, my uncle taught there."

The President's uncle, Dr. Ernest L. Nixon, was a professor of plant pathology at Penn State's School of Agriculture. He was known as "the potato wizard of Pennsylvania." Dr. Nixon died in March of 1969 and the President attended the funeral at State College, Pennsylvania.

But that didn't totally make up for what Penn State and Paterno had gone through because of the President's actions. However, everyone involved with Penn State football had the knowledge of what they had done during the exciting and great 1969 season—that second straight year of going undefeated and untied.

President Nixon had the knowledge, too. When Paterno accepted the Lambert Trophy as the outstanding team in the East at a luncheon in New York, Mr. Nixon sent him the following telegram:

"My warmest congratulations go to Coach Joe Paterno and to all the men of the Penn State football team as they are awarded the Lambert Trophy for the third consecutive year, tying the record set by the legendary Blanchard-Davis Army teams of the mid-forties."

Paterno managed to get in his digs, though. He told the assemblage at the luncheon, "I couldn't feel better about this trophy even if it were presented to me on national television by the President."

Earlier, when Mr. Nixon received the National Football Foundation and Hall of Fame Gold Medal Award, Joe had sent him a wire that said:

"Although we may disagree with your football analysis, Penn Staters have no doubt as to who is the nation's No. 1 football fan. Congratulations on receiving the highest honor we in college football can bestow."

This interchange was going through Joe's mind, too, as he

stood in the White House office. But all went well enough to calm down Paterno. He wasn't sent back to Sicily, or even to Brooklyn. The President even jokingly discussed the differences between himself and the Penn State coach. But, as Joe remembers, "He didn't change his mind."

Eventually the coaches left the White House and Paterno returned to the hotel—this time riding in the No. 1 limousine. For once he was No. 1.

Paterno had plenty of time to return to his office and answer the mail he received, including hundreds of letters from Texans. A few of them were unkind in tone, yet Paterno answered each of them, explaining generally his feelings and actions in the controversy.

Joe Paterno has strong loyalties to anyone who works with and for him. He expects the same in return as well as hard work, since he works harder than anyone in his circle of coaches and players. His feeling has always been that "I owe my players so much that I have to stick up for them. What would I be worth if I hadn't backed them up in this when they felt, as strongly as I, that we deserved to be No. 1, particularly after we beat Missouri in the Orange Bowl?"

After the victory over Missouri, Joe Paterno had one last word. "I don't like to keep pushing this thing," he said calmly, "but I still think we have as much right to be No. 1 as Texas or anybody else. Why should I sit back and let the President of the United States say that so-and-so is No. 1 when I've got fifty kids who've worked their tails off for me for three years. People can say it's sour grapes, but I'd be a lousy coach if I didn't argue for my team."

This is the nature of the man who took on the President for a reason of pride and would take on another President if the situation were repeated. Paterno, for his part, was his usual flip self when the matter came up on the banquet circuit during the winter months. He quipped, "At least I was fighting with Nixon before it became fashionable."

Texas Coach Darrell Royal explained it. "When Mr. Nixon talked to me on the phone a couple of days before the game with Arkansas, he asked if I'd accept such a trophy for No. 1 if Texas won the game. Naturally I was delighted for the chance. Then the President said, "That's fine because it's probably the last No. 1 plaque I'll ever give."

The flak from Pennsylvania was just too great for Mr. Nixon to want to go through that again.

2: The Man Who Won't Conform

Even before Joe Paterno's controversy over No. 1 with President Nixon, he had become a college football celebrity. Although, in 1969, his head coaching career had spanned only four years, his remarkable accomplishments had already marked him as a man who was rapidly ascending to the elite group in his chosen profession. Joe Paterno was being mentioned in the same breath with the Bear Bryants, Woody Hayeses, Darrell Royals, Frank Broyleses, John McKays, Bob Devaneys and Ara Parseghians, coaches whom many believed to be among the best in the country.

Consider Joe Paterno's accomplishments in his first four seasons since he succeeded Charles A. "Rip" Engle, his former college coach and longtime mentor, in 1966 as the head coach at Penn State after having served as Engle's assistant for sixteen years: two successive unbeaten and untied teams in 1968 and 1969; three bowl teams, two of them winners in the coveted Orange Bowl; college football's longest current winning streak—twenty-two games—and longest current unbeaten streak—thirty games (these streaks were later extended to twenty-three and thirty-one games before they ended); his teams had won the Lambert Trophy for "outstanding performance" in the East three years in a row; he had been selected by his peers in the American Football Coaches Association as Coach of the Year in 1968, only his third year as a head coach, in recognition of an unbeaten season; he had twice been named Eastern Coach of the Year by the New York Football Writers Association and he had already turned down a fat, long-term contract to coach a pro football team.

More than that, Joe Paterno, then forty-three years old, was the most refreshing young coach to come along in years. He had the charisma that is so rare in football coaches. Aside from the fact that his style of football was exciting and unorthodox, his attitudes toward big-time college football, as well as the myriad of problems in dealing with the New Generation on college campuses and with black athletes, were so different that older coaches sometimes shuddered when they heard him say things like "Football should be fun" or "There are other things in life besides football" or "I want my players to get involved in campus life" or "Athletic dormitories should be abolished" or "Football scholarships should be limited."

Paterno is a tough disciplinarian on the football field, but he doesn't think it matters much how long a boy's hair is or where his sideburns end, provided it is within reason. "I get exasperated when people who are supposed to be our leaders get excited over the length of a boy's hair. I think it's ridiculous," snorts Joe.

An admitted nonconformist in a profession that abounds with single-minded conservatives who generally are somewhere to the right of Spiro Agnew and Barry Goldwater, Joe Paterno doesn't indulge in coaching clichés. No bromides for success, no gimmicks, no emotion-stirring signs and posters, no passionate locker room speeches, no weeping and wailing over losses. He doesn't talk loudly about pride, patriotism, perfectionism, dedication, loyalty or character building. That doesn't necessarily mean that Paterno doesn't believe in those ideals, but he is more interested in relating to the sophisticated and intellectually eager football players of the present and to contributing to the broadening of their horizons.

Joe Paterno has taken on the President of the United States publicly; he has blasted the National Football Foundation and

Hall of Fame for ignoring his two unbeaten teams when that organization awarded its MacArthur Bowl for the national championship; he has often taken exception with his colleagues in the American Football Coaches Association; he has been a loudly vocal critic of wire service football polls; he has criticized Ivy League football; he staunchly defends Eastern football and is highly critical of some Eastern sportswriters for their lack of chauvinism; he has barred the press, even those members who regularly cover Penn State, from some of his practice sessions and then in an unusual display of open-handedness, has called them in for a frank briefing on special offensive and defensive plans for an important opponent. He lets his players call him by his first name, a radical departure from the traditional player-coach protocol. "Better they call me Joe than something else," he reasons.

This is Joe Paterno—a maverick in every sense of the word—and this is what makes him as refreshing as a summer breeze in a profession that is satiated with conformity and dullness.

To some, Paterno's philosophy of football is heresy. For years, success in college football has usually been equated with a football-is-everything and win-at-any-cost policy. Authoritarian coaches ran their squads with an iron hand and only the tough guys were supposed to be able to survive in the marketplace that big-time college football has become. Now along comes a self-styled "little Italian boy from Brooklyn" with an approach that some people find hard to believe. The truth of the matter is that Joe Paterno is unique among most of his coaching colleagues in almost every way possible.

For one thing, Paterno's appearance is hardly that of the big-time college football coach who used to be glorified by Hollywood in the oldtime Jack Oakie movies. About 5-feet-11, slender, with a prominent nose and eye glasses, Joe Paterno isn't likely to be mistaken for Rock Hudson—or even Darrell Royal. Some insist that he looks more like a New York detective or "the saxophone player at an Italian wedding." Joe's speech is pure, unadulterated Brooklynese and one would never guess that he was Ivy League educated—at Brown, no less, where he was an English literature major. Except, of course, when he talks about Romantic poets, expounds on medieval history and Greek mythology, quotes Browning and animatedly discusses the issues of the day, which is frequently.

A personable, extremely articulate man with a sharp sense of humor, Paterno is quick with a quip. Once when he was asked how a player named Lincoln Lippincott III happened to be on the Penn State squad, he whipped back, "He was on his way to Princeton and got lost." Another time, when Joe was asked if he favored a plan that would put a dome on Penn State's Beaver Stadium, he replied quickly, "I'm against it. I don't want anything that people can hang things from." When he was asked what his handicap was in golf, his answer was "My swing." In reply to a question on whether his quarterback, Chuck Burkhart, then a second-stringer, would perform better playing with the varsity, Joe asked, "Would Lyndon Johnson do a better job if the Congress were all Texans?" After his team lost its second straight game to Army in the rain in 1966, the Penn State equipment manager told Paterno he was ordering waterproof jackets for the squad. Joe suggested, "Better make mine bulletproof." When he was asked if his team would be affected by a high pre-season ranking, he said, "I told them publicity is like poison. It won't hurt if you don't swallow it." After his team lost its third game of the season to Syracuse 24-7 in 1970, Paterno was asked how people in State College were reacting. He replied, "I don't know. I haven't been out of the house lately." At the end of the 1970 season, Joe told people, "We had a 9-1 team with a 7-3 coach."

Paterno is outspoken and continually astounds his coaching colleagues and members of the working press with his frankness. A question always gets a direct, straightforward—and occasionally unpredictable—answer. He never minces words, nor does he try to evade a question. He has the ability to come directly to the point, and it is almost always a well-taken point.

"Joe is sometimes brutally honest," says Jim Tarman, now the Associate Athletic Director and Assistant to the Dean at Penn State and perhaps Paterno's closest friend, "and occasionally it provokes people. But he can't be a hypocrite, saying one thing and meaning something else. He is just not a phony."

Bright, intelligent and perceptive to the point of being almost clairvoyant, Paterno has a quick, analytical mind that is constantly working. A riverboat gambler at heart, he thrives on taking chances and his style of football constantly demonstrates that trait. "Be reckless," Joe tells his players, "gamble, take chances." Paterno has been called bold, even audacious, and he admits that he is sometimes brash. Although he is admired and respected for his keen football mind, he isn't loved by all of his players. That is all right with Joe, too. His answer is, "Coaching isn't a popularity contest."

Charlie Pittman, an All-America halfback on Penn State's unbeaten 1968 and 1969 teams, agrees with his former coach. "Some coaches try to get you to love and respect them so you'll do anything for them," says Charlie. "Joe's not loved, but he is respected for the type of person he is. He's really tough and he's intelligent. You're afraid not to respect him."

"He was kind of loud at times, he yelled a lot," says Dennis Onkotz, the All-America linebacker. "He didn't have to do that. We knew what we had to do."

Bobby Campbell, a halfback who was the running star of the 1967 and 1968 teams, wasn't happy with Paterno's discipline. He frequently questioned the coach's decision and more than once felt Paterno's wrath even though he was one of the stars of the team. In 1968, Campbell had a particularly spectacular day in a 30-12 victory over Syracuse that gave Penn State an unbeaten season. He scored two touchdowns, one on an 87-yard run, and rushed for 239 yards. After one of his scores, Campbell exuberantly threw the ball high into the air when he crossed the goal line in defiance of Paterno's strict rule that all players hand the ball to an official. Bobby got chewed out to a fare-thee-well for his showboating. In his anger, Joe threatened, "You're gonna pay for that football."

"It was worth it," snapped back Bobby, who was always ready with a quick retort.

Later, when Campbell was with the pro Pittsburgh Steelers, he blasted Paterno for his discipline. "He's a great football coach," Bobby admitted, "but I wasn't happy playing for him. I couldn't stand his discipline. I'm a free spirit."

However, another incident involving Frank Spaziani, who came to Penn State as a quarterback but was shifted to several other positions before finally winding up as a fine defensive end in 1967 and 1968, resulted in a more positive attitude. Following his last season as a player but while he was still in school, Spaziani came into the football office one day sporting a full set of muttonchop sideburns, a Fu Manchu mustache a la Joe Willie Namath and a little goatee.

Paterno took one look at Spaziani and said quietly, "Hey Spaz, shave."

"What do you mean, shave? I don't play for you anymore. You can't tell me what to do. Who do you think you are, a dictator? You can't make me shave," stormed Spaziani as he bolted out of the office, slamming the door behind him.

A week or so later, Paterno was walking down a corridor outside the football office when along came Frank Spaziani, completely clean shaven.

"Hi, Spaz," Joe greeted him, with a little smile.

"Hi, Coach," replied Spaziani, walking right past Paterno.

Ten minutes later, Paterno looked up from his desk to find Spaziani standing there. "Yeah, Spaz, what is it?" asked Joe.

Spaziani thought a minute, then blurted out, "I just couldn't stand to have you mad at me."

Paterno has an insatiable intellectual curiosity that requires constant stimulation. He finds some of this necessary stimulation in football but, while most college coaches are preoccupied with X's and O's and little else, Joe often can be found roaming the Penn State campus to seek out a professor for a bull session on the humanities. Or chatting with a group of students on campus problems. An intellectual football coach? Sounds silly, doesn't it, but Joe Paterno is as different from the usual image of a big-time, winning football coach as Phyllis Diller is from Raquel Welch.

While many coaches implore their players to "eat, drink, sleep and think" football twenty-four hours a day to the exclusion of everything else, Paterno firmly believes there is more to college life than playing football for Penn State.

"I want my players to enjoy the experience of going to college," says Paterno. "It should be the four greatest years of their lives. It's the only time in their lives when they're free, when they have the opportunity to choose what to do and when they want to do it. We don't want the student-athletes who come to Penn State to be just tied down to a football program. I tell the kids, *enjoy*

yourselves. There is so much besides football. Art, history, literature, music, politics, the changing society. I consider football
merely as just another extra-curricular activity, like debating, the
band or anything else on campus. It should never be taken out
of that context.

"Look at it this way. All of a sudden a kid comes out of a little
area, like I did out of Twenty-sixth Street and Avenue R in
Brooklyn, where everybody had the same dialect, everybody
thought the same way, everybody was a Dodger fan. Suddenly,
you're thrown into a college community where there are a
thousand things going on you never knew about. Football should
never supersede those things.

"Football is *not* the most important thing in this country. If
football suddenly disappeared from the scene tomorrow, we
would never miss it. European countries get along without it and
they still exist.

"I don't want my players to have a carpeted athletic dorm like
Bear Bryant has at Alabama," says Paterno, "or to be bunched
together where they can't associate with all types of students.
I want them to have other interests. I want them to get involved
in campus life. When a kid takes a look around Penn State and
says, 'Gee, there's nothing to do,' I tell him I suppose there was
nothing for the Romantic poets to do in the Lake Country of
England.

"I'm always after them. I tell them, 'Get involved. Don't let the
world pass you by. Get into it. Go after life. Attack it. Ten years
from now I want you to be able to look back on your college life
as a wonderful experience, not just four years of playing
football.' "

The Penn State campus, a large, sprawling complex tucked
away at the base of Mount Nittany, is splendidly isolated from
almost anywhere in the state of Pennsylvania. Ninety miles from
Harrisburg, the state capital, to the south, 140 miles from Pittsburgh to the southwest and approximately 250 miles from New
York City to the east, the school is situated in State College, a
bustling little town of 28,000 population, but the campus area is
officially known as University Park, complete with its own post
office.

On the easterly edge of the campus stands Beaver Stadium, a
handsome steel structure which, in 1960, was moved section by

section in 700 pieces one and a half miles from its former location near the Nittany Lion Inn to its present site. The move also involved an expansion of from 30,000 to more than 45,000 seats, and the stadium has since been enlarged to 61,017 seats, with the addition of almost 16,000 for the 1978 season. In a rare structural feat, the old portion of the stadium was reassembled beneath a new superstructure, which towers seventy rows high on each side from goal line to goal line. The stadium is named for General James A. Beaver, a former governor of Pennsylvania who served for many years as president of the Penn State Board of Trustees.

During the fall, Beaver Stadium has become the rallying point for some 60,000 students, parents, faculty members, old grads, townspeople and just plain fans every Saturday afternoon the Nittany Lions of Penn State are playing at home. People never cease to be amazed at how so many folks can find their way to Beaver Stadium on the few access roads which converge on State College and University Park. But they come, nevertheless, mostly by automobile, and Penn State probably could fill a 100,000-seat stadium—just so long as Joe Paterno's teams keep winning. In fact, university authorities are so sure that Paterno's Nittany Lions will continue to prosper that plans are already on the drawing board to expand the capacity of Beaver.

The university population of some 26,000 students lives in pastoral splendor on one of the most beautiful college campuses in the country. A combination of old and new with ivy-covered buildings vying for attention with modern brick high-rise dormitories, the campus covers an area of 14,775 acres. The Nittany Lion, carved out of white stone by famed sculptor Heinz Warneke in 1942, stands proudly near Recreation Hall, which contains the gym and athletic offices. The crouching Nittany Lion is Penn State's symbol. Recreational facilities for the students include an ice-skating rink, recently constructed plush indoor and outdoor swimming pools, tennis courts, intramural fields in profusion and two eighteen-hole golf courses. For the less sports inclined, the university bursts with cultural activity. Students can occupy their extra-curricular time with music and drama groups, lectures and the many other facets of the academic and cultural world. It is in these directions that Paterno points his football players.

Many of Paterno's players have profited by his advice. Mike

Reid, an All-America defensive tackle in 1968 and 1969 and winner of the Outland Award as the best interior lineman in the country in '69, was one who took his coach literally. Mike, who went on to pro football to become a starting defensive tackle for the Cincinnati Bengals, was a talented concert pianist who spent his off-football hours studying music and giving organ recitals. He was as much at home with Beethoven, Bach and Mozart as he was on the football field and he played the piano well enough to be invited to give concerts at the Mormon Tabernacle in Salt Lake City and in New York, Cincinnati and Miami.

"When I was disgusted or disappointed, I turned to the piano," Reid once said. "Quite a few great composers expressed deep sadness in music. Beethoven suffered and it comes out in his music. I don't mean to sound melodramatic but when I got word that I had to undergo a second knee operation in 1967, I turned to the piano. It gave me much comfort."

While music gave Reid comfort, he did not return the favor to his opponents. Mike, along with Steve Smear, made up the best defensive tackle combination in all of college football in 1968 and 1969. The point was, though, that Mike, despite the hours he had to spend perfecting his skills on the football field, still found time to pursue his music to become proficient in an artistic field so far removed from football.

Like most coaches, Paterno takes great pride in the academic achievements of his players. Coach Woody Hayes of Ohio State, for example, is always pointing out how many of his football players get their degrees or go on to medical school. The difference, however, is that Paterno insists that football should not interfere with the pursuit of players' studies and it is a fact that, in the last five years, Penn State players—overall—have surpassed the average of the rest of the male student body in their academic averages. Their majors have been as diverse as those of football players at Yale, Harvard or Princeton, running the gamut from biophysics to engineering to pre-law to pre-dental.

Dennis Onkotz was a biophysics major and was graduated with a 3.5 average on a 4.0 scale. Don Abbey, the fullback on the 1968 and 1969 teams, was a pre-dental honor student. Neal Smith, a defensive back who was a civil engineering major, also won honors.

Bob Holuba, a handsome 6-foot-3, 238-pound starting offensive guard for two seasons and an accounting major, made the Dean's List for five straight terms and had a 3.65 average. He was elected to Beta Gamma Sigma, the highest honor a student can receive in Penn State's College of Business Administration. Holuba, incidentally, chose Penn State over Yale after having won All-State honors at Bergen Catholic High School in Oradell, New Jersey, and was picked on the All-East team after the 1970 season. He also received a $1,000 NCAA Scholar-Athlete postgraduate award in January, 1971.

Holuba came by his choice naturally. His dad, Stan, owner of a large detergent manufacturing company in New Jersey, is a Penn State alumnus who was a member of the Nittany Lions' boxing team in the 1920's. Bob Holuba's choice of Penn State also paid dividends for Sue Paterno, Joe's wife. Through the generosity of Stan Holuba and his wife, Angela, Sue had what was probably a greater stock of detergents than most supermarkets in Centre County, where Penn State is situated.

Academic achievements by football players aren't unusual, of course. It happens at many good schools, but what is unique is that while most other coaches moan and complain bitterly when their athletes have scheduled classes that conflict with football practice, Paterno prefers that his players have classes to attend the morning of a home game. That isn't a put-on, either. "I like the idea of Saturday morning classes," he says. "It takes their minds off football."

There was one instance a few years ago when a premier linebacker wanted to take a Saturday morning physics examination on the day of the year's biggest game. Paterno agreed readily. The player took his exam and admitted later that he thought he was more relaxed during that day's game because he didn't have time to worry about the impending struggle until he got to the stadium.

Can you imagine Bear Bryant or Nebraska's Bob Devaney encouraging Saturday morning classes for their football players? But that is simply one more attitude that sets Joe Paterno apart from the majority of his fellow coaches.

3: Football for Fun, Paterno Style

Joe Paterno likes to talk about football being fun at Penn State, another departure that causes most other coaches to raise a suspicious eyebrow or two and to view him with wonderment. It also has caused some consternation in the ranks of his contemporaries.

Football was just never designed to be fun, they say. If we don't make our players work their guts out every minute of the football season, how can we win? And, if we don't win, how can we fill our massive stadiums every Saturday afternoon, how can we get those lucrative television games, how can we keep our jobs? That Paterno must be some kind of a nut, they say. Fair enough questions and fair enough assumptions, considering that college football has become a big business.

Darrell Royal of Texas, for example, says, "The only way I know to keep football fun is to win. There's no laughter in losing."

Many coaches agree with Royal. In 1970, when Coach Bob Odell of the University of Pennsylvania was blasted by four of his players, including the team's leading ground gainer, who quit his squad in midseason because, they claimed, "He took all the fun out of football," he reacted sharply.

"Football isn't a funsy game," snapped Odell. "You go out and knock the hell out of each other and that's not fun."

Odell, incidentally, decided at the end of the season that football at Penn, in particular, wasn't "funsy" for him, either, and he resigned. Odell then took the head coaching job at little Williams College.

Joe Paterno, however, thinks that's all a lot of foolishness. Football can be fun, he says, and you can still win. But, he admits, that football, even Joe Paterno style, isn't *all* fun.

"I figure that football has two seasons," Joe explains. "First, there is the pre-season practice. We have about ten dog days when the players work their tails off and maybe even wonder why they ever got involved in this crazy game. I think we probably work them harder than anybody else in the country. Then, after that is over, we want to get the kids rested up so they can enjoy the season. After all, they are only going to play about thirty college football games in their lifetime, and they ought to enjoy them.

"Practice isn't fun, either. But it's something the kids have to put up with in order to get the enjoyment out of football. Once the season starts, we don't ever scrimmage. We don't want to bang up anybody and besides, if we haven't made a boy a football player in spring practice and during the pre-season drills, then it's all over. We have failed and we'll never make him one. But we do want them to work hard in practice at perfecting their techniques and executing their plays. I don't want our practices to be as they are at some schools where eleven coaches concentrate on coaching eleven players and, when someone makes a mistake, his coach jumps all over him and chews him out. We don't do that."

Some coaches do, however. Alabama's Bear Bryant and Jim Owens, when he coached at the University of Washington, were of the hard-nosed school. They used what they called the "challenge" system to stimulate competition. At Washington, for instance, if a second teamer thought he was better than the player ranked ahead of him by the coaches, he could challenge him to a contest. Usually, it was brutal, sometimes bloody, one-on-one block and tackle combat. If the challenger bested his man, he got the first-team job. The only trouble was, players occasionally were injured in the warfare and could not play the next Saturday.

Practices are even rougher at Arizona State University, where Coach Frank Kush has attained and maintained a reputation for toughness. Kush believes that all football players should be treated equally—like animals. Woe to the Arizona State player who makes a mistake! Kush has been known to slam the side of a player's helmet hard enough to deck him. And, if the mistake is repeated, the victim must contend with "Mount Kush," a 300-foot, 45-degree slope covered with loose shale that stands next to the ASU practice field. The offender is forced to climb the hill at double time, an effort which usually results in his slipping and sliding and a profusion of scrapes and black and blue marks. Then there is the hamburger drill. If a receiver drops a pass, he is tackled by every member of the defensive team as he holds the ball on his fingertips. If, by chance, someone shows any mercy, he becomes the hamburger.

Coach Bo Schembechler of the University of Michigan also believes that practices should be the equivalent of a Marine boot camp. And he likes his reputation as a mean coach. "We run their tails off," says Bo. "Maybe three miles of sprints on Mondays. Then Tuesday and Wednesday we really hit. We bring the reserves in and we go after them for a full two hours."

On the other hand, Bobby Dodd, when he coached at Georgia Tech, used to seek out a natural comedian on the squad and encourage him to keep the players loose. Michigan State's Duffy Daugherty, perhaps the most impish of all coaches, has a special award called the "Oil Can," which he presents each year to the squad member with the best sense of humor. Duffy, one of the truly humorous men in college football, should win it himself each year.

Lee Corso, the young coach at Indiana University, is another one who likes to make his football fun and games. Lee, who played for and coached under Tom Nugent, another madcap innovator, at Florida State and Maryland, had a long-haired, barefoot, hippie punter on his 1970 Louisville team and his boys rollicked their way to the Missouri Valley Conference championship and a place in the Little Rose Bowl at Pasadena, California.

"There's no reason you can't keep your sense of humor and be human and still play football," says Corso. "We've had hamburger-eating contests, Italian nights at the training table, and I passed around cigars after we won one game. With all that we still expect them to be gentlemen and we give them responsibility. We don't have bedchecks. We don't have an athlete's dormitory. We don't have a hair code. I encourage them to talk to newspapermen, to be themselves, to communicate. You can't lock kids up and tell them you're giving them responsibility."

When Corso took his team to Pasadena, he said, "A bowl game should be fun and we're going to have fun. I'm going to turn them loose and say, 'By the way, if you can get in by two Saturday, we got a game to play.'"

Joe Paterno is tough on the practice field, certainly a lot tougher than his predecessor, Rip Engle, but he is smart enough to realize that practice can be boring and he has an antidote for that, too. He permits some clowning around and there is a lot of give-and-take between the coaches and the players. Joe, who didn't always feel that way, doesn't want his athletes to feel that practice is a drudgery. Frequently he will give his squad some new plays to work on during the week. Most times, the new plays never see the light of a game, but Joe feels that the diversion and anticipation give his players the welcome change of pace they need to relieve boredom.

Paterno realizes that even college football players have to be kept interested in what they are doing. It isn't enough simply to tell them that football is the most important thing in their lives and expect them to believe it. "With everything that is going on these days," Joe says, "you've got to compete for their interests."

Another thing that Paterno, unlike the majority of his colleagues, doesn't believe in is long meetings for his players. Most other coaches insist on a meeting the night before a game and another one the next morning to go over strategy and assignments and to remind the players what they are supposed to do in certain situations. Not Joe Paterno.

"If our kids don't know what they are supposed to do by Thursday night, after going over it and over it in practice all week, they'll never know it," Paterno reasons. "I don't go through a long checklist. What's the sense of cluttering up their minds? I want them mentally rested and ready to get some fun out of the game."

So, where does the fun come in football at Penn State?

"Playing the game on Saturday is when we have our fun," replies Paterno. "That's when all the hard work pays off. The fun is to be relaxed, to be loose, just to play as if it's a sandlot game. We tell our players, 'Don't worry about losing. Just relax and do your best. Enjoy it.' "

Paterno's philosophy is that nothing in life, including football, is worthwhile unless you enjoy it and gain something from the experience. He likens playing a football game to a skier going down a slope. "You should be doing it for the sheer enjoyment you get out of it," he says, "not because you have to win or you're afraid to lose."

Dennis Onkotz agrees that practice at Penn State was no picnic. "It was work," he remembers. "Anyone who thinks you can have fun and still win, well, they're dead wrong." But, Denny admits, "The games were fun. We enjoyed playing on Saturdays. We were loose, we never worried about making mistakes, we were encouraged by Joe to think for ourselves and to take chances."

Make no mistake, fun and all, winning *is* just as important at Penn State as it is at Ohio State, Notre Dame, Texas or Southern California. Paterno's thinking is never geared to losing but he is realistic enough to recognize the fact that, despite the late Vince Lombardi's football catechism, winning *isn't* everything. There are other things in life just as or even more important.

"Sure, we're trying to win football games and we're not going to be satisfied with anything less than a 10-0 season," says Paterno, "but I don't want it to ruin our lives if we lose. I don't want Penn State to become the kind of a place where an 8-2 season is a tragedy. You can't tell kids that a football loss is a tragedy. It's not. All I ask them to do is to give it their best. If we win, great. If we lose, it's not the end of the world. There will be another game next Saturday and the Saturday after that. I don't want my players crying. I want them to feel bad, but I don't want them to be ashamed. I'll never buy that stuff some coaches are always saying, that if a boy loses a football game, he's a loser in life.

"The coaches with that attitude, the ones who try to make their players believe that winning is the only thing, that nothing else matters, don't belong in football. As a matter of fact, there are too many men in college football today who don't belong working with young people. They don't relate to them at all. And that also goes for some people running universities and a lot of trustees and alumni who use athletics for their personal satisfaction.

"I tell our kids never to be afraid to lose. Think about winning. I don't ever want anybody playing for me who is afraid when he walks out on that football field that he's going to make a mistake that will cost us a football game. All I want them to do is pull up their pants, look the other guy in the eye and say, 'Let's go. Let's find out which of us is the better man.' I tell them either they can do it or they can't. What's the sense of worrying about it? Give it your best and if you can't do it, why you can't. If the other guy is better, then he should win.

"I always remember what Winston Churchill once said. 'Success is never final, failure is never fatal.' I think maybe that best explains my philosophy of football as well as life in general."

Just in case anybody has the idea that Joe Paterno doesn't mind losing once in a while, his record speaks for itself and so does Joe.

"Don't get me wrong. I *don't* like to lose. I think I take a loss as hard as any coach and a lot harder than I hope my players take it. They shouldn't have that kind of a commitment. If we lose, it's my fault. That's my responsibility as the head coach. I don't brood over a game but I do second-guess myself, analyzing where I made my mistakes. After all, I have more control of the game than the players. I have to prepare them. I have to design the game plan. I run the game from the sidelines. Sure, the players on the field do or don't make the big play but it's my job to give them the tools to win."

It is clearly obvious that Paterno has been able to get this philosophy across to his players. At least, Dennis Onkotz thinks so. "We never worried about losing," says Denny. "If we lost a game, we lost it, that's all. Why worry?"

Pete Johnson, a defensive back and tight end on the '68 and '69 Nittany Lion teams, says, "No one at Penn State even thinks of losing any more. Even in the '69 season, against Syracuse, when we were down by so much [14-0 at halftime], we figured that some way we'd pull it out." Penn State did indeed, 15-14, with a 2-point conversion late in the game to keep its winning streak alive.

When Colorado finally ended Penn State's thirty-one game non-losing streak, 41-13 in Boulder, Colorado, in the second game of the 1970 season, Paterno's reaction was typical. After the game ended, he ran briskly off the field with his squad and into the locker room, where the deadly silence was broken only by the roar of the celebration from the nearby quarters of the Colorado team. There was no nonsense about being good losers, no ranting and raving about mistakes—and there had been plenty by the Nittany Lions—no warmed-over clichés about bad breaks or the officiating, no self-flagellation over the ending of college football's longest winning streak. Joe simply told his team, referring to the jubilant shouts coming from the Colorado locker room, "Listen to them—let them have their glory. We've had our share."

Paterno chatted amiably with members of the press and, when asked about the crushing defeat by the Buffs, said straightforwardly, "Colorado was just a better football team. It's as simple as that."

Then, Joe added good-humoredly, "The trip wasn't a total loss, though. My wife got to see the Rockies. Sue woke me up this morning pointing and saying, 'Have you seen those *mountains?*' "

Later Paterno told Jack Newcombe, an old friend and a writer for *Life* magazine, "There's an elation to winning and when you get beaten too often you get angry. But when you haven't lost in a long time you find out just how ignominious it is. But look at me. I've finally acquired character. That feels good."

There was one more little post-game touch that pointed up the kind of a man Joe Paterno is. Despite his disappointment, he took the time to drop by the Colorado locker room to congratulate the winning players and to wish them luck over the rest of the season. When he left, two burly Colorado linemen looked at each other in astonishment.

"Can you believe that?" asked one of them. "Can you believe that after what just happened out there that he could come over and say that?"

"That's why they win, man, that's why they win," replied the other player. "That's class."

That, perhaps more than anything else, best describes Joe Paterno. He has class and style, two commodities that are fast disappearing from civilization. Paterno has something else—humility. The kind of humility that makes it automatic for him to give credit to his coaches and players when he wins and to claim the blame when he loses.

Most coaches would disagree with Paterno's views on winning and losing. They *want* their players to suffer when they lose. They *want* them to be afraid to lose. That is the price of big-time college football at most schools these days and that is why Joe Paterno's approach is so refreshing. He calls it the "Grand Experiment," a term which has had an exhilarating effect on the entire athletic program at Penn State. Obviously, it has paid off for the Nittany Lions.

Paterno, however, didn't always have this philosophy. When he was an assistant coach at Penn State under Rip Engle, he was more concerned with winning. "I was very ambitious," reflects Joe, "and I wanted to make sure I would get to the top. I thought the only way I was going to get ahead was by the success of the team."

Engle, a white-haired, fatherly man, always worried that perhaps he was pushing his players too hard. He felt that football was only a game and that he wanted his players to get something constructive out of their playing experience. Paterno often disagreed vocally with Engle's approach, insisting that he was too soft on the players, but later Joe was to admit that Engle was right and he was wrong.

In 1966, his first year as the head coach after Engle's retirement, Paterno pushed his team to the limit and beyond. He worked them hard in practice and insisted on complete concentration on football. There was a lot of dark muttering among the members of the squad and it was evident that the players were not happy with their new head coach, even though almost all of them had played under him when he was Engle's chief assistant. The result was that Penn State lost three of its first five games, including a 42-8 pasting by powerful Michigan State, which went on to tie Notre Dame for the national championship; a 49-11 loss to UCLA; and an unexpected 11-0 defeat by Army.

"Suddenly, I began to see that Rip had been right," says Joe.

"My approach had been totally wrong, I realized that I had lost some of the players because I was too concerned with my own record. I had lost sight of the fact that this was *their* team. My attitude had been that the players had better do it my way, or else. We were all unhappy, the players, the assistant coaches and everybody connected with the team."

To Paterno's credit, and an indication that he is intelligent enough to adjust his thinking when he recognizes that it is wrong, he began to reevaluate the situation. "I spent a lot of time talking to some of the kids," he recalls, "and I suddenly realized that we weren't getting the kind of enthusiasm we should out of them. I had not been taking their feelings into consideration. I decided right then and there that I had better see to it they got something out of football, that they ought to have some fun out of playing the game or I had better forget about being a coach."

Paterno's attitude and approach to football promptly changed. Practice sessions weren't nearly as tough as they had been. He had more rapport with his coaches and players, there was a spirit of give-and-take and the team, as a whole, began to loosen up. Penn State lost two more games that season, to superior teams from Syracuse and Georgia Tech, to break even, 5-5, but Paterno and his players had learned a great deal from the experience.

In retrospect, Joe reflects, "I think I was kind of overreacting. I wanted to make sure that people didn't think I was going to be exactly like Rip Engle. I wanted to let them know I would do things my way. But, I learned that any time you are dealing with people with different cultures you had better have the ability to change and adjust your thinking. I don't think I have all the answers forever."

This incident in his career, perhaps more than any other, provides a keen insight into the character of Joe Paterno. A man of lesser acumen, a man of lesser intelligence would not have been able to cope with the situation, nor would he have had the humility to admit that he had erred and to change his tactics. Thus, the idea of football for fun—Paterno style—was born out of adversity and through the hard fact that even a football coach can be wrong in his attitude and approach.

It is Paterno's contention that no team, regardless of its physical capabilities, can win unless its members have togetherness and a mutual love for one another. Although Joe would be the last to admit it, in this respect at least, there is great similarity between him and Coach Vince Lombardi. Vince, a tough, biting taskmaster who would accept nothing less than perfection from his players, always insisted that what made his Green Bay Packers so great in the 1960's was not his coaching genius but their genuine love for one another. He once said, "Coaches who can outline plays on a blackboard are a dime a dozen. The ones who win get inside their players and motivate them."

Paterno's method of motivating his players is not quite the same as Lombardi's, but the end result is the same. Vince's aim was to get his players to subordinate their individuality for the good of the group. His approach was to be tough and direct and to instill fear in his players. How well he succeeded was clearly evident during his nine seasons as the Green Bay coach when his Packers were the scourge of the National Football League and the nemesis of the fledgling American Football League in two Super Bowls, and later, just before his untimely death of cancer at the age of fifty-seven, in a single season as coach of the Washington Redskins.

Paterno, too, has succeeded in achieving this same kind of team respect and love for one another—he calls it "we" and "us"— but with a different approach. His way is a softer sell, an appeal to the best instincts of his players, a plea that no one individual should ever do anything to embarrass another one on the team. Like Lombardi, Paterno stresses togetherness, people doing things together and for one another.

"I think this is something people don't really understand about team sports," says Paterno. "They don't quite get it. But those of us who are close to it can see it. When you look at your team praying together before a game you can actually *feel* their genuine love, respect and admiration for each other. Here are people who have lost their individuality and their personal interest in something that is for the good of the team. They want to do well so their team can win. They don't care about how much publicity they're going to get. As a coach, you just know when they go out on the field with that much love and respect for each other, this losing themselves in something they think is a little bit bigger than they are, they will be tough to beat."

Proof of how well Paterno succeeds in getting his message across to his players is something that Steve Smear, outstanding defensive tackle of the 1967, 1968 and 1969 teams, once said. Steve spoke of the defensive team with a sort of primitive passion. "Three years we played together and never a voice was raised in anger," he said. "It was no fake. We worked together like the Celtics and the Packers. It all boiled down to team pride and this was what Coach Paterno tried to instill in us. He would say, 'Would you like to go to war with the guy next to you?' I know what he meant."

The defensive unit that Smear refers to was the same one that terrorized foes mercilessly during the long Penn State winning streak. Four of its members—Smear, Dennis Onkotz, Mike Reid and Halfback Neal Smith—were All-America selections, while three others—Linebacker Jim Kates, End John Ebersole and Halfback Paul Johnson—were named to the All-East team. Extremely intelligent young men, they were not merely caught up in emotional pyrotechnics that so many coaches use as their stock-in-trade. Indeed, the day is past when college players blindly accept fiery appeals from their coaches. But Steve Smear and his teammates, at least then, believed in and were dedicated to Joe Paterno's logical philosophy.

"If we could get that feeling—that 'we' and 'us' instead of 'I' and 'me'—into our society we wouldn't have as many problems and we would be able to lick those we have," claims Paterno. "Maybe we can't solve the national problems but I think that if we can make it work on the level of a football team, maybe some of it will spill over onto the campus, and maybe from the campus to the community, from the community to the county, from the county to the state and from the state to the nation. But people have to work at it."

Paterno's preoccupation and success with instilling this feeling in his football team has already attracted some recognition in national circles. The "we" and "us" at Penn State was the theme of Joe's acceptance speech when he was given the Congressional Medal Award by the Pennsylvania Association of Radio and Television Broadcasters at a dinner in Washington, D.C., early in 1970. Following his remarks, Paterno was given a standing ovation by the audience, which included Pennsylvania's two United States Senators and most of the state's congressmen.

Senator Richard S. Schweiker was so impressed, that when he spoke at the annual Penn State football banquet a month later, he called on the nation's leaders to learn from Paterno. "Why is Joe Paterno a great coach?" asked Senator Schweiker. "He listens to young people and he listens quietly. The channels are always open. Then he decides, based on what he has learned by listening and communicating. That's what we need more of in our country today. We need more of Joe Paterno's 'we' and 'us' instead of the 'I' and 'me' we have now. Joe has taught the country and certainly his profession. We should listen to what he has to say and learn from him."

Jim Tarman, who has had the opportunity to witness, first-hand, Paterno work his magic at Penn State, is convinced it is Joe's personality and intelligence—his charisma, if you will—that is mainly responsible for his ability to sell his players on his philosophy.

"Joe has this great ability to motivate and inspire his players," says Jim. "He is so intelligent, so bright and so quick mentally. He convinces them that they are something special, that they're just a little bit different from other football players in the country because at Penn State it's just not all football. It's all the things he wants them to be in addition to being football players.

"Through his personality and ability to sell people on his ideas, Joe has really gotten through to his players on this 'we' and 'us' idea that he stresses. You can see it among the players. They honestly believe that they *are* different from players on other teams. You hear them referring to themselves and the team as 'we' and 'us!' "

Oddly enough, for all his theories on subordinating individuality on the football field, Joe Paterno is very much an individualist when it comes to coaching. His proclivity for doing the unexpected and his penchant for gambling have rightly earned him a reputation as an unorthodox coach and one that the other coaches usually view with suspicion. It also has made him an innovator in a profession where most people find it easier to imitate what has been successful for others. In college football, as in

anything else, there are leaders and there are followers. There
are college coaches who faithfully imitate whatever is fashionable, whatever other coaches win with. Their number is legion.
Then, there are those coaches who innovate, who dream up new
variations of offenses and defenses to confound their enemies.
Coach Johnny McKay of Southern California is one. Back in 1962,
John took the old I formation that former Maryland Coach Tom
Nugent claims credit for introducing back in the 1950's, changed
it into what he called a power-I or shifting-T and won the national championship with it. Coach Darrell Royal of Texas is
another. In 1968, he was so intrigued by the triple option of Veer
offense devised by Coach Bill Yeoman of Houston that he studied
it, made a few twitches here and there and came up with his
wishbone version that was so successful it earned the Longhorns
the national championship in 1969—despite a justified protest by
Joe Paterno and Penn State.

One indication of Paterno's talent as an innovator was the de-

Joe Paterno belongs with the leaders. During his days as an
assistant coach under Rip Engle he was always thinking of new
variations in offense and defense, and Engle usually listened to
him because he recognized that Joe had a keen and unusual football mind. As a head coach, Paterno has on several occasions
changed his entire offense or defense to surprise an unsuspecting
opponent.

One indication of Paterno's talent as an innovator was the defense he devised for his Penn State team in 1967. Because he
wanted to do something different, something that would give
opposing coaches a pause, Joe spent an entire summer working
on some defensive ideas he had long been thinking about, including several that through the years Rip Engle had permitted
him to try. He also had been impressed with the defenses used
by Dee Andros of Oregon State and Hal Lahar of Colgate and
spent a lot of time talking with Dee and Hal about it. The result
was that Paterno came up with some novel ideas for pass coverage and up-front stunts that permitted his linebackers and players in the secondary to gamble. After discussion with Jim O'Hora,
his defensive coach, and other members of the staff, Paterno put
his plan into operation. The defense worked so well that Joe has
been deluged with phone calls and spring practice visits from
other coaches who want to learn it.

Coach Vince Dooley of Georgia, Coach Bill Dooley of North Carolina and members of the Auburn, Georgia Tech, Dartmouth, Virginia Military Institute, Villanova and Boston University coaching staffs, among others, have visited the Penn State campus to discuss the defense with Paterno and his assistants. Other coaches of big-time college football powers, some now out of the sport, also have made inquiries. Coach Bob Blackman, when he was at Dartmouth, and Coach Bud Carson of Georgia Tech even went so far as to pay Assistant Coaches Jim O'Hora and Frank Patrick a fee to come to their respective schools to teach them the elements of the defense. There are other coaches, though, like Chuck Fairbanks when he was at Oklahoma, who think it is too unorthodox.

Paterno is glad to hear that people think he is unorthodox. "You've got to be unorthodox in college football," claims Joe. "You just can't do the same things all the time and still win. There's another thing. Once a coach gets a reputation for being unorthodox, you have the other guy worried. He tells his team, 'They may do this, they may do that, watch out.' Now, when a coach and his team are spending that kind of time worrying about other things, they're just not going to be properly prepared for your team. Psychologically, it has a lot of advantages. Besides, just by nature, I have to try new things. I have to be stimulated intellectually. It makes coaching more challenging and more interesting.

"I think, too, the kids like being in the middle of something that's a little different," adds Joe.

One exercise in intellectual stimulation indulged in by Paterno was in Penn State's game with North Carolina State in 1967. The Atlantic Coast Conference team, then coached by Earl Edwards, a former Penn Stater, was undefeated in eight games and ranked No. 3 in the country when it came to University Park. The Wolfpack was bigger and more experienced than Penn State's mostly sophomore team, which had lost two games, and the visitors were favored to win.

The week before the game, Paterno decided that if his Nittany Lions were to have a chance against North Carolina State, he would have to do something drastic. He pondered the problem and then came up with a plan to discard his usual wing-T offense and open the game in a short punt formation. His assistant coaches demurred and the arguing went far into the night. But Paterno stubbornly persisted. "Naturally, I had my way," he says with a grin. "After all, I was the head coach."

Penn State did come out in a short punt formation, threw a screen pass to its slot man on the first series of downs and N.C. State was astounded. This was something they didn't expect and hadn't worked against. There were other surprises in store for the confused Wolfpack, too, and the result was a 13-8 win for Penn State in one of the season's outstanding upsets.

"We disrupted their game plan," recalls Paterno. "They were disorganized and we dominated the game in the first half."

That same season, against Syracuse, Penn State ran its first three plays without a huddle and from short punt formation. "People asked me, 'Why the hell do you do those damn crazy things?' " says Paterno. "Well, I think it's good to get opponents a little bit off balance. You get them wondering. I think our kids get a kick out of it, too. That's part of the fun."

Later that year, against Florida State in the post-season Gator Bowl game in Jacksonville, Florida, Paterno figured he had to make another unexpected move to get an edge over the favored Seminoles. "I was convinced that if we had used our regular offense and defense, Florida State would have annihilated us," says Joe.

So, out went the regular offense and in came a new alignment. Practice sessions were secret and Joe put his team into a V formation, hardly an innovation, but he also moved Ted Kwalick, his All-America tight end, into the backfield and shifted him up both ways—sometimes to slotback, sometimes to wingback in much the same type of offense that Coach Hank Stram of the Kansas City Chiefs began to use much later. That was new and it created havoc with the Florida State defense. Paterno also made some cute adjustments in his defense designed to stop Florida State's prolific passing attack, which had obliterated opponents all season long.

"Not everybody agreed with that, either, but there we were sitting on a 17-0 lead over Florida State in the third quarter. Then I blew the game with that now famous '4th and 1' call on our own 15 yard line," remembers Joe ruefully.

What happened on that "4th and 1" call by Paterno was that Penn State elected to go for the first down instead of punting, missed it by mere inches—according to the officials—and gave up the ball deep in its own territory. Florida State rallied to score two touchdowns, then kicked a field goal and the disappointed Nittany Lions had to settle for a 17-17 tie, the only non-winning effort in a thirty-one game streak.

Paterno readily admitted that his gamble undoubtedly cost Penn State the game but, he explained, "I had told our kids to be reckless in the second half, not to worry about sitting on that lead. So, the first time we had a chance to gamble, I just had to go for it."

Paterno's fatefull call in that game aroused a storm of muttering and criticism from Penn State alumni and fans around the country. It also earned him dubious recognition from *Sports Illustrated* for the "bonehead play" of all that year's post-season bowl games.

He was ribbed unmercifully by fans, friends and sportswriters but he took it all in typical stride. With his knack for poking fun at himself, he turned it to his advantage.

On the post-season banquet circuit, he was usually the first to bring up the subject of the "4th and 1" call in the Gator Bowl. He insisted that he would do it again in similar circumstances and he boldly told his critics, "You'd better get used to it, because that's how we're going to be at Penn State. We're going to be reckless, we're going to take chances. I made up my mind when I got this job I was not going to be a stereotyped coach. Lousy maybe, but not stereotyped."

That is how Joe Paterno is. He's the guy who would try to steal home in the World Series while the pitcher is holding the ball. He would go for a birdie rather than a safe par and tie in the U.S. Open. He would go for the home run pass on first down while deep in his own territory. He's the guy who would—and did against Kansas in the 1969 Orange Bowl—go for 2 points on the last play of the game rather than settle for a tie.

The gambler in Joe Paterno has added an exciting new dimension to Penn State football, one that the fans have learned to expect and love and opposing coaches have learned to dread. Penn State football players, in the era of Joe Paterno, are encouraged to be reckless, to take chances, to do the unexpected. It is a refreshing attitude in contrast to the majority of college football coaches who play the game by the book.

"Don't stand around and wait for something to happen," Paterno is constantly telling his players. "Don't be afraid to take chances. Gamble. Be reckless. Make things happen! Force a fumble, get an interception, block a kick, create confusion in the other team. We want to make our opponent afraid to make a mistake. That's when they make 'em and we'll take advantage of it."

Joe even encourages his players to defy him. "I say to them, 'Look, if you're a defensive halfback and you're playing in a zone defense and I tell you to play deep, but you just know that the next pass is going to be a short flat one—and there will be times when you just *know* it—and you don't go against everything I've told you, if you don't gamble for the interception, then you're no damn good. You're stupid, you're lousy, you're not a good football player. I can get a robot to play that position.'

"That's the way life is," says Paterno. "People aren't just lucky. Things happen to them because they are willing to gamble, to take chances. I don't want to ever think about ties. If kids at eighteen, nineteen and twenty, in the prime of their lives, have to settle for a tie, I feel sorry for them later on in life. If a boy gets to be a doctor, I don't want him going for a tie. What the hell, if you don't make it, you don't make it, but at least you have the experience of going for something, of making something happen through your own efforts.

"You've got to believe deep inside yourself that you're destined to do great things. I also believe that if I don't have the guts to take a chance, then I'm never going to be a good coach."

Paterno practices what he preaches in his personal life, too. More than once, he has taken gambles that influenced his own life. His first one was when he elected to pass up law school, following his graduation from Brown in 1950, to try his hand at coaching under Rip Engle, his college coach, at Penn State. Later in his career, he turned down assistant coaching jobs in professional football with Baltimore, Philadelphia and Oakland and several college head-coaching opportunities, including a highly coveted job at Yale, on the gamble that one day he would be the head coach at Penn State.

How well Paterno's Penn State teams have responded to his "go for broke" attitude was perhaps best demonstrated in 1969, when the Nittany Lions' defense, which Paterno—and many others—called "maybe the best college defensive team of all time," literally turned around game after game with its hell-for-leather style of play. Time and again during that unforgettable season, the defense, gambling with reckless abandon, came up with the big plays—an interception here, a blocked kick there, a fumble here. The result was Penn State's second straight undefeated season.

Many have tried to describe Joe Paterno and his style of coaching and the reactions have ranged from "refreshing" to "incredible" to "unbelievable." Dan Jenkins wrote in *Sports Illustrated* after the Army game in 1968: "While Paterno should be fretting about his team's possible climb toward No. 1 or an Orange Bowl bid, he stares at the boutique-colored leaves of the pastoral Alleghenies, thinks about Romantic poets and longs to drive his kids over to Waddle or Martha Furnace or Tusseyville so they can sit down and talk to a cow. Is this the atmosphere that has produced the best college football team the East has seen in years? You can bust everybody in Potters Mills if it isn't."

Ernie Accorsi, a former assistant sports information director at Penn State and now Assistant General Manager of the Baltimore Colts, wrote in *The Sporting News*: "He coaches the way Jackie Robinson played baseball, the way Arnold Palmer plays the Masters."

Jack Newcombe wrote in *Life* magazine: "In three seasons of nearly total conquest, he carved for himself an appealing image: a talkative, nervy plunger, always ready to go beyond the percentages and for making moves from the bench that contain more refreshing surprise than logic."

This, then, is Joe Paterno. Football coach, intellectual, maverick, philosopher, social worker, leader, gambler, idealist, Romanticist, humanist, activist.

4: What Is a Coach?

IN THE WORLD OF COLLEGE and professional athletics, the title "Coach" is the one that has become both glamorous and, more lately, a target for aggressions which have become part of a way of life. The coach is honored and glamorized when he wins, maligned and frequently fired when he loses. It is a precarious profession at best and only the very good ones survive.

Webster's New Collegiate Dictionary defines a coach as merely "an instructor in athletics" and one who prepares "for an athletic or other contest." But the true definition of a college football coach today is not that simple. His function is much more complex and the qualifications for the job are considerably more demanding. It is no longer sufficient that he be an expert in football. The X's and O's, the teaching of techniques, the master-minding of strategy, have become the least important tasks that a successful coach must perform better than other people to reach the top in his chosen profession.

He must be a super-saleman to compete successfully in the recruiting rat-race and to sell his program to the administration of his school, the players, faculty, students and alumni, not to mention the media; he must be a master psychologist and sociologist to handle the many and diverse individual problems associated with his players and the members of his usually large coaching staff; he must be able to relate with people; he must be an expert in public relations; he has to be a radio and television personality; a public speaker and very often a politician. He lives in a glass house, his every word and action subject to critical scrutiny. He is a father confessor, hero and scapegoat.

What is a coach? The definition has changed with the times. Where once the coach was a gruff, old-fashioned conservative who only had to direct himself to the game as it was played on the football field, today's new breed of coach must necessarily be a man for all seasons. There were few distractions for football coaches and players in the days of Amos Alonzo Stagg, Pop Warner, Knute Rockne, Bud Wilkinson and Colonel Earl Blaik, or even in the early days of Bear Bryant, Woody Hayes and Ben Schwartzwalder of Syracuse, who retired just a few years ago. The age of the authoritarian who ruled with an unyielding iron hand is over. Those who have not kept up with the times, who have not broadened their horizons and who persist in living in the dark ages will soon be extinct. Their demise from the world of college football is as certain as death and taxes. Joe Paterno puts it in even stronger words. He says, "If they can't adjust, they ought to get out of coaching."

It is still true, however, that a coach must first know his football and be able to teach it to his players. But, there is more to coaching today than mere technical knowledge, as many an ill-fated college football coach discovered in the 1960's and early 1970's. Bob Ward was fired by the University of Maryland after his players called for his dismissal on the grounds that he was too tough on them. Jim Miller of Boston College, Bill Elias of Navy, Johnny Coatta of Wisconsin, Ray Nagle of Iowa and Tom Harp of Duke, among many others, were fired for not winning often enough. In 1970, in a real "bush" move, the University of Illinois summarily fired Coach Jim Valek only hours before his team's sixth game with Ohio State, but the school was forced to back down and reinstate Valek for the remainder of the season when the Illini players voted to strike over the action. Charlie Tate of the University of Miami resigned in midseason because of "outside pressures." The "pressures" included late-night obscene phone calls to his family and repeated second-guessing by Miami fans. And the list of casualties goes on and on.

Joe Paterno was so alarmed by Bob Ward's forced dismissal at Maryland that he fired off a letter to Paul Dietzel, then president of the American Football Coaches Association, demanding an investigation.

"I don't know who's right or wrong," said Joe, "but I think it is the proper function of our association to ask Maryland why it let Ward go. I don't think it's a good thing for a squad to fire a coach. As an association, we ought to know what happened. If a university fired an English professor because his class didn't like the way he was doing things, I know darn well that the American Association of University Professors would want to know what happened."

Some coaches have become casualties for other reasons. Like Dave Puddington of Kent State, a proud young man who tried desperately to counteract the pall that descended on the campus of the Ohio school after the tragic killing of four students by the National Guard in the spring of 1970. Puddington resigned, citing the "prevailing contagious negativism on campus and in the community." He added sadly, "The fatalism around us and the current tendency to politicize every facet of life, even sports, has affected the young men in our football program."

Then there are coaches who are attacked when they leave one post for another. Paul Dietzel was torn apart by critical New York sportswriters when he left Army to take a job as athletic director and football coach at the University of South Carolina. Paul felt so keenly about the treatment he received that he wrote an article entitled "I Have Never Broken a Contract" for *Sports Illustrated*.

When Doug Rickey, once the toast of the University of Tennessee, left Knoxville to take the head coaching post at the University of Florida, his Alma Mater, he was vilified in living rooms all over town. And, when Dickey returned to Knoxville to play his former team, he was roundly booed by his onetime supporters and greeted with a new Tennessee battle song—"Tricky Dickey."

Many other coaches have become deeply involved with racial problems. Jim Owens at the University of Washington, Ray Willsey at the University of California at Berkeley, Lloyd Eaton at Wyoming, Johnny Pont at Indiana, Ray Nagle at Iowa, Ed Cavanaugh at Idaho State and Ben Schwartzwalder at Syracuse all were hit with revolts by their black athletes. After a similar uprising; Minnesota Coach Murray Warmath was ordered by his administration to take a course in a sensitivity program.

Life has become more complex and more difficult for college football coaches, and college administrators have not helped. Dan Devine, before he left Missouri to coach the Green Bay Packers, said, "The administrators who will stand up for a good coach are few and far between. They just take the easy way out and don't take into consideration whether or not he is a good teacher or a good man. Administrators talk out of both sides of their mouths."

Some coaches adjusted admirably to the new demands of their profession. John McKay, one of the top college coaches in the country before he left the University of Southern California for the pros, kept up with the times. There were others, too, like Tommy Prothro, when he was at UCLA, Ara Parseghian at Notre Dame, Frank Broyles at Arkansas, Darrell Royal at Texas, Dan Devine, during his time at Missouri, Bob Devaney at Nebraska, Bear Bryant at Alabama, John Bateman at Rutgers and Woody Hayes at Ohio State. (Unfortunately, many of these men are now out of coaching.) Joe Paterno has adjusted perhaps better than most, largely because he didn't have much adjusting to do. He always had a deep feeling for his athletes and he has a keen understanding of the times in which we live and a great sympathy for the problems which bother the young. He make an effort to identify with them.

But there are dozens and dozens of coaches who have not adjusted and they never will. Joe Paterno has no patience with them. He tells them the old authoritarian approach is out of step with the times, you can no longer tell young men to do something and expect them to follow you blindly. "They want to know why," says Paterno, "and they are entitled to know.

Coaches have to humanize their approach to football and their players," Joe insists. "The smart ones who can tune themselves in to the new generation are the only ones who will survive. Those who can't, don't belong in coaching any more."

Paterno admits that there is no tried and true formula which every coach can apply to particular situations. Nor does he have a panacea to offer hopeful coaches.

"There are ways to get hold of a group of today's young men," Joe says. "Sometimes you have to do it through your young assistant coaches. Individuals have different personalities and you have to be alert enough to recognize the differences in people. The coaches who do it best are the ones who have strength. An excellent example is Woody Hayes. He is the rare bird among college coaches. Although he is a throwback to the old-time coach and rules his roost with an iron hand, at the same time he has an awareness of what is going on in the world. Woody keeps himself so well informed, he is up-to-date on everything. He has great strength."

Most coaches agree on what a coach must be but they have varying opinions on the relative importance of qualifications and standards. Take Darrell Royal, who thinks that the development of pride is the primary function of a football coach. In his book, *Darrell Royal Talks Football,* he wrote:

"Pride is what causes a team's winning performance. . . . What's a fellow got to lose after he's had his pants dusted several times? It's just old shoe to him. When you lose your pride—and defeats will drain it like a leech—then you just can't generate much firepower.

"That's what I consider the primary task of a head football coach. Plant, fertilize, groom and develop that pride. The Texas football team would fare just as well if I didn't coach a lick. Our staff handles most of the instructing. But a head coach is guided by this main objective: dog, claw, wheedle, coax that fanatical effort out of the players. You want them to play every Saturday as if they were planting the flag on Iwo Jima."

Woody Hayes puts it another way. In his book, *Hot Line to Victory,* Woody says: "There are two qualities that a coach must have to far greater degree. . . . He must have an intense and continuing interest in the welfare and in the all-around development of each player and he must have an extremely strong desire to win. However, it must be a 'we' win attitude, not an 'I' win attitude."

Duffy Daugherty said, "Every coach worth his practice cap must believe in himself and he must believe in his players. . . . and he must be able to communicate this belief in his players. . . . and he must be able to communicate this belief in his coaching."

Joe Paterno's definition of a coach and what he must be and what he must do is not that simple. He differs from most of his colleagues, but that is not unusual because Paterno's thinking on most issues rarely conforms with that of other coaches. As one opposing coach puts it, "If we say it's black, he'll say it's white. And, you know, I'm beginning to think he's right, dammit!"

Here is Joe Paterno's definition of a coach, what qualifications he should have in today's world, what he has to be and how he has to conduct himself.

"First of all, a coach has to think of himself as a teacher and an educator. He has to feel that he has a vocation, not just a job, that he really has a 'calling' for coaching. Too many coaches are so concerned with winning that they neglect the teaching aspects of their vocation. I consider myself an educator in charge of an area of responsibility in the university, just as the head of the English or History departments. I am supposed to be developing certain character qualities and teaching the young people who come under my influence some values in life.

"At Penn State, coaches are given faculty rank and they are considered to be educators. I am a full professor and two of my assistant coaches are associate professors. But there are so many colleges that refuse to recognize the football coach as anything more than a man who is in charge of jocks. Yet they put him in control of a large group of young men, give him the responsibility of molding their character and all they care about is how many football games he wins or loses. This is demeaning.

"Another thing, I feel very strongly about coaches' contracts, although I don't have one at Penn State and I like it that way. I firmly believe that no coach should have less than a four-year contract when he takes a job at a new school. The first year, he's working with his predecessor's material and that's not a fair test. The second year, his recruits are sophomores and still learning. The third year is when he should find out whether or not he can do the job. The fourth year is the real test, and if he can't win then, he should move on.

"I deplore the fact that the American Football Coaches Association has not taken steps to upgrade the status of all of its members. Instead of worrying about things like who is going to be Coach of the Year or how we can get to be No. 1, our membership should be taking a stand to achieve faculty status and dignity for every college coach in the country and to get assurances that he will be given a fair opportunity to do his job. Our jobs should not depend upon the whim of the alumni or the vagaries of the administration. I am afraid that I have probably made myself unpopular in some quarters by speaking up at AFCA meetings but I am going to continue to do it until there is some action.

"A coach has to be a leader, not only by word but by example. He has to be a leader for the things *kids* think are important, things they can identify with, not only with what *he* thinks is important. And he has to make them identify with him. He has to be able to get people to do things. He has to be a leader to develop morale, not only among his players but among his assistant coaches. And he must remember that everybody is responsible for morale—his assistant, the sports information director, the trainer, the equipment man, the team doctors, the managers—it must be a total team effort.

"And morale doesn't mean only among the members of the first team. It's easy for first-stringers to have good morale, especially when you're winning, but a team is only as good as its poorest man. You have to worry about every member of your squad. Woody Hayes once said, 'I'm not worried about the morale of my top guys. I'm concerned about the morale of the guys at the bottom of the squad.' Woody is 100 percent right. If my sixtieth player, the guy who almost never gets to play, has good morale, then everybody has it. The only way you're going to have it is if everybody on your squad believes he has had a fair shake.

"A coach has to set high goals. He has to aim high, think big and then make sure that his players aspire to the highest goals they can achieve. He has to be able to get people to reach up. As Browning wrote, 'A man's reach should exceed his grasp, or what's a heaven for?'

"A coach should never underestimate himself or sell himself short on his abilities. He should take chances when the opportunity presents itself. He shouldn't have to say ten years later, 'I could have done that, but I was afraid to take a chance. I didn't think I could do it.'

"A head coach should make each of his assistants feel that his job is the important one. Just like in the management of a big company, he has to hire people who can do the job, have confidence in them and then let them do it. Each assistant has to have pride in his position, to be made to feel that it is a challenge and that he is an integral part of a leadership team.

"I always remember something I once read when I was preparing to give a talk on management. One expert in the field offered several pieces of advice. First, hire people who are smarter than you are. Then, give them a job they can do and let them do it. Thirdly, give them credit for doing it. And, lastly, you pray.

"A coach has to be as demanding of himself as he is of his players. He has to believe in what he is doing and then convince his players, not merely by demanding, but by instruction and example, that he is right. He has to assist his players. Maybe he has to chew out one boy to help him. Maybe he has to invite another boy out to his home, sit him down and say to him, 'Look, son, look how good you can be, what's available to you, not only as an athlete but as a person.' The coach has to inspire and drive them and help them get everything that's coming to them. He has to help them overcome their shortcomings. I think that is one of the most important functions of a coach—he has to help a boy get better, both as a player and as a man.

"Another thing a coach has to be able to do is help his players gain character qualities which will help them toward a better and successful life. He has to show them and prove to them that hard work, discipline, quality and ability will pay off, not only in football but in later life.

"A coach must be able to develop three things in an athlete: pride, poise and confidence in himself. I tell my players, 'You're either going to get better or worse, both as a football player and a person.' Kids have to realize that they change all the time and either they're going to reach greater heights or they are going to go downhill. It's the same way in life. You come in contact with people who influence you and you either become better for them or you get worse. It's the same way with a team. If they keep hustling, keep their poise, something good will happen.

"A coach has to be the boss on the field. He has to assert himself and take command, whether it's during practice or a game. I am a firm believer in the theory that if a team practices well, it will play well on Saturday. As a coach, it's my job to see that we practice well. I don't think any coach is worth his salt if he doesn't have the guts to throw his team off the field if things are not going right in practice. I've done it at Penn State and I'll do it every time I don't think my players are putting out or if the practice is just not going well. And, maybe this is giving away a coaching secret, I will sometimes deliberately get angry and start to yell and shout just to stir up my players in practice.

"There is a little bit of an actor in every football coach and some of us do it a little better than others. There was one scene in the movie *Patton,* played superbly by actor George C. Scott, that impressed me. General Patton is telling his staff about a daring, and what sounds like an improbable, maneuver that he is going to make with his army. The men look at him in disbelief but Patton says he is going to do it even if it costs the life of every man. He is raving and ranting, chewing the men out and then he throws out everybody except his adjutant.

"Patton's adjutant looks at him and says, 'General, sometimes they don't know when you're acting.'

"Patton answers, 'It isn't important for them to know, it's only important for me to know.'

"For example, on the sidelines during a game, I like to be up walking around. I like to make decisions, emotional decisions. I like the idea of being in charge. I want people around me. I want my squad up on their feet all through the game. People sometimes say to me, 'You're always pacing up and down the sidelines like a wild man.' Well, a lot of times things aren't going so well out on the field and I'll storm up and down the sidelines. Sure, sometimes it's an act, just to stir things up, to get my players emotionally charged up. Some coaches just stand there quietly. All coaches are different. You do what you do."

The movie *Patton,* incidentally, had a great impact on Joe Paterno, perhaps not for the same reasons that President Nixon reportedly found it an inspiration when he had to make military policy decisions. Paterno refers to it frequently in conversation, comparing General Patton's qualities as a leader with those which a good football coach must have. He is careful, however, to let people know that he is not passing judgment on some of the actions of the controversial World War II general.

"Every football coach ought to see the movie *Patton*," Paterno advises. "He had the ability to rally people around a cause, to get them to make greater sacrifices than they thought were possible. He had the ability to get people to do things by the sheer power of his personality, by his drive and his inspirational qualities. In that respect, he was fantastic. He paid attention to small details and felt that if you took care of the little things, the big things would take care of themselves. He was a bug on spirit and morale. He believed that he was destined for great things and there was never any doubt in his mind that he would succeed. That's the attitude a football coach must have.

"In the movie, he refers to something that Frederick the Great once said—*L'audace, l'audace, toujours l'audace*. Audacity. When his staff questions a decision, he tells them, 'You've got to take chances, you've got to be aggressive, you've got to go after things.' That appeals to me because that's the way I like to coach. I don't like to sit around and wait for something to happen. I like to make it happen.

"There is another analogy to be made between General Patton and football coaches. He said he always dreamed of leading a great army in a dangerous battle. I think all football coaches, on the day of a game, basically kind of think of themselves as leading their teams into great battles. I know this must sound cornball, but the coach who doesn't get stirred up ought to get out of the business and be something else, maybe a stockbroker or an insurance salesman. He isn't much of a coach.

"It is the job of a coach to gain respect but he can't worry about being popular and he can't sacrifice his personality just to be liked. He can't copy someone else. He's got to be himself, whether his style is being aloof or one of the boys, or whether he's a bitcher and a hollerer. Some coaches are charmers, others are tough guys. But, whatever he chooses to be, he must be consistent.

"The most important thing is for a coach to be fair. And it isn't enough just for him to *think* he is fair, he must *appear* to be fair to his players. If a boy complains that he isn't being given a fair shake, that he hasn't been given enough opportunity to make the team, hear him out, maybe he does have a legitimate gripe. Give him his chance. It's not very difficult to make adjustments. A coach's authority isn't necessarily being questioned or threatened if a boy thinks he is being treated unfairly. It is the coach's job, his obligation, to convince the boy that the treatment is fair.

"A coach must be morally ethical. He can't look for an unfair advantage or a way to beat the rules of the game. If he does, his players and the people around him will lose respect for him. For example, there was an incident that occurred several years ago when Rip Engle was the head coach and we played UCLA at our home field. Tommy Prothro was the UCLA coach and we knew he was a pretty sharp guy. Accidentally, some of our security people who had two-way radios discovered that UCLA coaches in the press box were giving instructions to Gary Beban, their quarterback, by radio. It was obvious that Beban had a receiver in his helmet. We knew which plays were coming because our people were tuned to the same wavelength. It would have been so simple to set up our defenses, yet Rip and I couldn't bring ourselves to take advantage of the information. There wouldn't have been any fun out of winning the game that way.

"A coach shouldn't ever complain about his kids. If all other things are equal, if they are practicing well, if they are doing just as well as they can, that's about all a coach has a right to expect. Maybe their talent is limited, or maybe it's the coach's fault and he has failed in getting them to fulfill their potential. One of the greatest signs I've ever seen hangs over the desk of Coach Johnny Devine of Peekskill (New York) High School. It says simply: DON'T BITCH ABOUT YOUR KIDS. THEY'RE THE ONLY ONES YOU HAVE.

"A coach must be adjustable to the times. Sure, he must have discipline and some rules and insist that they be adhered to by the players but they should never be the kind of rules that are oppressive or overbearing. Or unfair. Athletes and times have changed and a coach must be able to adjust his thinking and his rules to the times. He should never let himself get trapped into taking a position that is going to be publicly discussed. Or one that he isn't ready to defend logically to his players.

"A coach has to have a plan for everything. For when he's ahead, for when he's behind and when he's tied, for what he's going to say to his squad and to the press after the game. I don't go in for impassioned pep talks to my squad. You can't give kids today a pep talk, they're just too sophisticated and too knowledgeable to fall for that 'Win one for the Gipper' routine. You can't, all of a sudden, change things around with a thirty-minute talk.

"On the day before a game, I set aside an hour to plan what I'm going to say to my squad the next day. I plan my halftime talk and what I'm going to say after the game, win or lose. Maybe that sounds like being overprepared but, you know, there are people who say that Joe Paterno is never at a loss for words and I don't want to disappoint them.

"I have one final word of advice for coaches. Don't be a gimmick coach. If a coach has to use certain color locker rooms, or have wall-to-wall carpeting in his locker room, or have the band play Chinese music in order to get his kids to want to play football, he's going to get licked anyway. They're going to let him down in the clutch. I don't know any slogans or locker room signs that ever won a game for any coach. We don't put stars on helmets for special efforts like some coaches do, for an interception, a blocked kick and things of that nature. I say, if a kid has to have a star on his helmet in order to play well, then he's just no good anyway. I think some coaches overestimate their ability to influence kids when they do things like that instead of just letting them go out and play the game.

"Paul Dietzel, when he was at Army, was probably the greatest gimmick coach of all time. I remember once he sent his team out to play Navy and everybody wore white shoes. It didn't help the team's performance one bit. He called one of his three teams the 'Chinese Bandits' and every time they went into the game, the corps of cadets put on coolie hats, the band played Chinese music and a special flag was raised at one end of Michie Stadium. It was ridiculous. It was like Terry and the Pirates.

"Pepper Rodgers, when he was at Kansas, used artificial stimulation, like racing on to the field ahead of his team before the game and doing headstands. I don't think Pepper's team ever scored a touchdown because he stood on his head. Dave Hart, when he was at Pitt, was a gimmick coach and he wasn't around very long. When things are going badly for your team, there isn't a gimmick in the world that will help you win. And when things are going well, you don't need that junk, so why use it?

"I remember talking to Rip Engle one day about Dietzel's Chinese Bandits, the white shoes and all the rest of the things he was doing at Army. Rip told me, 'I have only one criterion for everything I've ever done. How would it look when you lose?' "

What is a coach?

There are a lot of good ones, proficient at their trade and winners, but there are few great ones. The great ones have special qualities—awareness and the ability to react quickly and automatically to situations on the field of play. More important, though, they have the intelligence and perceptiveness to relate to the people they coach. They are both activists and humanists, both compassionate and tough, both strong and adjustable. They endure and survive. They are the Vince Lombardis, the Woody Hayeses, the John McKays and the Bear Bryants.

Joe Paterno has all the qualities to be one of the great ones.

5: "He Is a Born Leader"

"I THINK my strongest suit as a football coach, aside from my ability to get people to do things, is that I can analyze an opponent and figure out a way we can beat them. If our style is not appropriate for a team we have to face, I won't hesitate to change it."

That's Joe Paterno talking. Immodest? Maybe, but it is probably the most accurate self-evaluation of the practical coaching philosophy of the man who has hit college football with the subtle impact of a sledgehammer. His style is "go" all the way. His daring and unorthodoxy on the field are admired by the coaches who don't have to play him and feared by those who do. He has a rare knowledge of the game that is unsurpassed by any other college coach, even those who have been at it much longer. More than that, he has the ability to communicate his knowledge to his players.

Joe Paterno lives and practices his definition of a coach. He aims high and won't be satisfied until he has achieved his goal. He demands a great deal, but gives more. He has lofty standards and insists that everyone associated with him—coaches and players alike—have high principles. To Joe Paterno, coaching is a way of life.

Off the field, Joe Paterno has raised the hackles of coaches, athletic directors and even a President with his honesty and frankness in speaking out for what he believes. What he believes is not always popular and frequently it hits people where they hurt most, but then, Paterno reasons, he isn't in a popularity contest. He has the courage of his convictions, a quality the coaching profession and the world at large could use a lot more of in these critical days. He is a nonconformist, and some folks, in the context of today's confused rhetoric, might even call him a radical or a revolutionary when it comes to his views on college football.

The greatest compliment to be paid Joe Paterno is that many coaches have begun to do some things his way, both technically and philosophically. They are copying Joe's defensive ideas, applying his offensive techniques and, more important, a few are even showing signs of adopting his philosophy of football. More coaches are gambling and taking chances. More of them are realizing that the length of a boy's hair or his sideburns or whether or not he has a mustache have nothing to do with discipline. A modest few are even encouraging their players to become involved in the life of their university. And a few have even discovered that football need not be a drudgery for them or their players, that they can stay loose about the game and that it can be fun. Consciously or unconsciously, they have been influenced by Joe Paterno's mod approach to football.

One of these is Indiana's Lee Corso, who says, "If you're going to play football, you can't coach scared or conservative. You've got to go, and that's the way we try to do it."

However, the true measure of a man who has achieved success in his chosen profession is how he is regarded by the people he has worked for, with and against. Few people are neutral about Joe Paterno. Some like him, others don't, including a few of his own players at Penn State, but almost everyone has an opinion about him. Almost no one is noncommittal. He has his supporters and his critics.

One of Joe Paterno's biggest boosters is Rip Engle, the man he succeeded as head coach at Penn State. Rip saw something in Paterno early on and he nurtured it by giving him unprecedented authority as an assistant coach. Engle, who had so much success in his own coaching career, is enjoying Paterno's rise to coaching fame.

"Joe has everything to be a great coach," says Rip. "He is quick to spot an opponent's weakness and he knows instantly what to do about it."

Opposing coaches have a rare appreciation of Paterno's talents. Not all agree with the way he does some things, but they have come to respect his coaching skill and to recognize him as one of the rising new leaders of their profession.

Woody Hayes, rarely unstinting in his praise of another coach and bluntly honest in his appraisal of men, says simply, "He's a student of the game. He's a good coach. Joe Paterno is good for football."

Coming from Woody Hayes, that is high praise indeed.

Pepper Rodgers, who found himself on the losing side against Paterno in the 1969 Orange Bowl, says, "He's tough to coach against. Joe seems to anticipate everything you're going to do and it's frustrating."

One thing Paterno didn't anticipate when his team played Kansas in the Orange Bowl was that Rodgers would have twelve men on the field when Penn State went for 2 points and a victory—and was stopped cold—on the last play of the game. But Pepper did, and it cost Kansas the game. The Jayhawks were penalized, Penn State got another chance and Paterno's team made it good to win, 15-14.

Tom Cahill, formerly of Army and now at little Union College, who feels a close kinship to the man who two years later followed him as Coach of the Year, says, "Joe is a smart fellow and he uses his talents to their fullest capacity. He has a sound understanding of the game and he has the personality to establish a good and natural rapport with his players. Joe also has the ability to get the maximum out of his squad."

John Bateman hasn't had the pleasure of competing against Paterno on the field, but he worked closely with him in the American Football Coaches Association when John coached at Rutgers, and the two men think alike. Bateman is open in his praise of Paterno. "There is no question about his ability as a coach, his record proves that," says John, "but I like the things he stands for and I like the fact that he doesn't pussyfoot about things he doesn't agree with. Joe Paterno is the best thing that has happened to college football in the last twenty years."

Dan Devine, whose Missouri team lost to Penn State in the 1970 Orange Bowl, demonstrated his feelings for Paterno as a coach after the game when he told people, "We knew his team was good, we knew they were well coached and we had seen the films of all their games, but we just weren't sure what to expect from Joe Paterno. He has a way of throwing opposing teams off balance by adjusting his offense and defense to take advantage of your weaknesses. It is a real challenge to coach against him."

Carmen Cozza of Yale and Bob Blackman, when he was at Dartmouth, often had their Ivy League fur rubbed the wrong way by former Ivy Leaguer Joe Paterno but, happily, they have never taken the darts he directs at their exclusive group personally. Cozza calls Paterno "the kind of coach everybody will be trying to imitate before very long."

Blackman, who had his feathers ruffled by Paterno at the end of the 1970 season when Joe challenged unbeaten Dartmouth to a post-season game to decide "which team is the best in the East," nevertheless says, "We're good friends and I have great appreciation for his ability as a coach. He does some things that surprise people, both on and off the field."

Paterno's challenge to Dartmouth wasn't really a surprise. He had been saying for years that, if Ivy League teams want to be considered as football equals with major independents in the East and other teams in the nation, they ought to play them "instead of staying in their own backyards and playing each other." He was annoyed by Dartmouth's claim that its undefeated team "could play with anybody in the country." All he wanted was to give Dartmouth a chance to play against somebody.

Ironically, Blackman got his chance to play Joe's Penn State team. Just a week after he was honored as Eastern Coach of the Year, Blackman left Dartmouth to take the head coaching job at the University of Illinois and the Illini were already on the Penn State schedule for 1972. The Lions won, 35-17.

What was a surprise, at least to Bob Blackman, was Paterno's appearance when the Dartmouth coach was presented with the Eastern Coach of the Year award by the New York Football

Writers Association at a cocktail party in New York in December of 1970. Joe, who had won the award for two previous years, came in from State College to lead the applause for Blackman. It was just one more way in which he showed his class.

Even Ben Schwartzwalder of Syracuse, who would have rather beat Penn State than any other team on his schedule and who constantly warned people that "you have to watch those guys in Pennsylvania or they'll trick you out of your uniform," admits that Joe Paterno's style is impressive. "He's a sound football technician," says Ben. "He's a good coach."

Al Davis, a former coach and the general managing partner of the pro Oakland Raiders who once sought Paterno as an assistant coach for his team, calls Paterno "one of the ten best young college coaches in the country."

Joe's own assistant coaches have perhaps an even better appreciation of his talents. The men who have worked with him and the members of his present staff never cease to marvel at his capacity for work and his thoroughness in preparing for an opponent.

Jim O'Hora, who handled the defensive line before he retired and the man on the coaching staff who is perhaps closest of all to Paterno, has a great regard for Joe's football mind. "Nothing ever escapes him," marvels O'Hora. "He is so quick to analyze the opponent's offense or defense and then react almost immediately to make the necessary adjustments. He knows both ends of the game, offense and defense, and he is always thinking."

George Welsh, now head coach at Navy, who took over the quarterbacks and offensive backs when Paterno moved up to the head coaching post, perhaps didn't have the same freedom that Joe had when he worked under Rip Engle, but George and the other assistant coaches, Frank Patrick, since retired, J. T. White, Bobby Phillips, Jim Weaver, Jerry Sandusky and John Chuckran, who replaced Earl Bruce as the freshman coach in 1970, are all sold on Paterno's way of doing things. Although they sometimes question his daring in doing the totally unexpected, they understand the nature of the man they work for.

Sever Toretti and Earl Bruce, both no longer coaching now, can look at Paterno in retrospect. Toretti thinks one of Joe's greatest assets as a coach is his ability to evaluate his players. "He has an instinct for picking the right man for the right position," says Tor, "and he has the courage to experiment and gamble on changing a boy's position if he feels that he would play a little better somewhere else, or if the team would benefit from it. Joe is tough, but fair and he is so thorough in his planning for a game."

"Paterno is a tireless worker," says Bruce. "He probably spends more time on football than most other coaches and he works his staff hard. But he never asks his assistants or his players to do anything he hasn't done. He also does his homework and his teams are always well prepared."

Other people close to the athletic picture at Penn State are even more enthusiastic in their praise of Joe Paterno. Richie Lucas, who was one of Paterno's quarterbacks, maybe the best one Joe ever had, says, "As a player, I learned so much from him. He has ideals and standards that many other people do not have. Everyone who comes in contact with him has to be just a little better for the experience. He would be a success in any field he chose to go into. Penn State's whole athletic program revolves around Joe, not so much for his success as a coach, but for the kind of man he is."

Jim Tarman, who has had the opportunity to watch Paterno operate on all levels, first as an assistant coach and then as the head man, when he lost and when he won, is deeply impressed by Joe's great ability to retain his cool in the heat of battle.

"As a tactician and a strategist, he has few equals," says Jim. "On the sidelines during a game, he's so calm and always knows what is going on and just what he is doing. On the day of a game, I really don't think there is a coach in the country who will ever outcoach him. Aside from his tactical knowledge of football, he also has a way of getting the most out of his players."

The late Ridge Riley, an old friend who was the alumni secretary until he retired in 1969 and who wrote the Alumni Association's weekly football letter, saw every Penn State football game since Paterno first came to University Park. He watched Joe grow from a fresh young assistant coach into a mature head coach and he knew how Paterno thought. "The great thing about Joe," said Ridge, "is the way he takes hold of a situation, whether it is on the field or in an area involving university policy. He is a born leader. As a friendly, and frequent, critic, I sometimes twit him about his moves on the football field but he usually turns out to be right."

Dr. Robert J. Scannell, the Dean of the College of Health, Physical Education and Recreation and Paterno's boss, is no stranger to big-time football. He played end at Notre Dame for three years and has a keen awareness of what Paterno means to Penn State and its football program. "Everybody knows about his greatness as a football coach," says Bob. "What he has done the past few years has proven that, but what we appreciate here is that he is a salesman for the university around the nation. Joe has a great knack for getting to the crux of a matter and for breaking it down into nickels and dimes so everybody understands it."

Ed Czekaj, the athletic director and Penn State football player in the early 1950's, concurs with Scannell. "Joe works so damn hard to get things done that he inspires the rest of us," says Ed. "He never looks for the easy way out and, if he has his way, we'll be playing schools like Notre Dame, Texas, Arkansas, Stanford and Ohio every year. He wants to win against the best."

Paterno's players, although some of them view him with mixed feelings, agree on his ability as a coach. Dennis Onkotz says, "I like Joe. He has to be a brilliant coach. He was so well organized and we were always so well prepared. We always knew what we were doing every minute. And he knows how to bring a team along and when it has reached its peak. He made mistakes, but he rarely made the same one twice.

"Joe was kind of a father figure to most of us. He was the coach and you had to have respect for him. You really couldn't get informal with him. He had to keep his distance to demonstrate his leadership.

"I think Paterno has put football in its proper place at Penn State, but I am sure there are probably some students on campus who think there is too much emphasis on football."

Despite all the accolades and kudos heaped on Paterno by the Penn State family, not all of Joe's players were exactly enchanted with him. In the summer of 1970, there was a slight rumble from the camp of the Washington Redskins, where three ex-Nittany

Lions were trying to make the pro squad. Jim Kates, Paul Johnson and Neal Smith were outspoken in their criticism of Joe Paterno and his style. One of them even questioned his image.

"The stress was always on football at Penn State," said Kates. "The only satisfaction I got was from winning." But, Kates admitted, "The coaching at Penn State was good. They schooled you in fundamentals."

"Paterno was tough," said Johnson. "He was a perfectionist, believing the game should be played with a minimum of mistakes. We were taught the way you practice is the way you play the game. If you practice hard you should win."

The most outspoken was Smith, who said, "Paterno wants the public to think he's concerned about his players' getting an education. Don't believe it. Like any other big-time coach, he's all football. I don't really know the coach's priorities but winning football games was right up there. You have to respect Paterno for his football knowledge, but not as a person."

It was tough talk but the facts belie some of Smith's comments. For one thing, in an era when only about half the college seniors entering professional football came out of school with their degrees, eight of the nine Penn State players—including Neal Smith—who were drafted after the 1969 season toted their diplomas off to pro camps. The percentage of the other senior members of the '69 team who received degrees was equally high. It is proof that Paterno and the athletic administration at Penn State do care about their players' getting an education.

Paterno, himself, was mildly shaken by the comments of Kates, Johnson and Smith. "I think this fun business is getting out of hand," said Joe. "It's getting to sound as if we go out on the practice field and sing and dance, that it's nothing but fun and games. People misunderstand what we're talking about. The fun part of it is in how you approach the ball game, the excitement of being different, of taking chances."

Joe Paterno is not perfect, but then, who is? A man who is so dedicated to change, to inspiring new thoughts about an old sport and to bringing a refreshing breath of air to college football is bound to bruise some feelings here and there. Perhaps Neal Smith didn't quite absorb as much as fast as some of the other young men who played under Paterno.

They say no man is a hero in his own home. But Sue Paterno, Joe's wife, has analyzed her husband better than most people.

"Joe demands so much of himself, he drives himself at a terrible pace. He thinks he can be a good coach as long as he works hard at his job, as long as he pays attention to details and he is a bug on that. He blames himself when we lose, that he didn't work hard enough, that he could have done something different if he had paid attention to one more little detail. I think his biggest fear in life is overlooking a detail.

"I think Joe feels that he always has to be better. He sees what he wants, he knows what he wants and he knows how to get people to do it."

It's a wise woman who knows her own husband.

6: It's a Long Way from Brooklyn to Brown

THE SAGA of precocious Joseph Vincent Paterno, football coach extraordinary, began on December 21, 1926, a day that was not particularly distinguished for any other great event, when he entered this world in a section of New York that many feel privileged to call the capital of their world. Fittingly enough, it happened in Brooklyn, that urban hamlet which never fails to draw laughs when mentioned on television and, conversely, is so staunchly upheld by its natives.

Joseph Vincent, a scrawny little fellow, was the first child of Angelo Lafayette and Florence de LaSalle Paterno, an Italian-American couple of modest means who also had been born and bred in Brooklyn and were then residing on Eighteenth Street. Except for some semi-stubborn resistance by Angelo Paterno, the new offspring might have wound up being called Angelo Lafayette Paterno, Jr. "That would have been a great name for a football coach," reflects Joe.

Mama Paterno thought it would have been just fine, especially since the career she was then envisioning for her first-born was hardly that of a football coach. What she had in mind was something like a doctor or a lawyer. But Dad Paterno persisted in his opposition, so it became Joseph Vincent.

Some twenty months later, the Paternos had their second child, George, who was to follow in his older brother's footsteps almost throughout his entire life. Then came a third son, Franklin, who was to die at the age of fifteen months. The fourth and last child in the family was, happily, a girl, and this time Mama Paterno got her way. The young lady was named Florence, after her mother, and she grew up to be pretty and feminine and a buffer between the rougher and tougher boys in the family. Florence is married to Phillip Middleman and lives in Forest Hills, New York. She is the mother of three children, Warren, Chris and Phillip Jr.

The elder Paterno was a modest, unassuming man who worked constantly to better himself. He had dropped out of high school to enlist in the Army soon after the United States entered World War I, but on his return he completed his high school education at night, went on to college and law school, also at night, and eventually passed his examination for the bar in 1941. Mr. Paterno rose to the position of Court Clerk in the Appellate Division of the New York State Supreme Court, a job which permitted him to raise his family in middle-class fashion. He also did a little legal work on the side. Unfortunately, he died suddenly of a heart attack in 1955 at the age of 58 and never lived to see his son's great success as a head football coach.

"Dad was a warm, wonderful human being who always saw only the best in people," says Joe. "He was always himself. Everybody who ever met him liked him. Dad was easygoing but he had a way of making you see his point. He liked to talk politics—he was an avid supporter of Franklin D. Roosevelt—and we really got into some warm discussions around the house. Dad was genuinely interested in what all of us did and we had a great family relationship."

Mama Paterno was the matriarch of the family, a strong-willed woman who was firm with her children. An extrovert, she was outspoken and her family always knew where she stood. Even today, with her three surviving children grown up and on their own, she continues to be a dominant figure in the family. She is proud of the accomplishments of her two coaching sons, Joe and

George, and rarely lets the occasion go by to extol them as "the best football coaches in the country."

In January of 1969, Mrs. Paterno stole the show when the New York Football Writers Association honored Joe as Eastern Coach of the Year at a cocktail party in the New York University Club in New York City after Penn State had completed an unbeaten season with a victory over Kansas in the Orange Bowl. Mrs. Paterno unabashedly reminded the large gathering that she had brought her boys up to be winners (George had just completed an 8-1 season as the head coach at the United States Merchant Marine Academy in Kings Point, Long Island) and she wasn't surprised that "Joe was such a good coach." After all, she told the assembled writers and coaches, "He had good training at home."

A deeply religious woman, Mrs. Paterno has great faith in prayer and she firmly believes that she actually helped Joe and Penn State beat Kansas in the 1969 Orange Bowl. And maybe she did, at that.

Mrs. Paterno and George were watching the game on television back in Brooklyn and, with only a minute and a half remaining and Kansas leading 14-7, George observed, "It's all over, Mom, Joe can't win this game."

"It isn't over, Joey will win," replied Mrs. Paterno indignantly. With that, she grabbed her rosary beads, rushed into the bathroom and began to pray.

"She no sooner started on her first Hail Mary," reported George, "When Chuck Burkhart hit Bobby Campbell with a long pass and a minute later Burkhart scored. Mom was praying furiously by this time and then came the 2-point play which failed, but there was a penalty because Kansas had twelve men on the field. That gave Penn State another chance and this time the 2-point try was good and Joe's team won, 15-14. I tell you, she made a believer out of me right then and there."

Mrs. Paterno's reliance on prayer was not a one-shot thing for the Kansas game. Every day during the football season she makes novenas on the hour. She starts at 9 A.M. with a prayer to St. Jude, the patron saint of lost causes, and repeats it hourly for nine hours. Mrs. Paterno's favorite inspiration is the Infant Jesus of Prague and she fondly calls Him her "little guy." She frequently tells Joe, "Don't worry about your team. The 'little guy' will take care of you."

Once, when Mrs. Paterno was watching another Penn State game on television with George and things were not going too well for the Nittany Lions, she jumped up and exclaimed, "I'm going to tell that 'little guy' to get on the ball or I'll dump Him for St. Joseph!"

All of Joe Paterno's early childhood was spent in the Flatbush area, a middle-class section of Brooklyn that was particularly noted in those days for being the home of Ebbets Field and the beloved Dodgers of sainted memory. The Paternos lived in apartments in several different locations while the family was growing up, but most of Joe's early life was spent on Twenty-third Street, where he was a neighbor of George Shiebler, who was later to become the commissioner of the Eastern College Athletic Conference, and Jack Smith, who became a writer for the New York *Daily News.*

The Paternos were a close-knit family and visited often with many relatives who lived in the area. "My mother had six sisters and three brothers and we must have had a hundred cousins," remembers Joe fondly. "We used to visit and go out together, not like today when you go out with your friends. Our family were our friends."

Joe and his brother, George, attended St. Edmund's School and did most of their playing in nearby Marine Park, schoolyards or in the streets. They engaged in the usual street games—stickball, punchball, touch football in between the traffic and parked cars. "Georgie was always a better athlete than I," Joe admits, "but I was a hell of a stickball player. A two-sewer man."

There was very little in the way of organized sports for the Paternos but Joe played basketball for the St. Edmund's parish team and proved to be pretty good at the game. There was little opportunity to play football anywhere, except for the games of touch football, which were more tests of endurance and agility than skill. There were the usual filial rivalries and clashes between the Paterno brothers but for the most part they got along well.

"Joe was always the big brother, looking out for me. They used to call us the Katzenjammer Kids around the neighborhood but I was usually the one who got us into trouble," says George. "Joe was older and I guess I kind of looked up to him."

There were a couple of incidents though, when Joe wasn't exactly George's protector. "I was about eight or nine years old, I guess, and one day we got into some kind of an argument," recalls Joe. "I gave George a belt in the nose and drew blood. Just then a neighbor came along, grabbed me by the collar and called me a bully for punching my little brother in the nose. What he didn't know was that Georgie had kicked me in the shins to start the fight."

"We had our little scraps, like most kids do," says Joe, "but we stuck together. If anyone picked on either of us, we'd both go after him."

George remembers another time when he suddenly began to get the impression that his big brother wasn't going to be so tolerant and patient with him. "One day, at the corner of Avenue U and Twenty-fifth Street, in front of a shoe store, we got into a fight over something and I hit Joe with a chain. He grabbed the chain out of my hands and threw it at me. I ducked and the chain went through the plate glass window of the shoe store. Boy, we really took off then. But the police found out we were responsible and it cost my father the price of a new plate glass window."

Although the two youngsters were close, there was a marked difference in their personalities and their interests, aside from sports. George was impulsive and spirited and liked to spend his spare time hunting and fishing.

"Joe was the one with the sense of responsibility and he was much more idealistic," says George. "Even then, he was a thinker and he liked to read and listen to music when we weren't out playing ball."

When it came time for Joe to enter high school, the Paterno family had a big decision to make. Mrs. Paterno always wanted Joe to go to a Catholic school and the Paternos finally settled on Brooklyn Prep, a private school with a good academic reputation. The tuition, even in those days, was pretty high but Mr. Paterno thought he would be able to manage it, and Joe took the entrance examination, passed it and entered Brooklyn Prep in February, 1941.

Joe, a skinny 125-pounder and only fourteen years old, didn't go out for football as a freshman. He didn't think he was ready to compete against bigger and older kids but he developed an interest in the game. He attended all the games and used to imagine himself as the star player of the team.

Just before the start of the next season, Zev Graham, a former Fordham University star who had been coaching at Fordham Prep, was hired as the new football coach at Brooklyn Prep. Zev was a peppery little man with a good sense of humor, but even he looked surprised when he issued a call for candidates for the 1942 team. A little fellow with skinny, birdlike legs raised his hand and·lined up with the guards. "I was planning to go out for center," remembers Joe Paterno, "but when I got a look at the size of the other kids, I said to myself, 'Uuh, uuh, that's not for you.' I was afraid that I wouldn't center the ball back right. So I went out for guard."

Joe got into a few games as a member of the kickoff team and even played against a powerful Mount St. Michael's team that featured Artie Donovan, son of the old-time boxing referee, who later went on to star in professional football with the Baltimore Colts. Brooklyn Prep upset the favored Mount St. Michael's team and Paterno remembers the game vividly because he almost scored a touchdown.

"We kicked off to start the second half," recalls Joe, "and the ball went into the end zone. The Mount St. Michael's players let it bounce around and I went diving for it. I remember thinking, 'Gee, I'm only a sophomore and I'm going to score a touchdown.' But Bob Shaughnessy, one of my teammates who is now a successful lawyer in New York City, knocked me out of the way and fell on it. It was the first big disappointment of my football career."

The next season, Graham decided the fiery little kid deserved a chance to be a starter and he installed Joe at guard. Brooklyn Prep wasn't very good that year, winning only two games, but Joe Paterno made a lasting impression on his coach, not so much for his ability but, even then, for his intelligence and spirit. By this time, Joe's brother, George, was also enrolled at Brooklyn Prep and he showed signs of developing into an outstanding running back. George had a scholarship to St. Augustine's but that school didn't have a football team, and Mr. and Mrs. Paterno decided that George deserved a chance to play. So they tightened the family belt, made some sacrifices and sent George to join his older brother at Brooklyn Prep.

Meanwhile, Joe was making his mark at Brooklyn Prep in other areas despite some early difficulties. The student body was composed mostly of Irish Catholics and Joe had to take a lot of abuse. "Other kids would call me 'Wop' and 'Dago' and other names and I was always ready to fight them. But, after awhile, when I had proven myself, I was accepted."

Joe was elected president of the student body in his senior year and his father became president of the Father's Guild.

One day, in the spring of 1944, Joe was watching Brooklyn Prep play a baseball game when Coach Graham, who also coached the baseball team, called him over. Graham had been talking to two priests but he interrupted to say to young Paterno, "Hey, pull up your pants leg."

"You know, I always had skinny legs, like a bird," says Joe, "and I was embarrassed but I did as I was told."

Zev asked the two priests, "Do you think I can make a fullback out of a guy with legs like that?"

Graham and the two priests laughed heartily, but Joe thought to himself, "You son-of-a-gun, I'll show you whether or not I can play fullback."

So, the next season, Joe's senior year, he was the fullback in Brooklyn Prep's double wing offense. Coach Graham disdained the use of the huddle and Joe called the plays and signals from his fullback position. Brother George was a halfback and the team's best runner. He was strong, tough and a fierce competitor. Between them, the Paterno brothers made football history that year at Brooklyn Prep. Sportswriters called them the "Gold Dust Twins" and they lived up to the nickname. The Prep beat Mount St. Michael's, Fordham Prep, St. John's Prep, Poly Prep, among others, and lost only one game for an 8-1 season. The only loss was to St. Cecilia of Englewood, New Jersey, which was then coached by Vince Lombardi, just starting a career that was to make him one of the most renowned coaches in football history.

There were some problems, though, for the Paterno boys. Joe was very much aware that he might be accused of favoritism if he gave George the ball too often despite the fact that the younger Paterno was by far the team's best runner. There was one game in particular, against Poly Prep, when Joe was called down by his coach for using George on too many plays. During the game Joe noticed that the opposing tackle was playing inside of Brooklyn Prep's end, making the off-tackle play a natural call. So Joe called George's play and he ran 40 yards for a touchdown. The next time Brooklyn Prep got the ball, Joe looked up and saw the same defensive alignment. He called the obvious play and this time George ran 60 yards for a touchdown. Coach Graham took Joe out of the game and chided him for giving the ball to George too often. Joe protested that he wasn't just trying to make George look good. "Poly Prep was giving us the hole," said Joe, "and I had to call his play to take advantage of it."

It was apparent then that Joe Paterno was a born leader. It was no mere accident that Zev Graham decided to have Joe call the plays for his team. The older Paterno brother was smart, he had the ability to lift a team and there was never any doubt as to who was the boss on the field when he was in the game. The astute Zev Graham was the first to recognize these qualities in Joe Paterno, something that other coaches also would come to recognize in due time.

Brooklyn Prep's lone loss that year, to Vince Lombardi's St. Cecilia team, was a classic. Prep had just come off a tough game with Mount St. Michael's and several of its players were suffering from injuries. Also, St. Cecilia had one of the best Catholic high school teams in the East and was in the midst of a long winning streak. Among the Saints' stars were Dick Doheny and Billy White, a pair of quarterbacks who went on to star for Fordham; Larry Higgins, a hard-running, shifty fullback; halfback Joe "Hook" Cerruti; and Joe Lombardi, brother of the coach, who was an All-Metropolitan guard. It was a close, hard-fought contest and the underdog Brooklyn Prep team was more than holding its own until late in the game, when Higgins burst off tackle on his right side, bounced off guess who?—yes, Joe Paterno, who was backing up the line on that side—and ran 60 yards for the winning touchdown.

Despite Joe's success as a football player (both he and George made the New York City All-Met team), he always felt that he

was a better basketball player. He was a starting guard at
Brooklyn Prep and held his own against some outstanding high
school players. Some of his contemporaries were Johnny Bach,
now the basketball coach at Penn State, and Jack Kaiser, who
went on to play for St. John's University and now coaches the
baseball team there. They were the stars of St. John's Prep. Also,
George Kafton and Joe Mullaney of Chaminade, who later played
on Holy Cross' 1947 national championship team. Mullaney, after
a successful coaching career at Providence College and a term
with the Los Angeles Lakers, has also coached other pro teams.
Paterno also played against Fuzzy Levane, then at James
Madison High School, who became the coach of the New York
Knickerbockers.

After his last season of football, Joe Paterno was roundly ignored by college football coaches. None of them had been
impressed enough by this skinny, bird-legged little guy to recruit
him as a football player even though he had been picked for the
All-Met team. However, Holy Cross expressed mild interest in
him and Fordham thought enough of his basketball ability to
offer him a partial scholarship. Although he was an outstanding
student, it never occurred to Joe to think about Ivy League
schools because his parents were unable to afford the relatively
high tuition prevalent even then at the exclusive colleges in the
East. Joe's dad wanted him to go to Army but a visit to West
Point on a bleak, cold day in January drove the notion from
Joe's mind.

Then, something happened that perhaps changed the entire
course of Joe Paterno's life.

Joe, then eighteen, had been graduated from Brooklyn Prep
in February, 1945, and he expected to be called in the military
draft momentarily. While waiting, he worked for Reverend
Francis Xavier Brock, the moderator of athletics at Brooklyn
Prep. His job was a rather innocuous one and included such
trivial tasks as picking up attendance slips and handing out volley
balls. Meanwhile, Coach Zev Graham had become friendly with
a man named Everett M. "Busy" Arnold, an alumnus of Brown
University who was a prominent publisher of comic books.
Arnold was actively recruiting football players for Brown at the
time and Coach Graham suggested that he might be interested in

Joe Paterno, the young man who had led his team to such a successful season in 1944. Arnold was indeed and he invited Joe to visit the Brown campus in Providence, Rhode Island. The football coach there was a man named Charles A. "Rip" Engle, a former high school coach who was in his first college head coaching job. The elder Paterno was impressed with Arnold. Joe liked what he saw at Brown but there were several hitches. First, the Paternos couldn't afford the luxury of an Ivy League education for their son. No problem, says "Busy." He would take care of all the expenses for tuition, books, room and board. Secondly, Joe was waiting to be drafted for military service.

As it turned out, Joe was not called up in the draft immediately and he enrolled at Brown in June. He was greeted by Coach Rip Engle and little did either of them know at the time that this was to be the beginning of a relationship that was to endure for more than twenty years. However, after Joe had been at Brown for about six weeks, he was suddenly called up by the military and left school, to serve in the Army, before classes began.

Joe's military career was undistinguished. On VJ day he was peeling potatoes on KP at Fort Dix, New Jersey, crying like a baby because he knew he was missing a great time celebrating with his family and friends back in New York. Eventually he was sent to Korea and then released from the Army in late August, 1946, just in time to return to Brown to begin his freshman year. By this time Joe's brother, George, also had been graduated from Brooklyn Prep and was being wooed by eight or ten colleges. "Busy" Arnold wanted both boys at Brown and Mr. Paterno agreed that would be a fine arrangement. So the Paterno brothers were united again, through the financial courtesy of Mr. Arnold, who footed all the bills during their college careers.

"I used to get the check from a foundation that Mr. Arnold had set up and I would take it down to the bursar's office," says Joe. "He must have been taking care of about eighteen or twenty players and we all appreciated his help. But that's all we got. Just the money for our tuition, room and board and books. Not another cent. It's illegal now for an individual to pay an athlete's college bills but I don't think there were any rules against it at the time."

As a returning GI, Joe was eligible for the varsity but George had to play for the freshman team. Coach Engle and his backfield coach, Weeb Ewbank, the same man who went on to coach the Baltimore Colts and New York Jets to pro football championships, were impressed with Joe's confidence but they decided that Paterno was to be a halfback who needed some seasoning before he would be ready for a starting job. Joe finally got his chance against Harvard and he promptly "distinguished" himself. He fumbled the opening kickoff, but recovered. Soon after, Harvard scored and kicked off. Paterno returned the kick to the 25-yard line, fumbled again and recovered. The kindest thing that happened to Joe after that grim experience was that Rip Engle virtually ignored him for the rest of the season.

Back in those days, the Ivy League was not quite as sanctimonious as it now claims to be and Brown had spring football practice like all other schools. In the spring of 1947, at the suggestion of Zev Graham, Paterno's old high school coach, Engle moved Joe to quarterback, where he was the backup man for Eddie Finn. He was also a starting defensive halfback. Joe saw some action at quarterback but not even that move saved Brown, and the Bruins had a mediocre season.

Things began to look up for Brown in 1948. Paterno was still a regular defensive halfback and the No. 2 quarterback but Rip Engle started a streak of winning seasons that lasted for the rest of his coaching career. The Bruins were 7-2, losing only to Rutgers and Harvard. While Joe was saving touchdowns on the defense, his brother, George, was one of the big guns in the Brown attack.

Joe's ability to quickly analyze a situation and react was directly responsible for one of those seven victories, a 23-20 decision over Princeton. In that game, the two teams were locked in a 20-20 tie with only minutes remaining and Brown was moving toward the winning touchdown. In an effort to stop the onrushing Bruins, Charlie Caldwell, the Princeton coach, put three wingbacks into the game to defend against Brown's passes. The maneuver worked when one of them intercepted a pass on the Princeton 4-yard line to stop the Brown drive. But then the strategy backfired. Princeton had the ball but the Tigers also had three defenders in their offensive backfield and no way to get them out. Princeton had used up all of its times out. Coach

Caldwell was in a dilemma: he could call an extra time out to get his running backs into the game, take a penalty back to the 1-yard line and risk a safety that could cost him the game or punt the ball on first down. Caldwell elected to kick, and that proved to be Princeton's undoing.

There was just about a minute left to play and Joe Paterno was the Brown safety man. He knew he somehow had to stop the clock to give Brown a chance to score. He quickly remembered that a fair catch would give Brown an automatic time out and, as the Princeton punt came sailing through the air, he raised his hands in the fair-catch signal. That little piece of brilliance by Paterno gave Brown time to move the ball within field goal range on a couple of passes and, with nine seconds to play, Joe Condon kicked the 39-yard field goal to beat the Tigers, 23-20.

Although Joe had considered basketball to be his best sport, his court career at Brown had its ups and downs. In his freshman year, Weeb Ewbank was the coach and Joe got his big chance when Brown played a great Holy Cross team that went on to win the national championship that year. The Crusaders were well-stocked with prominent stars, notably Bob Cousy, Joe Mullaney and George Kafton, Paterno's old high school adversaries. Joe found himself playing Cousy during the game. Cousy, even then a master at ball-handling, passing and shooting, practiced his legerdemain on the young rookie and scored 12 points in about a minute and a half. Holy Cross won the game by a lopsided score and young Joe Paterno learned one of the rude facts of life. He wasn't quite as good a basketball player as he thought he was!

But Joe stuck it out. Bob Morris, who had been a highly successful high school coach in Pawtucket, Rhode Island, where one of his prize players was Ernie Calverly, who went on to become a star at the University of Rhode Island, was the new coach the next season and he was impressed with Joe Paterno's zeal. Not his shooting, just his zeal.

"We used a weave a lot in those days," recalls Joe, "and any time we were in a jam, when the game seemed to slow down, Bob would send me in with instructions 'to get that damned team fired up.' I'd get in there, yell a lot and run around like a crazy man and the team really began to move. We'd never score much, but at least I would get them juiced up and out I'd come.

"In fact I was such a great shooter that the coach used to send me in so the other guys on the team could have rebound practice. I could always drive and I'd hustle in there with the ball, put it up and, boom, everybody would go to midcourt for the rebound. I guess I was what you'd call a playmaker."

Joe's basketball career at Brown finally ended after his junior year but he played often enough and well enough to win his letter in each of the three seasons. However, between playing football and basketball and his studies, Joe had little time for other extra-curricular activities. He was a good student and he had switched his major a couple of times, finally winding up in English literature. He joined Delta Kappa Epsilon, a fraternity which has since been thrown off the Brown campus. He occasionally tended bar at the fraternity house to pick up a few dollars for spending money and his idea of a big time was going up to Boston to watch Ted Williams play for the Red Sox. Joe was never much of a social lion, even in his college days, and his dating was restricted because of a lack of money.

"I had an occasional date, usually with a girl from back home," says Joe. "I didn't think the girls over at Pembroke were interested in a poor little guy from Brooklyn."

However, Joe did enjoy several close friendships with members of his fraternity and football teammates, some of which have endured through the years. Among his intimates were Pat Flynn, the son of the late Edward J. "Boss" Flynn, the famed New York politico, and Don Colo, a football teammate who went on to play with the Cleveland Browns.

Joe really came into his own as a college football player in 1949, his senior year, when Brown rolled to an 8-1 record and was considered one of the powers in the East. He was now the starting quarterback in Rip Engle's wing-T formation and played both ways, doubling as a defensive halfback when the opposing team had the ball. In all fairness, however, it must be pointed out that Joe Paterno rarely drew rave notices as a passer. He was no threat to the great passing quarterbacks of that time, like Arnold Galiffa of Army and Babe Parilli of Kentucky. In fact, Stanley Woodward, the late sports editor of the *New York Herald*

Tribune, once wrote about Paterno: "He can't run, and he can't pass. All he can do is think—and win."

Although Paterno was left-handed in everything he did, he threw the ball right-handed. He explains that easily enough. "When I was a kid I had only a right-handed baseball glove, so I had to throw righty."

Once, when Mel Allen, the former sportscaster, was describing a Brown-Columbia game on television, he went into ecstasy over the pass-catching of Frankie Mahoney, a Brown end who had gone to Brooklyn Prep. "Mahoney is a fantastic receiver," gushed Allen. "That ball is coming at him from all directions and still he catches it."

The passer, of course, was Joe Paterno. Joe's passes wobbled, fluttered, came end over end and almost never spiraled but, somehow, they managed to find their target. Brown's passing game, by necessity, was confined to short passes—hooks, down-and-outs, little flares—that rarely traveled more than 15 yards. Paterno, however, was a fairly good runner. He carried the ball a lot on bootleg action plays. He also had supreme confidence in himself. "I always felt I could move a team," Joe says.

What impressed Rip Engle about Joe Paterno as a quarterback was his brilliance as a play-caller, his tremendous leadership qualities, his ability to think quickly and clearly under pressure, his poise and confidence in himself and, above all, his knack for inspiring a team to greater heights. Consequently, Rip usually let Joe run the team during a game. "He was like having another coach on the field," recalls Engle.

Even then, Engle knew that this brash young man from Brooklyn had a mind of his own. Once, when Brown was playing Yale, Rip sent Freddie Kozak in with a play that he wanted Joe to run. Kozak dutifully relayed the message to the quarterback but he was greeted with a stony stare.

"We're not going to use it. We'll quick-kick."

"Quick-kick? What will I say to Rip?"

"Tell him I wouldn't listen to you. You quick-kick the football, they'll fumble, we'll get the ball back and score."

Then, while Engle fretted on the sidelines, Kozak quick-kicked to the Yale 3-yard line. Two plays later, just as Paterno had predicted, the Elis fumbled, Brown recovered and then went in for the touchdown. Rip never did register much of a complaint after the game.

Paterno also took great pride in his defensive ability but he had a couple of embarrassing moments in the Princeton game in 1949, the only game Brown lost that season.

Here is the way Joe tells it:

"Princeton put a skinny sophomore kid named Dick Kazmaier in the game. Nobody had ever heard of him. Well, the first time he got the ball, he came rolling out to his left, the side where I was playing defensive halfback, like he was going to pass. So I hung back and he kept the ball and ran for about 10 yards. A few plays later he came rolling around again and I figured to myself, 'This kid isn't going to catch me again.' This time I roared up the line of scrimmage, ready to destroy him with a crushing tackle. Just as I got there, he stopped short and threw a perfect pass over my head to John Emery for a touchdown. That score beat us."

That "skinny Kazmaier kid," of course, became All-America halfback and a Heisman Trophy winner!

Paterno's greatest game as a collegian, and the one he describes as the most thrilling he ever played in, was his last one, against Colgate on Thanksgiving Day. Brown had rolled over its Ivy League opponents to come up to its traditional closing game with a 7-1 record and was favored to end its season with a victory over the Red Raiders from the Chenango Valley. It had been a long, hard season for the Bruins and what they didn't know then was that this was to be Rip Engle's final game as the Brown coach.

While Brown fumbled and bumbled, Colgate attacked with unexpected ferocity and with only two minutes remaining in the third quarter the Red Raiders held a 26-7 lead. It seemed as if nothing would save Brown on this day and that Joe Paterno was going to finish his college playing career a loser. Even Coach Engle, morosely pacing up and down the sidelines with the members of his staff, was reconciled to a defeat.

Joe Paterno, however, was not ready to give up. The skinny kid from Brooklyn confidently told Engle, "Don't worry, coach. We'll get 'em." Then, during a time out, he got his team together and bawled the living daylights out of them. He cajoled, threatened, berated, shouted, implored, begged, even called on long-forgotten ancestors, and within minutes had roused his team to a fighting pitch.

What happened after that is one of the brightest chapters in Brown football history. With Joe Paterno lashing them, and George Paterno slashing through the line on run after run, the fighting-mad Bruins scored 34 points in the next seventeen minutes to overtake Colgate, 41-26. Brown fans were astounded and Colgate fans were shocked by the sudden turn of events. The "Gold Dust Twins" from Brooklyn had pulled off a comeback that every old Bruin would long remember.

Joe decided to forgo basketball in his senior year and he thought that his athletic career had come to an end. He was looking forward to going on to law school and his mother and father were delighted when he was accepted by Boston University. George still had his military service ahead of him and he was going to enlist in the Marine Corps after graduation in June. It seemed that the football world had seen the last of the Paterno brothers.

Then, one day just before spring practice—in those days even Ivy League schools had six weeks of spring drills—was to begin at Brown, Coach Engle sought out Joe and asked, "How would you like to help out in spring practice? I would like you to work with a young freshman quarterback who I think has some potential."

Paterno agreed, mostly because he thought it would give him something to do in the spring. He had never given any thought to coaching as a possible career and, even then, it did not occur to him. However, typically, he tried to read every book on quarterbacks he could lay hands on, trying to learn how to coach the young Brown quarterback.

Shortly before the end of spring practice, a rumor swept the Brown campus that Rip Engle had been offered the head coaching job at Pennsylvania State University, a school somewhere up in the hills of central Pennsylvania. Paterno didn't pay much attention to all the talk because, after all, it didn't affect him; he was going to law school at Boston University. He was going to be a lawyer and he dreamed of becoming a big wheel back in Brooklyn. Maybe even District Attorney.

It turned out that the rumor was true. Penn State, in a coaching turmoil after the retirement of Bob Higgins in 1948, had offered the job to Rip Engle and he had accepted it, much to the chagrin of the folks at Brown. In his six years as the head coach, Rip had turned the Bruins into a winner and the alumni hoped that he would remain to continue the tradition. During that time, Engle had turned down opportunities to go to Yale, Wisconsin and Pittsburgh. Rip, however, felt that the challenge at Penn State was so great that he had to take it to prove to himself that he could be a winning coach on a higher level.

Although Engle was committed to retaining the entire Penn State coaching staff, he got permission to bring along at least one of his assistants at Brown.

"Penn State had been using the single wing and I wanted to install the wing-T I had been using at Brown. I wanted someone with me at Penn State who knew the offense," explained Rip.

Engle, however, drew a blank response when he asked several of his assistant coaches to join him at Penn State. Gus Zitraides, Rip's No. 1 assistant, was going to succeed him as the head coach at Brown. Weeb Ewbank and Bill Doolittle, who went on to become an assistant coach at Army under Colonel Earl Blaik and later Dale Hall and Paul Dietzel before becoming head coach at Western Michigan, both elected to stay at Brown. The other assistants, Bob Preasy, Jimmy Dunn and Alex Nahigian, a part-time coach and scout who had been a baseball and football star at Holy Cross, weren't interested either. They were not intrigued by the prospect of going off to what they thought was some cow college in the sticks of Pennsylvania.

Perhaps in desperation, Engle turned to his young quarterback, Joe Paterno. He sought out Joe and asked, "Would you like to go to Penn State with me to be one of my assistant coaches?"

Paterno was flabbergasted by the offer and, when he told some of his friends that Engle wanted him to be one of his assistants at Penn State, they were reluctant to believe him. He called his parents and his Dad encouraged him to take the job. His mother, however, greeted the whole proposition with disdain. "A coach?"

Mom Paterno asked. "What did you go to college for? You didn't have to go to college to be a coach."

Joe now had to think seriously about his future. Up until then, he was planning a career as a lawyer and, suddenly, a whole new world had opened up for him. He wasn't sure that was what he wanted to do in life but, after wrestling with the problem, he decided to accept Engle's unexpected offer. He thought he could try it for a year or two and then, if he didn't like coaching, he would go on to law school as he had planned.

Some folks, including Joe Paterno, thought Rip Engle had made a serious mistake in taking this raw, cocky young man, whose only exposure to coaching had been a brief stint with a freshman quarterback in spring practice, on as a member of his staff. But Engle had seen something in Joe Paterno and was certain that he had made a wise choice. One thing he remembered vividly was how his quarterback had inspired the Brown team in that final game against Colgate.

"I liked his attitude and enthusiasm," recalls Engle. "Joe was intelligent, he was a clear thinker, he was articulate, he was a great competitor, he was enthusiastic about whatever he did, he knew his football, and I had confidence in him. He was a winner. What else do you want in a human being?"

So, the die was cast for young Joe Paterno. Although he had some doubts about whether or not he really wanted to make football coaching—instead of the law—his life's work, he decided to take a chance on his future. As it turned out, it was a fortuitous gamble.

7: The Making of a Coach

WHEN RIP ENGLE and his new young assistant, Joe Paterno, headed westward from Providence, Rhode Island, to State College, Pennsylvania, in 1950, they both had things to think about. For Rip, then forty-two years old, coaching at Penn State would be the greatest challenge he had yet faced in his career. For Joe, it was an exciting adventure for a twenty-three-year-old college quarterback who, only weeks before, had never even given a thought to coaching. For both of them, it would turn out to be a mutual appointment with destiny.

It also was in the nature of a homecoming for Rip Engle, who was a native of Salisbury, Pennsylvania, and had coached at Waynesboro (Pennsylvania) High School for eleven years before going to Brown. Rip had gone to Waynesboro immediately after his graduation in 1930 from Western Maryland College, where he had played under Coach Dick Harlow, who later coached at Penn State and Harvard. At Western Maryland, Engle had lettered in football, basketball, baseball and tennis, captained the baseball and basketball teams and had been named an All-Maryland end in 1929, when his team was unbeaten and untied in

eleven games. Rip's teams at Waynesboro High had enjoyed unusual success, winning eighty-six games while losing only seventeen and tying five in eleven years. Three of his teams had been
unbeaten and untied and he had won eight conference championships.

Engle had gone to Brown as an assistant coach in 1942 and
moved up to the head coaching job in 1944. Success had come
slowly at Brown, Rip had become intrigued with the possibilities
of the wing-T offense, then reasonably new to college football,
and he installed it at Brown when he took over as the head coach.
His first four teams lost more games than they won (the record
was an uninspiring 13-17-4), but Engle's 1948 and 1949 clubs
won fifteen of their eighteen games, the only Bruin football teams
to do that well since 1932. It was this, and a firm recommendation
from Dick Harlow, Engle's old college coach who had coached
at Penn State from 1915 to 1917, that brought Rip to the attention of Penn State.

Although some folks at Brown, and in other parts of the
Eastern seaboard, regarded Penn State as "that cow college
somewhere in Pennsylvania," the Nittany Lions even then enjoyed
a prestigious place in Eastern football. Penn State had been
playing the game since 1887 under a handful of coaches who had
been eminently successful in producing winning teams. The 1922
club, coached by Hugo Bezdek, had gone to the Rose Bowl,
where it lost to the University of Southern California, 14-3, and
the unbeaten and untied 1947 team, coached by Bob Higgins, tied
Southern Methodist University, 13-13, in the Cotton Bowl.

Higgins, an All-America end at Penn State in 1919 and one
of the Nittany Lions' most celebrated football heroes, became
the head coach in 1930, succeeding Bezdek, and after a slow
start he had built Penn State into a respected football power.
State was playing—and beating—teams like Syracuse, Iowa,
Pittsburgh, Harvard, Columbia, Penn, Army, Navy, New York
University, Fordham, Washington State, Michigan State and
Nebraska. Higgins' best team was the 1947 one, which set two
NCAA records that still exist. It held its opponents to an average
of 17 yards per game rushing and the fewest rushing yards per
play—0.64. Steve Suhey, a guard on the '47 team, earned All-
America honors.

Despite his great success, Bob Higgins coached only one more year. He led the 1948 team to a fine 7-1-1 season and then announced that he was retiring after having served for nineteen years as the head coach. Higgins' decision, unhappily, produced a situation that most old Penn Staters would like to forget.

Two members of Higgins' staff, Joe Bedenk, who played for Bezdek back in the 1920's and was also the school's baseball coach, and Earl Edwards, a Penn State player in the late 1920's and early 1930's, were both active candidates for the job. Both had their supporters and pretty soon Penn State was a divided camp. Edwards had nominal support from Higgins and he also was backed by Al Michaels, Jim O'Hora and Earl Bruce, three other assistant coaches. Bedenk, however, had been coaching at Penn State since 1932 and powerful forces were working behind the scenes to secure his appointment. Bedenk won the battle, was named head coach and Edwards left to become an assistant at Michigan State. He later became the head coach at North Carolina State.

With Edwards gone and resentment still smoldering among the remaining members of his coaching staff, Bedenk hired Sever Toretti, a Pennsylvania high school coach, to handle the line and Frank Patrick, a former Pitt star who had played for the Chicago Cardinals and was then backfield coach for the Pittsburgh Steelers, to work with the backs. Michaels, O'Hora and Bruce remained on the staff. It was not a happy year. Penn State lost to Villanova, Army, Michigan State and Pitt, and at the end of the season Bedenk resigned as head coach but insisted on remaining on the staff as an assistant. Earl Bruce was named interim coach and handled the squad during spring practice.

That was the situation at Penn State when Rip Engle and his young assistant, Joe Paterno, arrived in 1950. Rip had been told that one of the conditions of his new job was that he was to retain the entire coaching staff, Bedenk included.

"That was very unusual," said Rip, "because usually a new coach is permitted to bring in his own staff. But I thought we could somehow make things work."

To Engle's credit, he "made things work" so well that, except for Bedenk, who retired from football coaching a few years later, and Michaels, who left to go with Edwards when Earl got the head coaching job at North Carolina State, the rest of the staff remained virtually intact throughout Engle's coaching days at Penn State and most of the same men are still there under Paterno. J. T. White, a former Michigan player, joined the staff in 1954 when Bedenk quit, and Dan Radakovich, a former Penn State player, was added to coach the linebackers in 1960. Radakovich subsequently left after the 1969 season to become defensive coordinator at the University of Cincinnati.

There were only two changes in the staff during Engle's sixteen-year tenure. Both occurred in 1963, when Toretti, who handled the offensive line, was moved up to the post of assistant to the athletic director and became the Athletic Department's chief recruiter. Toretti was replaced by Joe McMullen, who had played for Engle at Brown in the 1940's. (McMullen left in 1969 to become the head coach at San Jose State.) Just before the start of the '63 season, George Welsh, former Navy quarterback, was added to the coaching staff. O'Hora, Patrick and Bruce all have retired but White is still at Penn State.

Joe Paterno, although a neophyte in coaching, had no compunction about inserting himself into this kind of a situation. Because of his previous close contact with Engle, he knew how Rip thought and felt about most things. When controversies arose in staff meetings, it was usually the cocky little guy from Brooklyn who spoke up, sometimes heatedly. "I was such a damn loudmouth, I couldn't keep quiet when I thought things weren't going right," remembers Joe.

There were many arguments between young Paterno and Bedenk, who very often did not see eye-to-eye with other members of the staff, either. "Joe never hesitated to speak his mind," says Jim O'Hora, "and frequently the discussions became quite heated. Bedenk would usually wind up calling Joe a 'young whippersnapper.' "

"Rip did a fantastic job of getting that staff to work together," says Paterno. "He never imposed himself on anybody. He always let everybody have his say until, after awhile, they all discovered they were agreeing with him and with each other. I learned a great deal from Rip about how to handle people."

Actually, the Engle-Paterno reign began at Penn State in the late spring of 1950. Rip had agreed to make the move just after the conclusion of spring practice at Brown, but while drills were still going on at Penn State under the direction of Earl Bruce, Engle took Joe down to Penn State with him and they lived together in a home that Rip had bought adjacent to the campus. Engle still hadn't moved his wife, Sunny, and son, Charles Jr., or their furniture to State College, so the two men slept in bunk beds in an otherwise empty house.

"I'll never forget Rip telling me on the way down how much I would like Penn State, how clean it was, you could even eat off the floors in the barns," Joe recalls. "I'd never been in a barn in my life. They didn't have any barns in Brooklyn, and I guess I was impressed anyway."

Life in State College proved to be a lot different than life in Brooklyn, or even Providence, for young Joe Paterno. His beloved Brooklyn Dodgers were several hundred miles away, no one would dream of playing stickball in the tree-lined streets and, since he wasn't much of a swinger anyway, night life was nonexistent.

After about three months of this monastic living, Paterno told Engle, "You'd better start looking around for another coach because I'm getting out of here. I'll go nuts in this town."

Then Joe moved in with Steve Suhey and his wife, Ginger, who was the daughter of Bob Higgins. The Suheys lived in a two-bedroom apartment on High Street. Suddenly things began to look up socially for Joe. Suhey, who had played awhile for the Pittsburgh Steelers, and Ginger had loads of friends, and many of Steve's former teammates used to drop by for a beer and some conversation. Paterno got to know a lot of people around town and he began to get a feel for Penn State and its football tradition. He was impressed with the kind of youngsters who attended the university and found them to be quite different from the usual run of students he had met at Brown.

"They were friendlier and more serious about getting an education," Joe says. "There was a much more wholesome attitude. Most of them came from poor or middle-class homes and they weren't snooty like so many kids I had come in contact with at Brown."

So Paterno decided to stick it out at Penn State with Rip Engle for at least a year. He was assigned to work with the quarterbacks and quickly showed how astute he was. When Engle asked him which one of three competing quarterbacks was the best, he replied, "I'll tell you one thing. Vince O'Bara will never be a starting quarterback."

O'Bara started at quarterback in evey game that year.

"That was my first great prediction," says Joe. "The second was that Jimmy Brown would never make it as a pro."

The 1959 season hardly started out as a howling success for the new Penn State regime. The Nittany Lions, still getting used to Coach Rip Engle's wing-T formation, beat Georgetown in their opening game but then lost three straight to Army, Syracuse and Nebraska before playing a 7-7 tie with Temple. Things improved after that and Penn State won its last four games, including a spectacular 21-20 victory over Pitt in the finale to finish with a 5-3-1 record.

It was after that first season that Paterno achieved his first notice as a quipster. Following the last game, he was asked to speak at a meeting of the Quarterback Club. Bob Higgins introduced him as one of the new coaches at Penn State and then needled, "By the way, son, what *do* you coach?"

"I'm the pass interception coach," replied Joe, and that broke up the gathering.

Joe's baptismal year as a football coach was over and now he had to make a decision about how he wanted to spend the rest of his life. He went home to Brooklyn for Christmas and talked over his problem with his father.

"What do you really want to do?" asked Mr. Paterno.

"I think I like coaching," replied Joe, "but there's no money in it. I'm only making $3,600 a year."

"Well," said Mr. Paterno, "I've never made any real money, but I'm doing what I want to do and I think that's more important than money. If you like coaching, Joe, stay with it."

Mr. Paterno's advice was what Joe wanted to hear. He returned to Penn State after Christmas vacation and told Engle that he had decided to make coaching his career. Naturally, Rip was delighted. He had seen something in this bright young man and was convinced that Paterno had the potential to become a good football coach.

The next season, 1951, Engle decided that he wanted his football players all together so that he could control their study habits and would always know where they were. Rip asked the administration to set aside two floors in a dormitory for them and, since Paterno was a bachelor, he made him the dorm counselor, or as some of the players called him, the "house mother." In addition to his policing duties, he was supposed to give tutoring aid to those who needed it, and in those days, even Joe admits that there were a lot of Penn State football players who needed help with their studies. The year turned out to be a nightmare for Joe and, more than anything else, convinced him that an athletic dorm for football players was a huge mistake.

Engle and his staff had recruited well and among the freshmen that year were players like Jesse Arnell, Rosey Grier and a big end named Joe Yukica. Arnell became one of the finest athletes in Penn State history while Grier gained fame as a pro tackle for the New York Giants and Los Angeles Rams before going into show business, and Yukica eventually was named the head football coach at Boston College. They were a hell-raising bunch and Paterno had his hands full riding herd on them. Poker was the favorite after-dark sport and some of them liked to play until the wee hours of the morning. But Joe, who was only a few years older than most of the players, banned the games.

Things were quiet for about two weeks and, then, one night Paterno was awakened about 3 A.M. by the sound of raucous laughter. He got out of bed, walked down the corridors, looking under the doors for a sign of light. It was all dark and Joe headed back for his room. Suddenly he heard a laugh and it seemed to be coming from the bathroom. He yanked open the door and there were about ten of his football players, enjoying their poker game. They had placed blankets on the floor of the shower stall, drawn the curtain and made it their own private gaming room.

"I found out that they had all been going to bed about eight o'clock every night, setting their alarm clocks for 1 A.M., and then playing poker in the shower for the rest of the night," said Joe. "I didn't get much sleep the rest of *that* year."

Paterno's experience soured him on athletic dorms. First, he learned that the players resented being set apart from the rest of the students. They referred to this dorm as "our cage" and to themselves as "animals." They had the idea, too, that they were entitled to and were being given special treatment, when this was not the case. Also, they seemed to resent the supervision.

"The players rarely got a chance to mingle with their fellow students," complained Joe. "It just wasn't right to deprive them of the best part of their college life. That's when I made up my mind that I would never have an athletic dorm if I ever became a head coach."

It also convinced Engle that his noble experiment was not so noble and the next season the whole idea was abandoned.

Meanwhile, Paterno was busy coaching the Penn State quarterbacks, for better or for worse. Tony Rados, a transfer from Notre Dame, was the quarterback in 1951, 1952 and 1953. Rados, a tall boy with a great arm, still holds Penn State career records for the most passes (425) and the most completions (199). But he was not much of a runner. He was too slow and, besides, had a bad knee. Rados was still learning his trade, under Paterno's tutelage, in 1951 when the Lions had a 5-4 season, but Tony began to develop the next year and so did football at Penn State. The Lions lost only to Michigan State and Syracuse and tied Purdue while winning seven games.

Just about then, Rip Engle got his first superstar, a quick, slippery runner named Lenny Moore, who teamed up with Rados in the backfield in 1953 to give Penn State a one-two punch it had lacked up until then. Also, the football rules committee decided to outlaw two-platoon football that same year and it forced some changes in the way Penn State played the game. Rados, suddenly, had to play both ways and he was placed at halfback on defense.

"Rados had problems," recollects Paterno. "He had that bad knee and he was so slow anyway that, when the ball was snapped, he would begin back-pedaling toward his own goal line. He wasn't going to let anyone get behind him."

Penn State opened the 1953 season with Wisconsin and the Badgers had the great Alan "The Horse" Ameche, an All-America, at fullback. But Ameche also had to play defense for the first time and Coach Ivy Williamson made him an outside linebacker in his 5-3 defense. The Penn State coaches heard about it and they decided that their game plan would be to run at Ameche early and often, hoping that he would get so weary he wouldn't be able to run the ball at full speed against them. Rados was given his instructions by Paterno, who then went up to the press box to work on the phones. Rados followed the game plan to the letter. On the first play, he called for a line back on Ameche's side and, zap, the Nittany Lions had second down and 12 yards to go. On the next play, Penn State's wingback and end double-teamed Ameche on a power play off tackle. No gain. Then Rados called for a trap play but Ameche broke through to nail the ball carrier for a 3-yard loss.

Rados came out of the game, rushed to the phone and yelled to Paterno up in the press box, "Hey coach, you know what you can do with your game plan!"

Wisconsin beat Penn State 20-0 that day and the Lions also lost their second game, to Penn, 13-7. But then Rados began clicking on his passes and Moore began to show the great talent that later was to make him one of the most feared runners in the National Football League when he played for the Baltimore Colts. The Lions lost only one more game, a 20-19 decision to West Virginia.

However, Coach Engle, Paterno, his quarterback coach, and Rados were criticized by sportswriters and Penn State fans because Tony wouldn't throw passes to Moore. Rip defended both Paterno and Rados, saying lamely, "Lenny can't catch the ball. His hands are too small."

Moore's hands weren't "too small" when he got to the Baltimore Colts. He turned out to be one of the NFL's most talented pass receivers. The truth of the matter, though, was that Engle was really trying to protect Moore. Lenny, who frequently played as flanker in a double wing formation, just wouldn't run pass patterns when he was at Penn State.

"Lenny loafed going out of the backfield," says Paterno, "and Rados could never judge his speed. So, he just wouldn't throw to him."

Despite this, Lenny Moore turned out to be one of the greatest runners in Penn State football history before he finished his varsity career in 1955. He still holds five school rushing records—1,082 yards for one season; 2,380 yards for his career; 19.8-yard average for a single game; 8-yard per carry average for one season; and a 6.2-yard per carry average for his career. Two more of his career records—25 touchdowns and 454 rushing attempts—lasted for fourteen years until they were broken by Charlie Pittman in 1969.

Paterno, meanwhile, had become quite friendly with Jim O'Hora, his coaching colleague, and accepted an invitation to live with him and his wife, Bets. The O'Horas had just moved into a small new home and, although their living space was limited, they made room for Joe. It was a liaison that lasted for almost ten years and, during that time, the two men became close friends. They were a contrast in moods and temperaments. O'Hora, ten years older, was easygoing, more passive in nature and inclined to be conciliatory rather than combative. Paterno was impetuous, impatient and critical of those who did not agree with him. He had a fiery temper and a short fuse, which usually became ignited at the slightest provocation. There were many times when Jim had to calm down his younger friend and he never hesitated to tell him when he thought he was wrong or out of line.

Their common interest in football bound them together in a fast friendship that has endured even though Paterno later became O'Hora's boss. The two men spent endless hours discussing football, replaying games, evaluating players, figuring out strategy and new techniques and arguing the relative merits of offenses and defenses. Since O'Hora was coaching the defense and Paterno was involved with the offense, they learned from each other. They rejoiced together when Penn State won and agonized together when the Nittany Lions lost.

In fact, even now, as the head coach, Joe often seeks out Jim to discuss problems with him. "Jim probably is the one guy who has had more influence on my coaching and my personality than anyone else," Joe claims. "Without Jim O'Hora I never would have survived at Penn State. He fought battles for me, he defended me, he even gave up friendships for me. I know that some people stopped inviting Bets and Jim because they felt they would have to invite me, too, and they didn't want me around. I'm certain there were some folks who thought I was too cocky, too outspoken. In those early days, I was frustrated because we couldn't get things going faster. I wanted Rip to move faster, to get rid of people, to change things. I felt we weren't driving hard enough, that we weren't doing enough things fast enough. I was impatient for success and always moaning and complaining. Rip was doing it his way, which proved to be the right way in the long haul. Jim would sit and listen to me while I poured out my heart. He would point out where I was wrong. He encouraged me to be patient."

Despite O'Hora's encouragement, Paterno's patience wasn't always evident. Nor was he always tactful in his criticism of others. But now that he had decided to make coaching his life's work, the intensity of his interest in football increased. He spent all of his waking moments thinking about and learning football. He watched game films for hours every night. He analyzed every mistake and knew the capabilities of each member of the squad. Bright and questioning, he absorbed things quickly and his inventive imagination worked overtime in developing new ideas and techniques.

"Joe was always a step ahead of the rest of us," says O'Hora. "He was probably the best prepared among the assistant coaches. He did his homework well."

Bets O'Hora, a kind, thoughtful woman, and the O'Hora children, Jimmy, Peggy and Donny, adopted Joe as a member of their family. They ate together, went out together, shared family secrets and, when the O'Horas moved to a larger home, Joe Paterno moved along with them. He was a bachelor but he still enjoyed all the comforts and warmth of family life. As the years went on, Joe's bachelorhood became a matter of concern to the O'Horas. He dated occasionally but never seriously and he never permitted his social life to interfere with his football. Finally, in 1961, Jim tactfully suggested to Joe that perhaps now was the proper time for him to have a home of his own. O'Hora told him, "When I was a kid I remember relatives coming over from Ireland and moving in with my family. They would stay a year and then leave us to get married." Paterno took the hint and quickly found an apartment. As it turned out, he had also found a girl friend.

"I know it was a move I should have made a lot earlier," reflects Joe, "but the O'Horas were like my own family and I liked living with them. I will always be grateful to Bets and Jim for their kindness and understanding. They got me over a lot of rough spots."

Paterno continued to work with the Penn State quarterbacks. He was given complete charge by Engle, who made it a practice never to interfere with the areas assigned to his assistant coaches. A stickler for the smallest of details, Joe worked his charges hard. Rados' successor in 1954 was to be a young sophomore named Milt Plum, who later persuaded Tom Cahill, the present Army coach, to come to River Dell High School in New Jersey when Wayne was the superintendent of schools there. Joe was sent to Woodbury to recruit Plum and he was impressed by the strapping 6-foot-2, 195-pound youngster who could throw the ball a country mile.

Plum was invited to visit Penn State for a weekend and he stayed overnight at the Phi Delta Theta fraternity house. The next day Paterno took him over to Rip Engle's house to introduce him to the head coach. After the usual conversation about the virtues of attending Penn State and playing football for the Nittany Lions, Rip asked Plum if he had any questions.

"Yes, Coach," replied Milt. "I saw some kids drinking and smoking in the fraternity house last night. I don't drink or smoke and I'm just wondering if I have to start doing that to get along in college."

Engle, one of the great teetotalers of all time but an expert connoisseur of soft drinks, looked at the young man in amazement. "I'm glad to hear you say that," said Rip. "That's a decision you're going to have to make all your life and you might as well start right now. I don't drink, but I have a lot of friends who do and I enjoy being with them. You're going to have friends who drink, too, but that doesn't mean you have to do it. You can do anything you want."

Despite his natural talent for throwing the ball, Plum was not an immediate superstar at Penn State. "He was a great natural thrower but he never knew where to throw the ball," says Paterno. "He had the same problems most big quarterbacks have, he didn't know how to use his legs. He didn't know how to stride properly and, as a result, he was always throwing off balance. His biggest problem, though, was that he was confused most of the time. He didn't have confidence in himself."

Plum's competition for the quarterback job in 1954 was a senior named Don Bailey, who had played for Nick Skorich at

Central Catholic High School in Pittsburgh. When Bailey came to Penn State for a tryout, which was permitted in those days, Paterno was not impressed. "He had the smallest hands you ever saw for a quarterback," says Joe. "His hands hardly came up to my knuckles."

Bailey had played defense for three years and Paterno still didn't think he could make the grade at quarterback. So Milt Plum was installed as the quarterback for the opening game against an Illinois team that had J. C. Caroline and Nate Woodson and was being touted as the national champion. Plum had trouble moving the team and Penn State was behind. Finally, in desperation, Engle decided to use Bailey over Paterno's protest.

"I didn't want to use him," said Joe. "You never knew what he was going to do. He was the kind of quarterback who would go back to pass, have perfect follow through and you'd be looking downfield for the ball but it had fallen off his small hand and was lying on the ground. He was a tough runner but the only trouble was we would be running an option play to the left and he'd come out of the backfield running to the right."

In spite of Paterno's dark prognosis, Bailey got the Nittany Lions moving and they upset Illinois, 14-12. From then on he was the starting quarterback and he led Penn State to a 7-2 season. West Virginia and Texas Christian University were the only teams to defeat the Lions that season. Still, Paterno was not impressed and he was surprised when Bailey was chosen to be the backup quarterback to Ralph Guglielmi, Notre Dame's All-America, in the East-West game in San Francisco. As luck would have it, Guglielmi became ill and couldn't play so Bailey was the East quarterback. All he did, while Paterno nervously watched the game with his brother, George, on television back in Brooklyn, was play so well that he was named the Most Valuable Player in the game!

"That really proved how much I knew about quarterbacks," laughs Joe.

Meanwhile, Paterno worked diligently with Milt Plum, trying to correct his faults and to instill some confidence in him. He corrected his stride, taught him how to pick out his receivers and encouraged him to believe in himself. Joe was tough on his pupil, though, and there were times when Plum wondered if it was worth the effort. There were even more doubts in Milt's mind when Penn State barely managed to break even in its first six games in 1955. Plum hardly looked like the quarterback who was to go on to enjoy a long career with the Cleveland Browns.

Milt finally emerged from his shell of mediocrity in the seventh game of the season, against Syracuse, in one of the greatest contests ever played on old Beaver Field. That was the game that pitted Lenny Moore against Jimmy Brown in a spectacular running duel. The ball went up and down the field like a yo-yo as Moore and Brown tore up the turf. Lenny run for 142 yards, Brown piled up 132 yards, but it was Plum's direction and passing that contributed to a 21-20 victory for Penn State.

From that game on, Milt Plum was a big-league quarterback, thanks to Paterno's patience and coaching. Under the constant prodding of Paterno, Plum acquired confidence in himself as well as the confidence of his teammates. In 1956, Milt had his finest hour against Ohio State in Columbus. Coach Woody Hayes' Buckeyes were unbeaten and ranked among the leaders in the country. They were heavily favored to beat the lightly regarded visitors from the East. A great Penn State defense, led by Sam Valentine, an All-America guard, held Ohio State to a single touchdown and the Nittany Lions upset the shocked Bucks, 7-6. Plum was a big factor in the game, running 20 yards on a quarterback sneak to set up a touchdown and then kicking the winning extra point. Penn State lost to Army and Syracuse and was tied by Pitt, but its final record was 6-2-1.

Perhaps the best of all the Penn State quarterbacks coached by Joe Paterno was Richie Lucas, the only one to make All-America. Richie, a handsome, dark-haired young man, was overlooked by most schools when he played for Glassport (Pennsylvania) High School. The No. 1 prospect in the state was Jerry Eisman of Bethel High, who was being chased by dozens of schools. Another highly regarded quarterback was Ross Fichtner of McKeesport. However, Paterno was looking at films of Eisman's games when, suddenly, he saw this rangy youngster from Bethel running, passing and playing defense. He looked mighty good and Paterno reported this information back to Coach Engle. "Let's go after both of them," declared Rip.

By this time the word got around that Penn State was interested in Richie Lucas. Pitt also wanted him, so the chase was on for Eisman, Fichtner and Lucas. Eisman had already told Penn State he was coming to University Park and Paterno practically attached himself to the Lucas family. Joe would drop in from time to time, just to see how Richie was getting along and, hopefully, to discourage the opposition. Many times, however, he met Vic Fusia, then an assistant coach at Pitt and later the head coach at the University of Massachusetts, coming or going. Joe appeared in the Lucas' kitchen so often that Mrs. Lucas got to consider him a regular at her dinner table. The perseverance paid off. Richie decided on Penn State, leaving Fusia and Pitt empty-handed, but Eisman changed his mind in August and went to Kentucky. Jerry is now an assistant coach at the University of Cincinnati. Fichtner had decided on the University of Miami but switched his allegiance to Purdue, where he made the Big Ten all-star team and then went on to become an outstanding defensive back with the professional Cleveland Browns.

"I made up my mind early that I wanted to go to Penn State," recalls Lucas. "For one thing, I liked Joe Paterno very much. He never tried to high-pressure me and I felt he was really interested in my welfare."

Joe was delighted with his new recruit. What he liked most about Richie was his daring, his willingness to gamble. Perhaps Paterno saw a bit of himself in Richie. Joe worked long hours with him, correcting his passing flaws, sharpening up his play-calling and polishing his technique.

In 1957, Lucas began his sophomore year as the backup quarterback to Al Jacks, an unspectacular but highly efficient player who did everything mechanically right. However, Jacks hurt his shoulder and Lucas got his big chance against Syracuse in a game which was shown on national television. Richie, who had a flair for making the big play, made the most of the opportunity. He was not an especially talented passer but he managed to get the ball on target. He was particularly deadly on short passes. His forte was running and he did that like a halfback. Quick and tough, he could hammer the line inside or go outside on sweeps and options with equal skill. Richie also played defense and was the surest tackler on the team. Just to keep busy, he did the punting, too.

Lucas tore off a couple of long runs against Syracuse, tantalized the Orange with his short passes and led Penn State to a 20-12 win. After that, the starting job was his but it wasn't all roses for Richie. The last game of the season, against Pitt, was a personal disaster. He couldn't do anything right and Pitt won, 14-13. The next year, though, when Penn State posted a 6-3-1 record, Richie Lucas began to receive some national recognition as one of the nation's premier quarterbacks.

Lucas' success was a personal triumph for Joe Paterno, but he was restless. Although Joe had been reasonably happy at Penn State, once he made up his mind that football coaching was to be his career, he was impatient to get ahead in his field. He had written to Jim Tatum at the University of North Carolina, Colonel Earl Blaik at Army and Bud Wilkinson at Oklahoma, inquiring about job possibilities, but no one seemed to be interested in him. However, in 1958 he saw a golden opportunity when the University of Southern California offered the head coaching job to Rip Engle. Rip considered the offer very seriously and even made a trip to Los Angeles to discuss the job. Upon his return, he talked it over with several members of his staff he thought he might take along with him. Among them were Paterno and O'Hora. Jim, after giving the matter due thought, decided that he preferred to remain at Penn State but Joe, bubbling with ambition, saw this as a chance to coach at a more prestigious football school.

Paterno tried desperately to persuade Engle that this was their chance to get into the big time. He was impressed by the glamour of Los Angeles and he cited the advantages, both professional and financial, of coaching at a university in a large city. But Rip decided to turn down the bid from USC and Joe was a sorely disappointed young man. But Paterno didn't let that interfere with his coaching. He thought he had an All-America in Richie Lucas and he set out to prove it.

The All-America bandwagon started when Coach Engle stated flatly, "Richie Lucas is the best all-around football player in the country." Jim Tarman, then Penn State's capable sports information director, took it from there. He nicknamed Lucas the "Riverboat Gambler," a tribute to his willingness to take chances, and had a publicity picture taken of Richie, an infectious grin splitting his boyish face, all decked out in a striped shirt, derby, garters on his sleeves and holding a royal flush in his hand. The picture, along with Engle's quote and a publicity blurb full of flowery prose describing Lucas' talent, was sent all over the country. What made the "Riverboat Gambler" tag a real natural was that Penn State's opening game in 1959 was to be played against Missouri in Columbia, hard by the Mississippi River. The All-America buildup was on.

Rip Engle, naturally, was more interested in taking full advantage of Lucas' skills as passer and runner. Paterno was full of ideas about that and he made some suggestions to Engle. The result was that Rip changed his entire offense. He went to a double slot formation so that Lucas could run the option play either way behind the excellent blocking of Fullback Pat Botula. Richie would sprint out wide and, if the opposing end was knocked down, he would keep the ball and run. If the defense came up, he would flip a short pass into the flat. It was a devastating type of offense, especially with someone like Richie Lucas handling the ball.

Lucas had one of his greatest days against Missouri. He dazzled the Tigers with his running, completed ten of eleven passes and Penn State won, 19-8. He had another big game against Army and the Nittany Lions beat the Cadets, 17-11, for the first time in sixty years. For that performance, Richie was picked as Back of the Week by *Sports Illustrated*. Penn State won its first seven games and then faced Syracuse, also unbeaten and pointing toward the national championship. Syracuse was ranked No. 4, Penn State No. 7.

The night before the game, Joe Paterno and Jim Tarman hosted a group of visiting sportswriters for dinner at Duffy's Tavern in Boalsburg, a neighboring community. Jesse Abramson of the *New York Herald Tribune* and Len Elliott of the *Newark Evening News* both said to Paterno, "On paper, tomorrow's game should be no contest. Syracuse should win. Do you think you have a chance?"

"Well," replied Joe, "here's what we have to do to stay with them. We have to intercept three passes, run back a kick for a touchdown, block a punt and get a quick score. If we do all that, we have a chance to beat Syracuse."

The next day, Penn State scored first. Roger Kochman ran back a kickoff 100 yards for a touchdown, the Nittany Lions blocked a punt and intercepted three passes, and Richie Lucas and his teammates almost spoiled Syracuse's chances for the national title. Penn State barely lost, 20-18, as Ernie Davis, another All-America, proved to be just a little too much for the aroused Lions. Syracuse, one of the finest teams ever put together, went on to a No. 1 ranking and the national championship.

Joe Paterno's clairvoyance in assessing what Penn State had to do to stay in the game astounded Abramson and Elliott. But Joe had forgotten to mention one other little thing—extra points —and that cost Penn State the game!

One thing Richie Lucas had was confidence. Although, inexplicably, he had never played well against Pitt, he assured Paterno that he had nothing to worry about as the team came up to its final game with its old rival.

"Don't worry, Coach, we're three touchdowns better than they are," said Richie confidently.

"That's what worries me," replied Paterno.

"Nah, we're not going to blow this one," said Lucas.

But Richie and his teammates did blow it. Only minutes after the opening kickoff, Lucas was nailed in his own end zone for a safety and Pitt led, 2-0. Then the Panthers got a touchdown for a 9-0 lead. Pitt won the game, 22-7, and even Richie Lucas was silent in the locker room.

Penn State's 8-2 record in 1959 earned it an invitation to play Alabama in the first Liberty Bowl in Philadelphia's Municipal Stadium on a freezing, blustery day in December. It was Coach Bear Bryant's first year at 'Bama and the Crimson Tide had lost only one game. Lucas was hurt early in the game, but not before he had saved the Lions, when they were backed up to their own 4-yard line, with a 40-yard run. Richie's sub, Galen Hall, threw a screen pass from a fake place-kick formation—which Coach Engle had put into the Penn State repertoire only the day before the game—and Penn State beat Alabama, 7-0.

Richie Lucas made almost every All-America team at the end of the season, was awarded the Maxwell Trophy as the outstanding college player of the year and acclaimed everywhere as one of the finest quarterbacks in Penn State history. The pros, however, had their own ideas about his abilities. Lucas was drafted by the Washington Redskins of the National Football League— as a defensive back. But the Buffalo Bills of the AFL also drafted him as a quarterback and he signed with them. After two unhappy years, he returned to Penn State to work on the Altoona campus and then came back to University Park to become Assistant Business Manager of Athletics.

Even now, Richie Lucas is effusive in his praise of Joe Paterno as his quarterback coach. "The thing I appreciated more than anything else is the fact that Joe never criticized me in front of the other players. We had a conversational relationship. If he disagreed with a play I called, he'd tell me about it privately and then he would hear out my reasons for it. It gave me confidence. Joe was a very basic person, even then. He didn't worry about what caused a problem, he was more concerned with getting to the root of it. Joe was always fair and he treated his players like responsible adults. All he asked from you was to give all you had to offer.

"I learned so much from him, not only about football but about life itself. He helped me to find out what I knew and who I was."

Many Penn State athletes in the last twenty years have felt the same way about Joe Paterno. He recruited extensively and frequently was the first contact a high school prospect had with Penn State. Some liked him, others disliked him, but most of them agree that they stood a little taller, learned a little more and were better men for their association with Joe Paterno.

8: The Quarterback Maker

RECRUITING WAS AN IMPORTANT PART of Joe Paterno's job at Penn State and one of his favorite antagonists was Vic Fusia, when Vic was an assistant at Pitt under Coach John Michelosen. Fusia was smooth in his approach, well-spoken, articulate and a worthy adversary. Because the two Pennsylvania schools were usually going after the same high school players, Paterno and Fusia often found themselves in head-to-head competition. They had one other thing in common. Joe and Vic both would go looking for good Italian restaurants whenever they were on the road.

On one occasion, Paterno and Fusia were both trying to recruit Matt Szykowny and Dick Turici, the stars of the North Catholic High School team in Pittsburgh. Szykowny, a quarterback, and Turici, a fullback, also were being heavily recruited by at least a dozen other schools, including the University of Iowa. Szykowny was the prize of the package and Paterno wanted him desperately. He was the kind of quarterback, Joe thought, who could win for Penn State.

One day Paterno got a phone call from Szykowny's high school coach, who told him, "I think Matt is leaning toward Penn State.

The senior prom is coming up and if you could get somebody to lend him a car, that would really clinch it for you."

In those days, less concerned with the niceties of recruiting than he is now, Paterno would have done almost anything to get a player. So Joe called a Penn State alumnus who owned a Dodge agency in Pittsburgh, explained the circumstances to him and asked if he had a car he could let Szykowny and Turici use for their senior prom.

"Sure," replied the alumnus. "I'll give them a fancy convertible to use."

Paterno was sure now that he was going to get Szykowny. The youngster would be impressed by the sharp car and would come rushing to Penn State. Well, it didn't quite work out that way. Several weeks later, Joe learned that both Szykowny and Turici were going to Iowa.

"I can't prove it," Joe says, "but I am certain that Iowa gave Szykowny a money deal to go there."

Shortly afterwards, Paterno bumped into his old friend, Fusia, on the recruiting trail and they were commiserating with each other over a bowl of spaghetti on the loss of Matt Szykowny, who went on to become one of the most prolific passers in Iowa history.

"Gee, I thought we had him," said Vic.

"You thought you had him?" countered Joe. "I was sure we had him. You know what I did for that kid? I even got him a car to use for his senior prom."

"You did?" replied Fusia. "Well, do you know where he went with that car after the prom? I sent those kids and their dates to the Holiday House, the most expensive night club in town, and told the manager to send me the bill!"

Obviously, Szykowny and Turici had not been impressed enough by either the car supplied by Paterno or the night club entertainment supplied by Fusia.

Recruiting was not always very subtle—or very legal—in Joe Paterno's early days at Penn State. For instance, in Paterno's first summer at State College, he got word from Chick Werner, then the track coach, that he ought to go after a lad named A. C. Jenkins from Mansfield, Ohio. In addition to being an outstanding football player, Jenkins was also a great hurdler and sprinter, and the boy's high school coach, an old college team-mate of Werner's at the University of Illinois, told Chick he thought Jenkins might like to go to Penn State. The only trouble was that Jenkins had spent the summer working out at the University of Toledo and the Rockets weren't about to let him off campus.

"I was just a fresh kid out of college," says Paterno, "and I didn't know anything about this big-time recruiting. But we were really desperate for football players and Rip Engle told me to go ahead and try to get him."

Paterno and Steve Suhey drove to Toledo, armed only with good intentions and the name of a Penn State alumnus, a former college wrestler, who was an attorney in the city. When they arrived, Joe called the Penn State grad, identified himself as one of Rip Engle's assistants and asked for help in recruiting A. C. Jenkins.

"I'd like to help you," replied the man, "but I don't think it would be ethical. You see, I'm also the wrestling coach at Toledo."

Now Paterno knew he had to act quickly. He located Jenkins in his dorm, made an appointment to meet him at a nearby drug-store and, when the boy arrived, invited him to go for a ride. The ride ended in Mansfield, where Paterno and Suhey talked to Jenkins' folks and got permission to take A. C. up to State College.

It was now late August and Joe stashed Jenkins away in a room with Earl Mundell, another football player. Mundell had strict instructions to let Paterno know if anyone came around asking about Jenkins. One day, A. C. didn't show up for practice and Mundell reported that he couldn't find him.

"What happened," says Paterno, "was that the Toledo folks had stolen him back from us."

Paterno and Earl Bruce, the freshman coach, spent endless hours on the road, scouring the hills and coal mines of Pennsylvania and the flatlands of New Jersey for promising high school football players. Earl, who was Paterno's senior by some twenty years, provided the father image while Joe was the youthful coach who had a knack for buddying up to prospective recruits. They made a good team.

One spring, Joe and Earl spent considerable time trying to recruit Emil Caprara, a tough fullback from Turtle Creek, Pennsylvania, who came from a talented football family. One brother had played at Notre Dame and another had been a star at Georgia. Caprara had shown some interest in Penn State but he also was considering the University of Maryland. In fact, he spent the next summer working in Washington, D.C., in a job secured for him by the Maryland people.

Meanwhile, Paterno and Bruce also had become impressed with Ron Markowitz, a youngster who played for nearby Braddock High. Markowitz had been the star of a summer all-star game in Pittsburgh but he had already announced that he, too, was going to Maryland.

Despite this, Paterno and Bruce decided late in the summer that they were going to try to steal Caprara and Markowitz away from Maryland. They drove down to Turtle Creek, invited Caprara to visit Penn State for the weekend, and he agreed. Emil also told them he thought Ron Markowitz would like to come, too.

That was all right with Joe and Earl. They put Caprara in the car and set out for Markowitz's home, twelve miles away. As they were driving along, another car approached from the opposite direction and Caprara suddenly ducked his head and hit the floor.

"Gee," he yelled, "that was Jack Hannameyer, the Maryland assistant coach. I bet he's up here to see Markowitz and me."

"We took off like a shot," recalls Paterno. "We raced over to Markowitz's house, bundled him into the car and then spent the next five or six hours driving all over the area. We rode past Ronnie's house a couple of times and, sure enough, Hannameyer's car was parked outside. We had lunch, ice cream sodas, hamburgers, dinner, anything to kill time until Hannameyer got tired of waiting for Ronnie."

Finally, the coast was clear and the party returned to Markowitz's house. Paterno and Bruce got permission from Ronnie's parents for him to spend the weekend at Penn State. The cloak-and-dagger ploy worked. Caprara and Markowitz enrolled at Penn State and they both had respectable football careers.

Paterno wasn't always so successful in spiriting players away from other schools. There was the case of Mike Ditka, a big, raw-boned end from Aliquippa, Pennsylvania, who told Joe that he was coming to Penn State. Paterno got him a high-paying summer job with Michael Baker, Jr., a Penn State alumnus who owned a consulting engineering firm in Rochester, Pennsylvania. But Pitt kept working on Ditka all summer long and Mike switched his allegiance to the hated Panthers. Penn State thus lost a player who went on to become an All-America and the best tight end in the National Football League for almost a decade.

The Ditka affair wasn't a total loss for Paterno, however. During the recruiting battle, he had the privilege of meeting Carroll "Beano" Cook, the Pitt sports information director and a legend in his own time among college publicists. Beano, who eventually left Pitt to become the press director for ABC-TV's college football telecasts, was chauvinistic about Pitt football in those days and wasn't one bit bashful about letting folks know his sentiments.

That summer, after a scholastic all-star game in Pittsburgh, Paterno hosted a small party for Ditka and his family in Frankie Gustine's, a local restaurant. Joe was standing outside Gustine's waiting for Mike's younger brother, when Red Mack, another widely sought Pennsylvania high school player, came along and stopped to chat. Red had decided to go to Notre Dame and Joe wished him well.

When Mack left, a big burly guy with a crew cut came over to Paterno and said, "You know, that was Red Mack and he couldn't get into Pitt."

"Gee," replied Joe, facetiously, "he must really be dumb if he can't get into Pitt."

Paterno's new friend took the bait. "The guy became furious. He wanted to punch me in the nose," laughs Paterno. "I found out later his name was Beano Cook."

Since that episode, Paterno and Cook have enjoyed a pleasant relationship. Beano admires Joe for his coaching ability and his integrity as a coach. In fact, when he was at Pitt and doing a weekly television show in Johnstown, Pennsylvania, the irrepressible Cook told his TV audience, "If I was an athletic director, I would hire Joe Paterno as my football coach."

Needless to say, that went over big with Pitt's coach, John Michelosen.

One famous Pennsylvania athlete Paterno didn't try to recruit was Joe Willie Namath of Beaver Falls, who has since gained some notoriety as the swingingest of all pro quarterbacks. Namath, even then a free-wheeler who did his own thing whenever it pleased him, was the best high school quarterback in the state and his coach, Larry Bruno, was one of Paterno's best friends. But Joe wasn't interested in Joe Willie and didn't even bother to stop by Beaver Falls to talk with him.

"He wasn't a good student," says Joe frankly.

Penn State's recruiting got a big boost in 1963 when Sever Toretti left his coaching assignment to become assistant athletic director under Ernie McCoy. Actually, Toretti was to be the Athletic Department's chief recruiter and, although his work included other sports, notably basketball, his major interest was football. Tor, a swarthy, handsome man who had served his apprenticeship in the Pennsylvania high school ranks, was well equipped for his new post. He was completely dedicated to the program at Penn State, had an engaging personality that usually captured the parents of a prospect and he was articulate.

Toretti, Paterno and the other Penn State assistants, taking their cue from Notre Dame, were not above enlisting religion in their recruiting efforts, and a couple of Catholic priests were largely responsible for the Nittany Lions' getting Dennis Onkotz and Steve Smear, two of the brightest stars of the superb defense that lost only two games from 1967 through 1969.

Onkotz's mother wanted him to go to a college that was more accessible to his home in Northampton, Pennsylvania, and Princeton was high on the list. However, when Denny came up to State College for a visit, Jim O'Hora took him to mass at Our Lady of Victory Church and introduced him to the Very Rev. Stephen J. Gergel, who, it turned out, had grown up with Mrs. Onkotz.

It was a stroke of good luck for Penn State.

Father Gergel got into the recruiting act and he spent a lot of time trying to convince Mrs. Onkotz that Penn State was the only place for Denny. He eventually succeeded and Onkotz became one of the Lions' brightest stars.

Smear, who came from Johnstown, was first called to Paterno's attention by Bill Shearer, an old friend who lived in Johnstown. Bill kept in close touch with Smear but he had lots of competition from Notre Dame, particularly since Steve was a Catholic. Smear's mother owned a bar near St. Andrew's Church and was very active in church affairs. Her pastor was the Rev. Joseph H. Fleming, whose brother, the Very Rev. Patrick V. Fleming, coincidentally, was the pastor of Joe Paterno's church in State College.

Not even Notre Dame could beat that kind of an alliance.

It didn't take long for the two Father Flemings, with some help from Bill Shearer, to invoke their priestly charm on Steve's mother, Mrs. Detko, and Steve wound up at Penn State.

Even now, as the head coach, Paterno has a big hand in the recruiting at Penn State. One of his conquests was Steve Joachim, a tall quarterback from Haverford, Pennsylvania, who broke almost every one of the state's high school passing records in 1969. Joachim was sought after by more than 100 schools, including Notre Dame and Alabama.

"I visited Notre Dame and Alabama, but there's such a great difference between Penn State and the other schools that I never really had a choice," said Joachim. "When I visited Notre Dame, I was given a time when I could see Coach Ara Parseghian and I had to wait in line for my turn. When I finally got to see him, it was so impersonal.

"At Alabama, I was impressed by the football dorm but there wasn't really a personal touch. At Penn State, it was completely different. The people there seemed to really care about me and Coach Paterno made me feel at home, like I was part of his family. I felt he was interested in me as a person and not just as another high school quarterback. It was a warm kind of feeling and I knew that I wanted to spend my college years with someone like Coach Paterno."

Paterno's recruiting eventually brought him into occasional competition with his brother, George. After his discharge from the Marines in 1953, George spent the next four and one-half years working as a New York City detective but in 1958 he suddenly decided that what he really wanted was to be a football coach. He had watched Joe's activities with increasing interest and his appetite for the profession was whetted. He got a job at Brooklyn Prep as an assistant to his old high school coach, Zev Graham, and three years later moved to Clark High School in Westbury, Long Island.

Ironically, George became a head coach before his older brother. He joined Coach Chuck Mills' staff at the United States Merchant Marine Academy in Kings Point, Long Island, in 1964 and a year later he succeeded Mills in the top job. The Paterno brothers burned up the telephone wires talking football and many of their ideas and techniques were similar, although George didn't have the same kind of players at Kings Point as Joe had at Penn State. There was a vast difference in both quantity and quality. George's first three seasons as a head coach were unspectacular but his coaching paid off in 1968, when Kings Point posted an 8-1 record. That was the same year that Joe had his first unbeaten season at Penn State. George was satisfied but he was also restless. After all, Kings Point wasn't exactly the big time. So he left to take a job as offensive backfield coach under Coach Duffy Daugherty at Michigan State. But, two years later, George returned to Kings Point as head football coach and assistant to the athletic director.

To many, it seemed odd that George didn't join his brother at Penn State. They got along well together, their football philosophy was pretty much the same and it seemed like a natural alliance. But the Paternos, after talking it over at great length, agreed that it would not be a good idea for George to be working for Joe. It wasn't a question of "Joe being a nice guy to visit but I wouldn't want to work for him." George wanted to make his own career and he thought his presence at Penn State might put Joe in a peculiar position with the rest of his coaching staff.

It was a wise decision, but circumstances change and if Joe Paterno ever decides to cast his lot with professional football, a distinct possibility some time in the future, the brothers Paterno probably will be united and working together.

After Richie Lucas, there was a procession of quarterbacks, all under Joe Paterno's wing. There was Galen Hall, a little, fat, balding fellow who looked more like a second-string guard than a quarterback. In fact, Joe had some reservations about Hall when he recruited him. Galen had rolls of fat around his waist, was top heavy in the rear and waddled when he walked. He was supposed to be 6-foot-1 but was closer to 5-foot-8.

"Galen was the first 6-foot-1 guy I ever saw who came up to my chest," laughs Joe.

Despite his physical appearance, Hall turned out to be a blue-chip quarterback. He could pass and run, was a constant threat on the rollout and had the kind of confidence that Paterno liked. In fact, at the time, Joe called him the best sophomore quarterback he ever had at Penn State. Hall led the 1960 team back to the Liberty Bowl, where the Lions beat Oregon, 41-12, and then, in 1961, took them to the Gator Bowl, where they surprised Georgia Tech, 30-15. One of the stars of that team was Bob Mitinger, a husky end who was picked for the All-America team.

Then there was Pete Liske. Tall and rangy, Liske was perhaps the best pure passer of all the Penn State quarterbacks coached by Joe Paterno. In addition, he was a superb ball handler. But Liske almost didn't make it to University Park. When he was recruiting, Joe had to make a decision between two New Jersey boys, Liske, who played at Plainfield High School, and Gary Cuozzo, who was the star at Glen Ridge. Paterno advised Rip Engle to take Liske because he felt Pete had played against tougher competition. Cuozzo, of course, became a star at the University of Virginia and then the quarterback for the Minnesota Vikings after having served an apprenticeship as Johnny Unitas' substitute with the Baltimore Colts. Liske, after playing pro football in Canada, went with the Denver Broncos.

Liske's first varsity year was 1962, and that was perhaps the best team Rip Engle ever had at Penn State. With Liske passing, Halfback Roger Kochman running and End Dave Robinson leading a tough, talented defense, the Nittany Lions lost only to Army, 9-6, in a 9-1 season and then went to the Gator Bowl, where Florida beat them, 17-7. Kochman, a very fast superrunner, and Robinson, who went on to become an All-Pro star with the Green Bay Packers, both made All-America.

Liske was the quarterback again in 1962 and Penn State didn't fare quite so well, losing to old nemesis Army 10-7, Syracuse 9-0 and Pitt 22-21. But Pete was throwing as well as ever and finished his career with four Penn State records which still stand: 19 completions in a single game; a 56.2 percent average for a season and 54.9 percent for his career; and 24 touchdowns for his career.

Joe Paterno's magic had produced five outstanding quarterbacks—two of them, Milt Plum and Pete Liske, had gone into the pros—in the fourteen years he had been coaching at Penn State but, in 1964, it seemed that his luck had run out. He decided to go with Gary Wydman, a tall boy from New York who seemed to have all the necessary tools for success but hadn't looked good in the pre-season drills. Despite this, Paterno was convinced that the team would be able to win with Wydman. Coach Engle had always given Joe complete authority over the quarterbacks. Rip had complete confidence in all his assistants, relying upon their judgment and evaluation of the players they coached. Engle was even more reliant upon Joe's opinion, especially since Joe had just been named Associate Coach, and he agreed to go along with his decision to play Wydman at quarterback. But there was general disagreement among the other assistants and the arguments in meetings waxed hot and heavy.

It was apparent early in the season that Wydman couldn't do the job at quarterback. He threw interceptions, fumbled handoffs and generally played badly. Even worse, Penn State lost four of its first five games—to Navy 21-8, UCLA 21-14, Oregon 22-14 and Syracuse 21-14. The only victory was a 6-2 decision over a sub-par Army team at West Point, and Wydman had hardly been sensational in that game.

The heat was on Paterno to make a change. The people in town were bugging him, the other assistant coaches were at him constantly, the players were dropping broad hints and even Coach Engle was beginning to ask questions. But Joe stubbornly refused to bench Wydman for another quarterback. Part of the problem was he didn't think there was anyone else on the squad who could do any better.

"The worst thing you can do when you're losing is to start messing around with your quarterback," Joe insisted. "If we drop Wydman now, we'll just be going backwards. I'm sure he'll get better. He has the talent and one day he'll put it all together."

Tempers, especially Paterno's, were on edge over the situation all over Penn State. Things got so bad that Joe even lashed out at Sunny Engle, Rip's wife, when she cornered him one night at a cocktail party and suggested that he ought to replace Wydman. It was an indication of the extent of the furor over Wydman that this was the only time Sunny Engle ever became involved in a coaching problem.

"Don't you put in your two cents, Sunny," raged Paterno. "You don't know what you're talking about. If Rip wants to change quarterbacks, you tell Rip to come and see me himself."

Paterno stood firm, despite the increasing criticism, which frequently became nasty and derisive. His ability as a coach was questioned in almost every living room in State College and even his colleagues on the coaching staff were beginning to wonder about his judgment.

Suddenly, against West Virginia, Gary Wydman began to put it all together. His passes were accurate, his running was sharp and he handled the ball like a pro. The Nittany Lions won that game, 37-8, and then beat Maryland, 17-9. But Ohio State, unbeaten and ranked No. 2 in the nation, was coming up next and there didn't seem to be any way that Penn State could beat the powerful Buckeyes. Coach Woody Hayes had fashioned a team that was obviously headed for the Big Ten title and maybe even the national championship. But, in the back of Woody's mind was the nagging memory of a 7-6 upset scored over the Bucks by Penn State in 1956 and the fact that Ohio State had *never* beaten the Nittany Lions in three previous games.

The night before the game, Paterno, Jim Tarman and Jim O'Hora were having a beer in the cocktail lounge of the motel where they were staying in Columbus. They were making small talk but, eventually, the conversation got around to the Ohio State game.

"I know we can't possibly win," said Tarman, "but we're not going to be humiliated, are we?"

"We're going to shut out Woody," replied Joe matter-of-factly.

Tarman looked in disbelief at Paterno and Joe repeated, "We're going to shut out Woody."

"How do you figure *that*?" asked Tarman.

"Well," said Joe. "We've had one of the greatest weeks of practice I've ever seen at Penn State. We've put in some changes that will neutralize some of the things they do best on offense and we've scrapped our regular offense. We're going to use only a few basic plays. I really think we're going to shut out Ohio State. But don't tell anybody before the game that I said it."

Paterno need not have feared that Tarman would dare repeat his words. On the face of it, Joe's predictions sounded ridiculous. Ohio State's defense was one of the best in the country and its linebackers, Ike Kelley and Tom Bugel, were All-Americas. They had been wrecking everybody's offenses all year long. Woody Hayes also had his usual collection of line-smashing backs who crunched out yardage in his "three yards and a cloud of dust" attack. It was sheer folly even to consider that Penn State, with a mediocre 3-4 record, could beat the Bucks, much less shut them out!

The next day, however, some 84,000 Ohio State fans in Ohio Stadium were in for the shock of their lives. So was irascible Woody Hayes, who had never beaten one of Rip Engle's Penn State teams. Gary Wydman ran the simple Nittany Lion offense perfectly, the Penn State blockers neutralized Kelley and Bugel so effectively that it seemed they weren't even in the game. The visitors' defense, led by Glenn Ressler, their All-America middle guard, was so good that Ohio State didn't get a first down until late in the third quarter, and that came on a penalty. It seemed that the Penn State defenders knew exactly where the Ohio State plays were going and they were always there to stop the surprised Bucks' runners. Ohio State got only four other first downs in the game and the Nittany Lions shut out Woody Hayes' team, 27-0. It was one of the greatest college football upsets of the decade.

When the word of Penn State's victory came over the wire in the sports department of *The New York Times*, an excited copy boy shouted for all to hear, "Penn State beat Ohio State!"

The late Joe Sheehan, assistant sports editor, never looking up from his desk, asked calmly, "Don't they always?"

After the game, Tarman came down from the press box and met Paterno, standing with Rip Engle and Jim O'Hora, at the door of the team bus. Paterno greeted Jim with a big grin.

"Well, now I'll tell you the truth, Jim," said Joe, "I really thought maybe Ohio State would get a field goal."

Later Paterno explained why he had been so certain of a victory. "Actually, Woody had gotten into a pattern with his offense. After studying the films and our scouting reports, we felt we could tell which side they were going to run without any chance for error. We changed our defense to put Ressler directly on the head of the Ohio State center and he had a fantastic day. We always knew where the play was going before the ball was snapped and our kids were always there. It was as simple as that."

There was no stopping Penn State after that. The Nittany Lions trampled Houston and Pitt in their last two games for a five-game winning streak that gave them a 6-4 record and they were voted the Lambert Trophy over an unbeaten Princeton team. There was a great hue and cry from the Ivy Leaguers but few people really disputed the fact that, at the end of the season, this Penn State team was truly the best in the East. As an indication of this, the Lions were invited to play in the Gator Bowl but the players voted to turn down the bid. They were satisfied to rest on their well-earned laurels.

It was vindication, too, for Joe Paterno, who had stood by his quarterback, Gary Wydman, when everyone else felt that he should be benched. Joe had refused to give in to criticism when he believed that the course he had taken was right. More important, he demonstrated that he didn't panic under pressure. He had survived his first major crisis as a football coach.

For Rip Engle, heading into the twilight of his career as a head coach, the 1964 season was one of the most gratifying he had ever experienced. Some of his teams had finished with better records but none had ever before come back from such a poor start to attain such splendid heights.

"Those kids were just wonderful," said Rip. "I've never had a team that gave as much as this one did. They never stopped trying, even when it seemed that the season was going to be a total failure."

Long before this, Joe Paterno's work with the Penn State quarterbacks and his imaginative coaching had attracted attention in other quarters. In 1959, his old backfield coach at Brown, Weeb Ewbank, whose Baltimore Colts had won the National Football League championship, invited Joe to join his staff. Two years later, Nick Skorich, then coaching the Philadelphia Eagles, offered him a job. Then Al Davis, a brilliant coach who had pulled the perennial last-place Oakland Raiders out of the dregs of the American Football League into respectability, made overtures to Paterno. Joe, whose goal always was to succeed Rip Engle as the head coach at Penn State, turned down all offers. However, he was sorely tempted by the Baltimore, Philadelphia and Oakland pro jobs.

Paterno discussed the Baltimore post with Engle, who told him that he would not stand in his way if he really wanted to leave but that he thought he had a good future at Penn State. Then Joe called Frank Lauterbur, who had left a job as an assistant coach with the Colts to join Colonel Blaik's staff at Army. He wanted to know why Lauterbur had left Baltimore. Frank's reasons were simple and to the point. He liked pro football, it was exciting, but he felt that college football provided a coach with more security and more opportunities to become a head coach. Lauterbur subsequently left Army to become an assistant at Pitt under Coach John Michelosen and then became the athletic director and head football coach at the University of Toledo, where he took the Rockets from obscurity in the Mid-America Conference to national fame. He produced two successive unbeaten and untied teams in 1969 and 1970 before he left to become head coach at the University of Iowa.

After mulling over Ewbank's offer, Paterno turned it down. Again in 1961, when Skorich tried to him to go to the Philadelphia Eagles, Joe thought very seriously about joining the pros. He was tempted again by the Oakland Raiders but he wasn't sure that he wanted to work for Al Davis, a strong willed man who insisted on total compliance from everybody who worked for him.

"I respected Al's ability as a coach and general manager and I was sure that he was going to be a big success at Oakland," says Joe, "but his personality was too strong. I knew I would be expected to give in to him on everything and I wasn't going to do that."

There were other job opportunities in the college ranks, too. Bill Flynn, the athletic director at Boston College, talked to Paterno before the Eagles hired Jim Miller in 1962. But Joe told Flynn he didn't want to coach at a Catholic school. He didn't like the idea of all those "assistant coaches with black, frocks" looking over his shoulder at practice every day. He had an interview at Yale when Jordan Olivar resigned after the 1962 season but the Elis decided to hire John Pont, who had been so successful at Miami of Ohio.

Just two years later, after the end of the 1964 season, Pont left Yale to gò to Indiana University and the Ivy League school came looking for Paterno. This proved to be the turning point in Joe's coaching career. Delaney Kiputh, the Yale athletic director, offered the job to Paterno and then Joe began to do some sincere soul-searching. The head coaching position at Yale was always considered to be one of the plums of the profession and it was hard to turn down. Joe went to Rip Engle and Ernie McCoy and put his cards on the table. What he wanted was assurance that when Rip Engle retired he would be named the head coach at Penn State. If he couldn't get that assurance, he was going to take the Yale job.

Engle, meanwhile, had begun to think seriously of retirement after the 1962 season—his best at Penn State. It had been a long, hard year, extended by the Gator Bowl game, and then Rip had gone to Honolulu to coach one of the teams in the Hula Bowl. He was weary physically and mentally. Engle discussed the future with his wife, Sunny, and they agreed that he would stay on a few more seasons. Rip also began to think about his eventual successor and his choice, naturally, was Joe Paterno.

Paterno knew that he was Engle's choice—Rip had made that clear when Joe was officially named Associate Coach in 1964— but he also knew that the decision wasn't Rip's to make. When the time came, it would be made by Dr. Eric A. Walker, the president of the university, and McCoy.

After a frank and open discussion with Joe on his future at Penn State, both men assured him that, barring any unforeseen circumstances, the head coaching job at Penn State would be his when Rip Engle elected to retire. Paterno rejected Yale's liberal offer and the Ivy League school gave the job to Carman Cozza, who had been Pont's assistant at both Miami of Ohio and Yale.

Yale's loss was Penn State's gain.

Although, ostensibly, Paterno was the quarterback coach and in charge of the offense, his influence had increased ten-fold since he came to Penn State with Rip Engle as a raw young assistant coach. Engle had quickly recognized that Joe had a fine football mind and slowly but surely he gave him added responsibilities. Although other members of the staff were older in age and experience, Engle began to depend more and more on Paterno as his chief aide even though the title didn't become official until 1964. But, long before then, Joe had become the co-architect, along with Engle, of Penn State's weekly game plans. He was the head assistant on the sidelines during the games and he was the one who sent in plays to the quarterbacks. Joe's dominant personality and his ambition to succeed had a lot to do with it, of course, but Rip was smart enough to know that he had a budding coaching genius on his hands and he encouraged him. More and more, as the years went on, Engle sought out Paterno's advice, not only on offense but on defense, too.

At many other schools, such an arrangement might have created hard feelings among other members of the coaching staff. But the Penn State staff was unusual in many respects. For one thing, it had remained virtually intact ever since Rip Engle took over in 1950. It was a close-knit group and the men worked well together. There was no back-biting, no maneuvering for position in the hierarchy or for credit. Engle always was very careful to be liberal with his praise of his assistants and decisions were made only after each man had his opportunity to be heard. It was more a partnership than a boss-assistant relationship.

A further indication of the unity that exists among the entire athletic family at Penn State is the longevity of its members. Ernie McCoy served for sixteen years as Athletic Director and Dean of the College of Health and Physical Education until his retirement in 1969. He was succeeded as Director of Athletics by Ed Czekaj, a former Penn State football player who joined the department in 1953 as assistant graduate manager of athletics and later became business manager. Jim Tarman, a key man in his double posts in the athletic department, joined up in 1958, while Trainer Chuck Medlar, another former Penn Stater, has been in his post since 1946 and Sports Information Director John Morris came aboard in 1970. Even the team doctor has been around a long time. Dr. Samuel Fleagle has been at it since 1966.

Unlike so many men who have been coaching a long time, Rip Engle was not stereotyped in his football. Although he was one of the pioneers of the wing-T formation, he was willing to make changes to suit his personnel, or even the times, and he did so throughout the years. Many of the changes, both offensively and defensively, were suggested by Joe Paterno, some successful and others not so successful in turn. Paterno constantly demonstrated his fierce loyalty to Engle and his dedication to his job. Sometimes, however, Joe's dedication got out of hand, especially in his early days at Penn State, when he was considered by many to be a "hot-headed young kid."

On one occasion, in 1956, Joe clashed publicly with Ernie McCoy over a matter of policy. McCoy, an astute administrator, found Penn State's athletic finances in a deplorable condition when he became Athletic Director in 1953. The athletic program was operating in the red and Ernie instituted some economies to correct the situation. Paterno didn't agree with McCoy and proceeded to tell Ernie so at a social gathering at his home.

What bothered Joe at the time was the lack of training table meals for the football squad and what he thought were second-class travel arrangements. The discussion raged hot and heavy and there was some name-calling. Cooler heads tried to calm down both men and, when Sunny Engle remonstrated with Joe, he turned on her and told her to shut up. Paterno concluded his tirade by brandishing his finger under McCoy's nose and shouting, "McCoy, we're going to win in spite of you!"

Then there was that other incident with Sunny Engle, when she suggested that perhaps Paterno ought to find another quarterback instead of Gary Wydman. There were others, too, as this impetuous young man tried desperately to make things happen. Along the way, his bluntness and directness bruised some egos and hurt some feelings. Fortunately for him, people tended to forgive his outbursts, writing them off as overenthusiasm.

"I was really a pain in the neck," admits Joe. "I thought I was smarter than everybody else and I had no patience for anyone who disagreed with me. I thought I had all the answers."

Eventually, Paterno got over being "smarter than everybody else." He matured, both in his job and his personality, and the change was noticeable as he grew older. A confirmed bachelor, he never went in much for dating although many folks around State College tried to arrange meetings with eligible girls. Smart, personable and good company, he was considered a prize catch.

But Joe was so busy thinking, discussing and coaching football, recruiting players and being Rip Engle's alter ego that he really didn't have much time for socializing, except with other members of the coaching staff and a few close friends. He was content to spend his leisure hours in an occasional poker game with Jim Tarman; Steve Garban, who captained the 1958 Penn State team and was then the assistant business manager of athletics; Ridge Riley, the alumni secretary and editor of the weekly football letter; Jack Brannigan and Jim O'Hora. When sportswriters and other media people visited Penn State during spring practice or came down to cover games in the fall, it was usually Paterno and Tarman who squired them around and went out to dinner with them. So, it was a fairly busy life for Paterno.

Also, because Joe was the only bachelor on the staff he drew extra-curricular assignments, like helping to monitor a study hall for freshman football players. During the winter of 1959, Joe was attracted to a young lady who was dating one of the freshman players. Always a friendly soul and never shy, Paterno got into a conversation with her one day and learned that her name was Suzanne Pohland, she was a freshman at Penn State and her home was in Latrobe, Pennsylvania. Sue, an attractive and very bright girl with a good sense of humor, was obviously unawed by the assistant football coach, who had become known around the campus as "that young maverick." They chatted for awhile, discussing the books which the observant Paterno noticed she was carrying under her arm. After that, they ran into each other from time to time on campus or at the football study hall.

"He was a friend, sort of a father confessor," says Sue. "The Paterno paternal instinct, I guess."

It wasn't long, however, before the paternal instinct developed into a budding romance. In the summer of 1961, Sue took a job in Avon on the New Jersey shore and, coincidentally, Joe rented a bungalow in nearby Belmar and brought his mother, sister and nephew down. Their paths crossed again and they spent a lot of time together, reading, talking and dating. She was pinned to a young man at Penn State but Joe, in his persuasive way, soon convinced her that she wasn't really in love with him.

Midway through the summer, Joe asked Sue to marry him but, by this time, she, too, was so filled up with Penn State football that her answer was, "You'd better think about beating Navy in the opening game."

Paterno persisted, though, and finally, at the end of the summer, Sue agreed to marry him. They planned the wedding for late August, just before the start of football practice. However, getting married wasn't as simple as it seemed to be under the bright sun on the beach at the Jersey shore. Joe, then thirty-four, was thirteen years older than Sue and that caused immediate complications with Sue's family.

Sue's parents wanted the couple to wait until after Sue's graduation from college in December. It was agreed that they would announce their engagement on Thanksgiving Day—after the final game of the season with Pitt—and they would be married in January or February. They also agreed that, since Sue was still a student, they would keep their relationship a secret.

Sue learned quickly that her life would have to be regulated by football. Immediately after the Pitt game, Penn State was invited to play Georgia Tech in the Gator Bowl in late December. That postponed the announcement of the engagement and, subsequently, the planned wedding. Then, it was the recruiting season and spring practice. Joe wasn't going to let a little thing like a wedding—even his own—interfere with his getting a hot quarterback prospect or a 260-pound tackle! Finally, Sue and Joe were married on May 12, 1962.

Their honeymoon had almost as many false starts as the wedding, but let Sue tell that story:

"Well, originally we planned to go to Europe for two months and then, after I had gotten my passport and shots, Joe said he didn't think he would have the time for that, what with all the recruiting he had to do, but how about going to Bermuda for a few weeks? Then it was the Virgin Islands for a couple of weeks and that soon became Florida for ten days. From there it dwindled to Sea Island, Georgia, for a week and we eventually wound up at Virginia Beach for five days.

"On the way to Virginia Beach, we stopped at Somerset, Pennsylvania, to see a player Joe was trying to recruit. I sat in the car for a half-hour while Joe talked to the boy and his family. But the whole thing was a waste. We didn't get him. He went to Ohio State. But we did send post cards from Virginia Beach to all the kids Joe was recruiting.

"I guess that was better than inviting them on our honeymoon."

Upon their return, the Paternos settled into Joe's former small bachelor apartment in State College and Sue soon found out that she would have to share her husband with his football friends. Joe's apartment continued to be the headquarters for visiting coaches, high school recruits and an occasional sportswriter, some invited and others uninvited. Sue quickly realized that this kind of informal entertaining was part of a coach's life—especially Joe Paterno's—and she was a gracious hostess.

For a guy who took so long to get married, Joe didn't waste any time putting together a family. Diana Lynn, the Paterno's first child, was born on April 7, 1963, followed by Mary Kathryn on January 13, 1965, David on July 1, 1966, Joseph Jr. on October 21, 1968, and George Scott on November 1, 1972. Only two of the youngsters, Joseph—the Paternos call him Jay because Joe says, "There aren't going to be any Juniors around our house"—and George were born during the football season, though Diana Lynn barely made it before the start of spring practice.

Despite his new family responsibilities, Paterno maintained his same breakneck pace. He continued to recruit extensively, worked with the quarterbacks, helped plan the offense and even got involved with the defensive planning. He assumed more and more responsibility and it was obvious to all that he was Rip Engle's heir apparent.

Engle had been talking about retiring for several years and he made up his mind after the 1965 season, when Penn State barely managed a 5-5 record, losing to Michigan State, UCLA, Syracuse, California and Pitt. Three of the losses were by a total of nine points and the season had been a particularly trying one for Rip. He suffered through the defeats, especially the close ones, and realized that football was taking too much out of him. He had been coaching for thirty-five years, was nearing sixty, and frankly was just plain weary. He felt that it was time for him to give up coaching.

"Once you reach fifty-five," observed Rip, "you have to work longer and harder to get the job done. If you work longer and harder, your health is going to suffer. If you don't do it, then the team suffers. In either case, you have to be hurt. So, you can't win and, if you get into a situation where you can't win, then you'd better get out."

So, Rip decided to get out. He went to Dr. Walker and Ernie McCoy in December, told them he wanted to retire and that he expected Joe Paterno to be his successor. Engle's resignation became official in February and it was accepted reluctantly. The administration was truly sorry to see Rip quit. He not only had been an outstanding coach but also had brought honor to the university as its representative.

McCoy's announcement that Joe Paterno would succeed Rip Engle as the head coach at Penn State came as no surprise to anyone. With it came a vote of confidence from the administration and a series of accolades that would turn any young man's head. Dr. Walker acclaimed Paterno as "an outstanding leader, both on and off the field." Ernie McCoy said, "We are extremely proud to have him as our head coach." Rip Engle was prophetic as he handed down his mantle to his protégé. Proclaimed Rip, "I'm confident that he will be one of the fine coaches to emerge from this era of outstanding young men in the coaching profession."

Joe Paterno was elated. It took about three seconds to accept the job and, during that brief interval, he was already planning what he was going to do in the next spring practice. "It's the only job I've ever really wanted in coaching," Joe said honestly.

At age thirty-nine, Joe Paterno, his early dreams of becoming a barrister long since forgotten, was finally where wanted to be.

9: The Year of the Orange Lion

Joe Paterno's first year as head coach was a struggle with himself and his beliefs in his sometimes taxing demands on those around him. That 1966 year was not a successful one by Penn State football standards and it wasn't until the Nittany Lions won their final game of the year that Penn State was assured of not having a losing season. No team at Penn State had been a loser over the season since 1938, when the Lions finished with a 3-4-1 record.

A 48-24 victory over a poor Pittsburgh team in the final game gave Joe Paterno a .500 mark for his first season as head coach but hardly much satisfaction. "I was not sure I was a good head coach and I was not sure of my future when that year ended," he says now.

Before the season ended, Sue Paterno wasn't sure of her husband's future either. She believed, as always, that whatever he did he would be successful at. But she was sure of one thing as the eighth game of the season approached, the game with the enemy from upstate New York, Syracuse. Sue, still an undergraduate in many ways, was sure "part of the problem here was the great lack of enthusiasm and great lack of spirit among the students with regard to the football Joe was trying to get going."

Sue began to develop as much of the pixy in her as Duffy Daugherty showed to Paterno on the ride to see President Nixon. But Sue's pixy way was a devilish little twitch in her mind that pictured the need for some get-up-and-go feeling among the locals in the valley of the Nittany Lion. Oh, that Nittany Lion. What a great symbol for a college. That honored hunk of statuary by Heinz Warneke standing just outside of Recreation Hall, the home of Penn State basketball, wrestling, gymnastics and all coaching offices.

There was that Nittany Lion, a mountain lion in solid stone, set to spring, with head twisted slightly to the left looking for the unwary enemy. Could it be the enemy was Ben Schwartzwalder and his Orange-clad Syracuse football players?

In that week when Sue Paterno began dreaming up trouble, Syracuse was the ENEMY! What better than to make Syracuse people the object of venom, at least through Saturday when the game would be played in Beaver Stadium, a mile or so from the beloved Nittany Lion statue.

Sue thought of her undergraduate dormitory days, not too far behind her at that. "I had a corner room and I could look at the Lion and, after coeds had to check in, the boys stayed and guarded the Lion all night to make sure nothing happened to it on Thursday and Friday nights before a home game. I remember in my sophomore year, the year we beat Army for something like the first time in a hundred years. That's when it started. Some cadets went after the Lion and that's when the guarding started."

But Sue didn't like it when in 1966 that spirit to protect and brag about Penn State seemed to have evaporated. It might have been gone in the move to the new generation of college undergraduates. But Sue was thinking. "I didn't see any of this spirit anymore—you know, the pep rallies."

So Sue began to conjecture. She needed co-conspirators for conjuring and she turned naturally to her favorite co-worker in the pixy department—Sandra Welsh, wife of George Welsh, offensive backfield assistant to Joe Paterno and the former Navy quarterback who led the Middies to victory in the Sugar Bowl game of 1955. Sandra was, herself, a recent undergraduate and still a bit of a freshman like Sue. They called in a needed third party to drive the escape car and to "ride shotgun." This turned out to be Nancy Radakovich, wife of Dan Radakovich, coach of the Penn State linebackers. The three little darlings came up with a sure-fire plan to get everyone at Penn State mad as hatters at Syracuse.

What the trio planned was a work of art designed to stimulate the dormant spirit at Penn State. They would paint the beloved Nittany Lion orange, the traditional sign of a strike in the night by the enemy—Syracuse—before football teams meet to strike on Saturday. A plan, as well organized as the great Brinks robbery, took shape in those three feminine heads with Coach Sue in charge. Sandra and Sue would do the dirty work while Nancy remained in the car for the quick getaway.

Thursday night was the time of the weekly coaches' cocktail party and dinner with wives. The host for that Thursday night before the 1966 Syracuse game was Earl Bruce, the freshman coach and senior member of the staff. Cocktails at the Bruces and then to dinner at the Tavern. It was also Earl's birthday, so Sue promised to bring a birthday cake for the mob at the Tavern.

The plan called for Sue to "forget" the cake when she arrived at Earl Bruce's house for pre-dinner cocktails. She would then ask Nancy and Sandra to drive her home for the cake while everyone else went to the Tavern, and the three little devils would rejoin the gang with cake in hand. But the conspiring trio had really left the cake in Nancy's car, a little white Renault. There was no need to go back to Sue's house for the cake. Just a quick stop at the Lion statue and Sue and Sandra could throw three cans of washable orange paint on the still animal. That would do it and Syracuse would be blamed.

The plan went just perfectly up to a point. After committing the act, aimed at reinstilling Penn State with football spirit, Sandra Welsh and Sue Paterno returned to the white Renault. ("You'd think she at least could have had a black car," Sue remembers.) There, looking Sue right in the eye, was John Doolittle, an assistant track coach. Nancy was so nervous she couldn't get the gear shift to move for her.

"Nancy had the lights out in the car, anyway," Sue claimed.

"We were a block and a half away from the Lion when I said to Nancy, 'Well, when are you going to turn the headlights back on?' She's very hyperactive, you know."

On went the car lights, inside and out, and Sue turned to Sandra in disgust and said, "Sandra, you have paint all over you." Sandra returned the look, saying, "Sue, so do you." So Nancy carried the cake into the Tavern while the paint throwers washed up but they forgot to wash the paint off their coats where it had also spilled.

Actually, the three little bottles of washable paint had covered only a bit of the Lion, and the orange paper streamers the girls added for a final touch weren't too harmful. But Sue had to return to the scene of the crime after dinner at the Tavern to see if students had caught on and were guarding or washing off the Lion. She talked Joe into driving by on the way home and sure enough, there was the Lion, smeared from jaw to tail in solid orange, a magnificent job of work by the ENEMY, Syracuse. Sue said nothing but Joe caught on quickly. He said, more as a statement than a question, "You did that, didn't you." They didn't speak again that night and the trouble began the next day.

Friday morning the local radio station issued the news that the police knew who had painted the Lion the orange of Syracuse. Sue worried and Joe worried, particularly after someone ran into his office to tell him, "They know the three who painted the Lion and they're going to go to jail." Joe's first reaction was, "If Sue's going to jail then who is going to mind Diana and Mary Kay?" Joe said his whole insides began churning.

Sue, too scared to leave the house, got a call from Joe, who, by this time, had calmed down a bit. He told her the culprits were going to go to jail and how do you like that for a coach's wife? Then the phone rang again and Sandra breathlessly related how she had gone by the lion a few minutes earlier and it was solid orange from head to tail and done in oil paint and "Oh, my god, what now?" The little paint the girls tossed had only splashed here and there on the poor animal.

George Welsh also knew the original artists of the Lion that Thursday night. Sandra never did get the orange out of her raincoat. George and Joe were doing a slow burn when the word came that the culprits had been caught and were in jail. They were three Syracuse students who had done the dastardly act with oil paint that covered the Lion and the original, less impressive Sue-Sandra-Nancy job. So, a trio of feisty Syracuse students spent the weekend in the cooler while the first culprits went scot free, trying to keep their secret known only to Joe Paterno and George Welsh.

Sue had to tell her mother. "She thought it was hysterical. Joe thought it was horrible. You see, I hadn't grown up yet and I did a lot of those pranks in college. You know, lovely pranks that don't really hurt."

Sue sat in misery during the Syracuse game the next day. She kept thinking, "If we lose it's my fault because I painted that lousy Lion." Penn State lost, 12-10, but it really wasn't Sue's fault.

Looking back, it was, in a way, worth it to Sue, since the spirit rose on Penn State's campus during ensuing years. Winning might just have had a little more to do with that than painting lions orange.

But when Joe Paterno took over as head coach before that 1966 season he needed more than spirit to get where he wanted to go with his Nittany Lion teams. He needed understanding with his coaching staff, with his players and the ability to run things properly according to his ideas of coaching. His big problem, especially after that 5-5 season, was "Can I do it, really?"

Paterno began his head coaching career not too sure how to work with his assistants. This wasn't a man coming in from outside to take over the top spot but this was a man who had worked with the staff for years as an equal, as another assistant coach. Now he was the boss, and for the first year Paterno had problems because "everyone was falling over backward not to hurt one another," according to Joe.

Paterno had retained Rip Engle's entire staff—Jim O'Hora, George Welsh, Frank Patrick, J. T. White, Joe McMullen, Earl Bruce and Dan Radakovich, the same men he had worked with for many years. When Joe moved up to head coach it left a vacancy on the staff and he hired Bob Phillips, who had been a successful Pennsylvania high school coach. Paterno's relationship with his colleagues had always been excellent but now it was on a different basis. He was the boss and Joe felt that he had to establish this fact but he also realized he had to do it gradually.

This caused some problems. In some instances, Joe was too reluctant to overrule his assistants when he thought his instinct was right. At other times he made decisions on his own when, perhap, he should have listened to the advice of his aides who might have been closer to a situation.

Looking back on the 1966 season during the winter of 1967, Paterno had ample time to study his errors. There was a long list of "never do agains" haunting this man whose pride was damaged by a mere .500 season in his first try at head coaching.

He had broken from the barrier in spring practice of 1966 with a major error. He worked his players too long and too hard. He continued this throughout spring practice, normally a boring and strenuous time for college football athletes who would much rather be walking with their girls around a nice campus smelling of spring or just lolling around on their free time. Practice is always work with Paterno or any good coach so spring practice is worse than in the fall, when, at least at the end of a week's practice, there is the fun of the game to look forward to.

Sue's spirit drive wasn't needed so much as Paterno's reassessing his own failings as a first-year head coach. The spirit of the Lion (orange- or stone-colored) would follow when Paterno settled into a more successful pattern that led only to winning, winning and more winning.

"For one thing, we had to get closer to the players on the team," Joe decided. "I had suddenly become too far from them, I think. We also had to get them back closer to their own families. That's so damn important."

So, first on the program was to rebuild morale, which had slipped after two successive 5-5 seasons. Another contributing factor was the plain fact that Paterno, the new boss, had become too aloof. Joe has never gone back to the close relationship level he worked at as an assistant and he never will. But all Joe had to do was retreat slightly from his former attitude to retain a still accessible position. What Paterno had forgotten was that a head coach is no longer like the president of a bank who can shun the personal concerns and problems of his staff and his players.

"We lost boys in that 1966 season by moving them up and down too much," Paterno recalls. "We were confused and there was doubt in the players' minds that we were doing the right things. We didn't make it work right."

Joe realized that he had been too impatient with some of his players and had not given them enough of an opportunity to develop at their positions. Instead of being loose, they were up-tight and afraid to make mistakes. "I learned that a young man must feel comfortable at his position in order to play well," says Joe, "and this takes time."

Paterno opened the year with an offense that he finally realized was not suited to his personnel. He went back to a more basic offense a bit too late to make the year a winning one but just in time to make it a non-losing season. Joe's error, he realized later, was "we just shouldn't have stuck with that I formation so long."

Jack White was the quarterback of that 1966 team when the season opened against Maryland. Penn State won, 15-7, and Lou Saban, the Maryland coach, also in his first year as head coach at College Park, called Paterno a couple of days later to say "You really stunk. We just stunk a lot more." Paterno remembers that as "damn near the truth."

The next game was "no chance in a million" at Michigan State, the place where Duffy Daugherty had a team that was to tie Notre Dame 10-10, in what was the classic buildup game of the decade. That Michigan State team had Bubba Smith and George Webster on defense. That team had everything. Bubba Smith almost tore Jack White in half on a blind-side tackle early in the game, which the Spartans won, 42-8. White bled from his kidneys after that shot and Tom Cahill, the man from the East who was also in a rookie head coaching year at Army in 1966, after watching films of the game, said, "That was the dirtiest tackle I've ever seen. Bubba should have been barred for life from football."

Paterno, however, disagreed with Cahill. "It was a legal tackle," said Joe. "But maybe one of the hardest tackles I've ever seen."

Penn State was operating from the I formation during those early games, which produced only one victory in three tries. After the slaughter at Michigan State, Paterno continued with the I as Penn State went up to meet always troublesome Army at West Point. Jack White, still hurting from contact with Bubba

Smith, was at quarterback at the outset of the game, which was played in a light rain.

Sitting in the press box was Ernie McCoy, the Penn State Athletic Director. Many persons heard him criticize Joe Paterno's continuing use of the I formation. McCoy wanted Penn State back in its fundamental offense, which stresses power running, but Paterno stubbornly decided to stay with the I for at least one more game. When Paterno heard of McCoy's remarks, Joe was none too pleased and he let McCoy know it.

Penn State lost to Army, 11-0, and, as it turned out, that game had a lot to do with the future of both Paterno and Army's coach Tom Cahill. Not because Paterno let McCoy influence him but because Paterno learned the hard way. Penn State later abandoned the I, leaving it on The Plain at West Point for more satisfactory offenses that could do the job a bit more successfully. Conversely, that Penn State-Army game was the making of the Army team for 1966. Cahill, who had been nothing more than the plebe (freshman) football coach for seven years, had been appointed head coach at Army in the spring of 1966 shortly after Paul Dietzel suddenly left Army to take the coaching job at the University of South Carolina. Cahill had no great talent on his squad but he had a bunch of eager sophomores and a personal desire to win despite believing he was only an interim coach.

When Army defeated Penn State, its stiffest opponent in its first three games, that game was the launching site for an 8-2 season and Cahill became the Coach of the Year for his amazing job in his first season as head coach of a college team.

Paterno, who was later to follow in Cahill's footsteps as Coach of the Year, was having more serious problems in his rookie year. He finally decided to toss away the I formation and with it went Jack White as quarterback. White, who went on to become a dentist, was described by Paterno as a "tough kid, a great competitor and the kind of boy you'd want as a son." But, Joe adds, "When we decided we didn't really have the kind of people for the I, we dropped it. White wasn't the kind of man to have at quarterback in the different type of offense where you had to throw back across the field, pitch back and do other things. Jack couldn't find the secondary receivers and do the job in the new offense."

Penn State switched to a more basic wing-T formation, with backs set apart behind the quarterback and a wide back, whereas the slot-I had two backs lined up directly back of the quarterback before the snap.

Tom Sherman, who started the season playing defense, moved in at quarterback for the next game, with Boston College at Newton, Massachusetts. Penn State won, 30-21, and Paterno, reflecting on the season later, said, "I think if we had had Sherman in there from the start of the season we might have been a 6-4 team, or better. Certainly better than 5-5. We went to Sherman and we started to move the ball."

So ended the playing career of Jack White, a young man who was the center of some problems among Penn State, Pittsburgh and Syracuse. White, a good student, had started his college career at the University of Florida. He had a brother at Florida but Jack decided to transfer to Penn State after the 1962-1963 academic year. This meant he had to sit out of football for a year but that he had three varsity years of eligibility remaining, from 1964 to 1966. NCAA rules required a transfer to be inactive for one year.

However, Syracuse, Penn State, Pittsburgh and West Virginia had an agreement among themselves that did not permit red-shirting unless a player was injured or ill. Uninjured and perfectly healthy, White was considered a red-shirt by Syracuse and Pittsburgh. The problem was settled, though, in Penn State's favor, and White got to play in 1966—but not for long.

During White's tenure as the quarterback, several things began to develop for Paterno and Penn State. The rookie head coach made the mistake of putting in a new pass coverage late in the week before the second game of the season, with Michigan State. "That's one thing I learned about coaching," Joe says. "We should have had a new coverage in there on Monday instead of Thursday. The kids were confused out there on the field. Of course, we weren't in the same class with Michigan State that day. We took a hell of a licking, about the worst beating Penn State has had in years and years. But I learned to put new things in early in a week, if ever."

One development for Penn State was the beginning of a great career by Mike Reid, who was a linebacker in 1966. He was important as Penn State, in a poorly played game, beat Maryland in the opener on three safeties. Reid had a "great game" in Paterno's estimation, but the coach says neither team played overall good football "by anyone's standards." But even with a victory over Maryland before the two losses, Paterno was beginning to hear those nasty sounds of "get rid of the coach."

A letter to Joe from a Penn State alumnus, a doctor in East Stroudsburg, Pennsylvania, informed Joe after the Maryland game, "If this is the kind of football I have to watch at Penn State for the next twenty years I want you to know I am going to start a campaign among alumni to bring in a Penn Stater to set football right with our university."

Joe answered, "That's fine, if you have any suggestions bring the people down and I'll be glad to talk to them for the job." In return, the doctor wrote a vicious letter to Joe, who wrote back once more: "Relax. If I can't do the job here, I'll be the first one to know it and the first to ask out of the job."

Many letters kept coming in to Paterno, who never has had a contract at Penn State. Joe doesn't think of most of these letters as vicious. "After all, vicious is only vicious to the guy who reads the letter. If he's sensitive the letter can be vicious. But I couldn't have cared less about those letters. I was just interested in getting things turned around."

This came about at Boston College, where the personnel was finally stabilized. Sherman did a fine job of picking the open receiver and the Nittany Lions won to even their record at 2-2.

But the next opponent was UCLA, which ran up even more points against Penn State than Michigan State had managed. "Here again, I made another of those mistakes," Joe remembers. "In my confidence that maybe I could outcoach and outthink people and outcircle and x them, Tuesday night I came up with a defense that I felt was just great on coverage. I tried to work it in on Wednesday and Thursday and on Friday we were still practicing it. When you practice something new on Friday you're out of business.

"We were going to be beaten but we probably shouldn't have been beaten that badly [49-11]. We just didn't know what we were doing out there." Besides, UCLA had Gary Beban at quarterback—the man who won the Heisman Trophy in 1967 as the best college player in the land.

A couple of victories over West Virginia and California fattened Penn State for the Syracuse match—that game every team has each year where the foe is an enemy.

It was a game with one big play Paterno remembers as the key, a play by Syracuse that Joe and his players knew was coming. But all the coaching by Paternos around the nation can't prevent what happened to Penn State.

Syracuse, on a fourth-down play at midfield, faked a punt. When Syracuse lined up, Tim Montgomery was the left defensive halfback for Penn State and he was stationed near the Penn State bench. Joe Paterno yelled to him, "They're going to pass. Timmy, they're going to pass."

"Yeh, I know, Coach. O.K."

Syracuse did just that, but Montgomery, covering the receiver, slipped and fell. Syracuse made the first down, went on to score and won the game 12-10. "But we played a good game in that one," Paterno insists.

As always seems to happen between football enemies, something happened prior to the game that irritated Ben Schwartzwalder, Syracuse's coach. The Syracuse coaching staff had been using closed-circuit TV for video replay in the press box, where assistant coaches watched the field action and reported back to the sidelines suggesting adjustments. This electronic coaching has since been outlawed. But Syracuse requested the right to use its TV replay set in the press box at Penn State.

Paterno put his foot down: "Absolutely no."

Ernie McCoy had to inform Syracuse that Penn State would not permit such coaching aids since Penn State didn't use them. Schwartzwalder was miffed, something he becomes at times just by the mere mention of Penn State. That Friday night, the usual pre-game press party was held at Penn State and Schwartzwalder boycotted the gathering. And he has not attended a press party at Penn State since.

Other colleges were using TV aid to watch the play repeated in slow motion to help the coaches decide just how to adjust to a situation. Paterno said, "It helps. UCLA was using it in those days. But they couldn't use it in their own conference [Pacific Eight] games because the league had ruled against it. But when we played out there at UCLA they used it against us. And they adjusted a lot quicker to things in games against people like us than they adjusted to conference opponents."

A year later, a national rule prohibited the use of any electronic coaching aids, something UCLA had a knack for using. The Bruins, when Beban was a sophomore in 1965, put transistor receivers in Beban's helmet. A UCLA coach up in the press box used the tiny microphone and transmitter like a walkie-talkie. Beban, who scrambled and rolled out most of the time, would get a message on his helmet radio, "Pass! Pass!" or "Run! Run!"

UCLA never admitted to this tricky radio maneuver but never strongly denied it, either. How long the Bruins had been using it, no one ever knew. But it was at Penn State that UCLA was caught red-handed.

The UCLA walkie-talkie setup happened to be on the same wavelength as the walkie-talkies being used by security police and parking attendants outside Beaver Stadium. Every now and then one of the men with the Penn State walkie-talkies would hear, "Run! Run!" Then, "Pass! Pass!"

Finally the security men put it together and reported it to Joe Paterno on the sideline. It was too late to save Penn State from a 24-22 loss to UCLA but it wasn't too late to expose Coach Tommy Prothro's latest trick. Despite UCLA's denial, Paterno insisted, "I heard the orders to Beban on that radio."

Neither Coach Rip Engle nor Joe Paterno mentioned the incident at the post-game conference, but the football world found out about it a few days later when Ridge Riley, then secretary of the Penn State Alumni Association, broke the story in his weekly football letter. Ridge gave all the details and the wire services and newspapers quickly picked it up. To Engle's credit, he never blamed his team's defeat on UCLA's unsponsored radio program.

Following the Syracuse game, people began to forget orange Lions and electronic problems and even the loss a little bit. But the head coach didn't forget anything about the next game—another defeat at Georgia Tech, 21-0.

"I learned another lesson down there," said Joe. "We had to get more speed. If you're not quick enough you're going to get hurt, primarily on defense. They had a sub quarterback in there who wasn't a real good runner but he sprinted around our ends all afternoon. I knew then we were going to have to reorganize our thinking and get another type of defense. We were going to have to get quick in there on defense if we were going to beat any people and that game proved it to me for sure."

That loss presented Paterno with the possibility of being the first losing coach at Penn State since 1938 and the team with the chance of becoming the first Nittany Lion squad to be a loser since well before the players were born. Penn State was taking a 4-5 record against Pittsburgh the next week.

"I'm sure the possibility bothered me going against Pitt," Paterno said. "But you have to go back to a basic philosophy of sports. You can't be afraid to lose. I think any time there's a situation where you're afraid to lose you just can't do as well as you should. That thing was in the back of my mind but, what the hell, it's going to happen sometime. My main concern was to beat Pitt, I wasn't worried about losing to them."

"I'm sure the kids were worried about it," said Joe, who went to the trouble to post letters from former players up on the dressing room wall during the week. In these letters the men wrote of how proud they were to have been part of the long streak on non-losing teams—the longest such streak in college football. Richie Lucas, the former All-America quarterback, turned out to lend a hand. He reminisced a bit and spoke to the players about the streak and what it meant to him and other former Penn Staters.

Penn State won, 48-24, and the streak remained intact. The Nittany Lions had completed their twenty-ninth straight non-losing season. For Joe Paterno, who felt the losing Army game was "the low point in our season," it was a welcome relief. He had learned some valuable lessons that were to pay off in future years.

10: "Authoritarians Have to Go"

"I DON'T THINK that our society would collapse if we didn't have football. I just don't think that football is all that damn important."

That's the kind of statement that brands Joe Paterno as a heretic in a field filled with starry-eyed advocates of football as a way of life. To Joe Paterno, football is merely part of our culture, derived from some Americans' personal need to be Walter Mittys, identifying with the glorious deeds of Saturdays' heroes.

"I don't agree with Chet La Roche [ex-president of the National Football Foundation and Hall of Fame] and others who get up at Hall of Fame dinners, pay homage to Homer and other Greek gods and kneel at the foot of the altar to college football. It isn't that important to our survival as a nation.

"Huzinga, in his book, *Homo Ludens* or *Man the Player*, talks about how sports are a product of the culture and sports do not change cultures. He is absolutely right. Bullfighting in Spain and Mexico, soccer in European countries, cricket in England are sports that came out of their culture, out of their need for something competitive.

"Football is an American game because we have certain national characteristics, certain ways we want to identify with a guy decked out in shining armor. Even the rituals of football —the helmet, the color, the pageantry, the bands—are almost like the medieval knights of old in a joust. American men come home, they're sick and tired of their boring, monotonous life at the office, they plop down in front of their television sets and then, all of a sudden, they have a chance to identify with Woody Hayes and Ohio State, Bear Bryant and Alabama, Don Shula and the Miami Dolphins, or Joe Namath, Dick Butkus and Johnny Unitas, and it kind of makes them feel good. Perhaps that's what sports are supposed to do, to satisfy a need in our culture.

"Is football relevant to society? That's up to society to decide. When society says we don't need football, then the sport will die. And it should expire when society no longer wants or needs it. If that day comes, it will have to die a natural death. Who knows, maybe it will be replaced by soccer or six-day bike racing or marathon dances.

"What bothers me, though, is that some people are trying to destroy football today as a way of getting at our society. They are trying to do it by breaking down the rules and trying to change the game without having anything better to offer in its place. If that happens, it will be a tragedy but not because football is so important to our way of life. Sure, it can be replaced but it should be replaced only by something that is better and more relevant.

"I am all for change, but I want to change what we already have until we make it better, whether it's football, our government, the world or anything else. But I don't want to destroy what we have and just have levels. You can't just say you're going to destroy something without having a replacement that's better.

"I don't think football has to be defended as being relevant to society today in the sense of what it does for the whole of society. What is more important is what it does for individuals. It should be considered only as another extra-curricular activity in our academic program and it should never be taken out of that context.

"One reason that football is so popular in this country now is because it epitomizes the competition that is so inherent in our society. You know, the 'To the victor belongs the spoils' thing. There are other things in football that relate directly to our way of life—loyalty, discipline and working together in a common cause. I think that in these respects football *is* relevant to our society, at least to a greater part of it."

The storm of protest and dissent that overtook college campuses and then spilled over into the once tidy world of athletics in the last few years has questioned the relevancy of football and brought consternation to coaches everywhere. Some have learned to adjust to the New Generation—or as some call it, the Now Generation. Others have tried to fight against the rising tide of free-thinking and free-speaking among athletes with the only weapons they know—the same old authoritarian approach with its rigidity and refusal to recognize the changing scene.

College athletes in this new "Age of Aquarius" no longer blindly accept the same ideals and principles that once seemed so relevant a decade ago. They have become outspoken in their attitudes toward what they feel are insensitive coaches and autocratic administrators. They protest loudly against athletic policy, the relationship between coach and athlete and the rights and privileges of athletes. They don't want to be told they can't wear beards or how long their hair and sideburns must be. They don't want to be told whom to associate with off the football field. They no longer want to be considered as chattels. "The system is wrong," they say. "We want to change it."

Some college football players are greatly disturbed by labels which have been attached to them through the years. They resent being referred to as "animals" or "jocks" or, as in the case of Kenneth Wyrick, captain and tackle of the 1970 Army football team, they feel demeaned when people have the wrong image of them as individuals or members of a group.

Wyrick, a thoughtful young man, told a newspaper interviewer, "It disturbs me very much that the image of an Army football player is the epitome of discipline and rigidity. People who don't know us personally think we go around thinking, 'Kill, Kill,' all the time. That's not so. I'd say the football players are the most liberal-thinking cadets in the whole academy. If you polled the football team and asked everybody about Vietnam, I think the feeling would be overwhelmingly in favor of getting out of there."

Wyrick's comments caused a major rumble that not only shook up the brass at West Point but traveled as far as the Pentagon in Washington. However, his coach, Tom Cahill, was more relaxed about it. "Kenny only spoke his mind," shrugged Tom, "and he is entitled to that privilege."

Larry DiNardo, Notre Dame's All-America guard in 1970, wrote a long, reflective article in one of his school's football programs about a summer trip he took with some other college players to visit soldiers and hospitals in Vietnam. He concluded with the following thought:

"Someone asked me if I was impressed. Impressed? Perhaps that's not the right word. I now have new impressions because of what I saw and what I did. And the foremost is that this war is a total waste."

At the University of Florida, Carlos Alvarez, an All-America end, led in the formation of a union of sixty athletes who sought a greater voice in athletic programs and policies. After the union was formed, John Parker, an assistant track coach who had helped the athletes organize, was fired. One student told Doug Dickey, the football coach, that hair length and mode of dress were a matter of personal preference and that perhaps Dickey's mode of dress offended people.

Dickey's answer was, "I'm sorry if I offend you with my clothes. They're some old things I'm trying to wear out. I can't wear my hair long because I have a dandruff problem."

Needless to say, Dickey's flip retort was not appreciated by the athletes or their student supporters, who were attempting to make a serious point.

The coming of the New Generation has brought a varied reaction from the men who coach them. Ben Schwartzwalder of Syracuse, who was embroiled in a revolt by eight of his black athletes, says, "Football is not a democracy on the field. We have rules and you look upon yourself as a kind of benevolent dictator."

Jim Carlen, when he was at Texas Tech, thought the athletic

process in the United States was failing. "We have money, we have education, but we have no discipline," he said. "It was annoying for me to listen to an Arkansas crowd boo Bill Montgomery, a quarterback who hadn't lost more than four games in his college career, the way they did in Little Rock when we played there. There's something sick about a generation that pulls a stunt like that."

Carlen, who was called "Morality Fats" on the Texas Tech campus because of his taboos on alcohol and smoking among Tech players and coaches, also challenges college protesters. He says, "All I know is that if someone tries to take over anything at Tech, they'd better be prepared to get physical."

Bear Bryant of Alabama says, "We want an athlete that football means a lot to, who hasn't forgotten the old basics of self-sacrifice and discipline."

Ara Parseghian told his Notre Dame squad in the spring of 1970, "The country is divided, the university is divided, the church is divided, the world is divided. Football is the last vestige of unity."

Frank Leahy, the former Notre Dame coach, was unhappy with the New Generation and he minced no words. "Too many coaches are allowing their players to take over. It's my studied conviction that young men in our nation today are thirsty, crying out for discipline. Self-discipline and deprivaton are the two commodities most lacking in our society today. We do not have the power to do wthout. So many youths desire to teach before they learn how. And some have desires to retire before they've learned to work. Unfortunately, they are only the kind of fruit that rotted before it ripened."

At little Coe College in Cedar Rapids, Iowa, Glenn Drahn, the athletic director and head football coach, and his entire staff of coaches resigned because the college refused to allow Drahn to enforce his "no long hair" rule for all athletes. Drahn charged, "Because of the agitation derived by a few verbal radical students, our president has seen fit to deny the academic freedom of the coaches to determine and conduct the athletic program and policies of the college."

Walter Byers, the executive director of the National Collegiate

Athletic Association, who has never been known as a particular fan of football coaches, suddenly turned up as a booster in a 1970 issue of the *NCAA News.*

"The next decade is respectfully dedicated to the C-O-A-C-H," wrote Byers. "History shows that he has been more than a match for the ongoing attacks of alumni (doesn't win enough) and faculty (wins too much). Now he must keep a weather eye out for the local humanities commission, which may conclude that he is 'insensitive' to the needs of the modern youth, or he is failing to 'communicate.' Then there is always the possibility that a cadre of disgruntled athletes (accompanied by reporters and photographers) may meet him for breakfast with a list of demands."

Despite the narrow outlook of some people in sports, things *have* changed. The New Generation is vocal, articulate and determined to affect changes, regardless of the consequences they face from men like Jim Carlen, Bear Bryant and Glenn Drahn or the bitter criticism they get from a Frank Leahy. Some college athletes, football players included, think other things are more important. Their values have changed and they are prepared to abdicate from sports if they don't get a sympathetic ear from coaches, athletic directors or administrators.

Among coaches who recognize the change, Texas' Darrell Royal says, "We realize we are dealing with a different breed now. We don't have the same ironclad control over the student-athlete we had fifteen years ago and this is something that all coaches must adjust to."

John McKay goes even further. "The older generation talks about conformity," John says, "and we're always thinking the kids must conform to our rules and standards. Let's give them a chance, too, and try their ideas some times."

Bob Blackman, when he was at Dartmouth, said, "We let our players decide how long they want to wear their hair and whether or not they want to have long sideburns or mustaches. It's their business, not ours. It has nothing to do with the way they play football."

To prove Blackman's point, his 1970 team had plenty of "long hairs," including Murry Bowden, the co-captain and All-America linebacker, and the Indians had an unbeaten season.

Ohio State's Woody Hayes also has reluctantly but realistically relaxed his code on hair and dress. "I'm sorry to admit it," says Woody, "but longer hair and dungarees are almost standard dress now. I don't want to make a rule I have to back down on. Besides, we don't have rules at Ohio State. We have attitudes."

John Ralston, when he was at Stanford, was always more relaxed than most coaches about his rules. "There's just no sense in trying to force athletes to do things that are not really important," John reasons. "I don't consider the length of a boy's hair very important."

Gary Pettigrew of the Philadelphia Eagles, a pretty good pro football player, put the case of the New Generation into its proper perspective when he said, "The jock-stupid-athlete syndrome is passing. More and more you're going to find athletes who are interested in things other than sports—who, in a sense, are contemporary men. Interested in the environment, in government, in the changing social mores. If you're going to get respect from them, then you have to treat them as individuals. The first coach who realizes there are changes—and understands those changes—will be a new kind of winner."

Joe Paterno, perhaps better than most college football coaches, understands those changes and he is sympathetic to the New Generation. In fact, his views on the New Generation make many of his colleagues cringe.

"I like this generation," says Joe. "The young people are questioning us and they deserve to be heard and listened to. They want to be able to identify with something that is meaningful to them and we have been in the habit of turning them off if we don't agree.

"I'm a lot like these kids myself. I want to change things. And I'm going to do my damnedest to speak up about the things I think are wrong, whether it's in the university, football or in the country. The only way you can bring about a change is to do something about it.

"Football coaches have to learn to understand and identify with the New Generation. They have to learn to relate to young people, they have to become familiar with the things young people like. Maybe it's music or how they dress. Or maybe it means wearing your hair and sideburns just a little longer. A football coach who wants to survive in today's way of life can no longer be a crew-cut square. I don't mean that he has to break out in long hair down to his shoulders or wear beads, but he has to identify himself with the things young people like and do.

"I believe in discipline but I think that a coach's rules have to be tempered to consider the player. What difference does it make how long a kid's hair is? That doesn't have one single thing to do with discipline. When it comes to hair, dress or living habits, I think college football players are old enough and men enough to handle these things themselves. There are some things, however, that must remain the prerogative of the coach, like how long we're going to practice, who's going to play and what we're going to do in a game. That is one area where I think a coach cannot be adjustable if football is to survive as a part of college life.

"The coach who permits himself to be forced to take a position that's going to be discussed publicly is a damn fool and he is asking for trouble. Too many coaches today are more concerned with their public image—what will the trustees say, what will the alumni think—than they are in understanding their players and relating to them. The authoritarian approach has gone out of style. You just can't tell a kid today that he has to do something and expect him to do it. He wants to know 'Why?' and he is entitled to know. An athlete will no longer buy this business that they'll do something just because you have 'Coach' in front of your name.

"This whole thing is really a partnership. You've got to tell the players that it's *their* team. This business about its being Joe Paterno's team is a lot of crap. It isn't my team. It's theirs. I tell them it doesn't make any difference whether we've got guys with long hair or short hair. That won't decide whether or not we're going to be a good football team. But there are certain things that will make it easier for us to get along, to be a unified group. Maybe if we all keep our hair a certain length it's a symbol of unity, a sacrifice we make for unity. It's something that identifies us as a 'we' and 'us' group, makes us stand out a little more, makes each player proud to be a member of a team.

"Some people like to use the word 'communicate,' but I don't think that's the proper word. I *consult* with my players. The fact that you do consult indicates that you have respect for them. I want to exchange ideas with my players. I want to hear their thoughts on things so that we can discuss them freely like adults. We may not always agree, but at least I listen and I hear. However, after consulting, I always reserve the right to make my own decisions. That prerogative belongs to the coach, and when he loses it, he no longer is a coach. But he has to have an open mind."

Paterno's enlightenment has not come about accidentally. He has made a genuine effort to analyze what the young people on college campuses are thinking and saying and he has found that, in many cases, they are right and the Establishment is wrong. Not many college coaches agree with him but that doesn't bother him one bit.

"Too many college coaches live in the dark ages," Joe charges. "They don't want to or aren't able to relate to their players. Men like Jim Owens of Washington, Murray Warmath of Minnesota, Ben Schwartzwalder of Syracuse and Lloyd Eaton of Wyoming had problems with their players and, in most cases, perhaps it was because they showed a lack of understanding.

"On the other hand, some coaches adjusted because they were smart enough to realize the old way was no longer valid. John McKay of USC, Darrell Royal of Texas, Woody Hayes of Ohio State, Bob Blackman of Illinois, John Ralston of Stanford and John Bateman of Rutgers are outstanding examples of men who became tuned in to the times. There are others, too, but there are far more who have let the parade pass them by. There is no longer any place for them in college football. The authoritarians have to go!

"I think we have to understand, when we talk about youth today and the way they feel, what they're saying to us. They're asking our generation, 'What have you done for America and for your fellow man and for what other reason besides making money?' I think that's why there is so much distrust of us by young people today. They think any time we try to do anything we're doing it for selfish reasons.

"We have tried to buy them off. We've given them cars and we think that's bought respect. All it has really done is make them feel that we think material things will satisfy them. That money can buy everything. Well, it can't and the kids have proven that by their actions lately.

"The trouble is, our generation, the ones who came through the Depression and the war years, want to protect their children, they want to give them everything. They've forgotten that one of the great joys of life is achieving. That is part of youth's problem today. They're bored to death when they get to college. They've had all the joys. They've had sex, cars and privileges when they were young. There's got to be something else for them to do. So they go on to things like drugs.

"A lot of people·say the kids are scared to death, but it's really we who are scared. We're afraid we're going to lose what we have, that a minority group, in this case the youth of our country, is going to take something away from us.

"Most people talk about campus dissent as if it was a disease that has to be stamped out. I think that much of what has happened on college campuses has been good. The young people have stirred up the universities and made them change for the better. They are sick and tired of the damned hypocrisy that we have in a lot of schools, and they're right.

"The part of the student unrest that I don't like on college campuses, including ours at Penn State, are groups like the Students for a Democratic Society—the SDS—the hard-core revolutionary group that numbers maybe twenty-five or thirty. They're like vultures, preying upon any situation so they can stir up the so-called silent majority, the great mass of kids who are just determined to get a good education. Any time the university does something, they criticize it. When we have something good, a change for the better, we have to outsell the SDS in presenting it to the great majority of students. If we don't do it, they're going to destroy us.

"You just can't ask kids to work as hard as they've had to in high school in order to get into college and then make them take some of the courses they've had to take, listen to some professors who are terrible teachers and to see people who are not really interested in them but who are more interested in making a reputation for themselves in research or in writing a book or in becoming the so-called star of a department. For years we've had professors in classrooms who have had the attitude toward kids that if you don't like the way we're doing things here, then get out. We have ten guys waiting to get in your seats. It's wrong, terribly wrong.

"Now the kids are fed up with that kind of attitude and they are standing up and dissenting. It's been our fault. We have to listen, we've got to be able to say and teach things that are meaningful to them. I'm not saying that we have to make everything in our curriculum relevant, but it's got to be relevant teaching.

"The kids today have more guts than we did. They're just determined not to have to inherit the same kind of hypocritical society, with its corruption, scandals and smooth-talking politicians, that we did. They want a better world than that and they're entitled to it. They think they can get it by shaking up some of our institutions and that has happened at so many universities lately. Aside from a handful, like those in the SDS, most of them want to change things from within. They are not out to destroy an entire system, they just want to make it better by changing it.

"I sympathize with that kind of dissent. I've always been a doer myself. I hate people who sit around and bitch and then don't go out and do something. We have let down the youth of today. We say to them we can't change that quickly, we say we can't give them everything they want, but we don't explain why we can't go faster, why we can't give them everything they want. We don't try to protect what's good about our universities by actually selling them on what's good. We don't listen to them. We don't consult with them.

"I blame college administrators for a great deal of the trouble. They were running scared. It is as if you're walking along and you see a little black cloud. And you say, 'Well, we might get a little rain, but it won't be much.' So you take a chance. All of a sudden you're in the damnedest thunderstorm you've ever seen. You have no plan, you don't know what to do, so you start running every which way, you don't know where you're going. That's what happened to college administrations. They saw a little trouble here, a little trouble there. All of a sudden this thing became a violent storm, they were caught in it, they didn't have any plans and they didn't know where the hell to go. So everybody got a chance to get underneath a shelter, now we're all together and starting to form up a bit. Some of them have found ways to develop methods and procedures to handle problems and I don't think we're running scared anymore.

"I honestly believe that Penn State, for example, is a better university today because of its problems. Anybody who is honest would have to say that almost every university, except maybe Kent State, Columbia and California at Berkeley, where situations were permitted to get out of hand, are probably better for what has happened. The ones that have avoided violence have to be a little bit better for it.

"We have to get the students involved in the university and make them responsible for certain things. When we can't go along with their demands, we have to consult with them and explain why not. There are a lot of demands for change that are right. Maybe we should have more liberal rules for girls in dormitories, maybe the quality of teaching isn't as good as it should be, maybe some courses are not relevant to this day and age and maybe we should be teaching other things. We have to listen to student dissenters and we have to relate to them.

"Most of these kids are trying to identify with something that can be meaningful to them. I know this may sound corny, but college football can supply that vehicle if it's handled properly. Everybody talks about polarization, they all want to solve the big problem in the entire country. If a bunch of kids playing football can live together when their noses bleed, when they ache, when they're dog-tired and when some coach is chewing them out and they can do things together and for each other, then there has to be some good in it.

"Kids on college campuses today are anti-war and I think they are 100 percent right. No nation that has ever fought a war did a poorer job of selling the action in Vietnam to the people than the United States. We just tried to slip into Vietnam without ever admitting what we were doing and, all of a sudden, we were caught with our pants down and with several hundred thousand troops fighting an unpopular war. We were gradually sneaking our way into Vietnam and, suddenly, we looked up and we were embarrassed. And now it's impossible for us to defend our position there.

"Then along came Cambodia, another unpopular move that triggered violence on college campuses. The students were angry and they reacted. I don't condone violence but I understand it. They don't want to be drafted to fight a war that our country has had trouble justifying. I'd hate to be a nineteen- or twenty-year-old kid and have to go to Vietnam. I'd go because of the way I was brought up, because of the discipline I have, but I'd hate like hell to get an arm shot off for what's going on in Vietnam.

"This anti-war feeling has distorted some people's views of football. They try to connect the violence of the war with the violence of football. Pro football, in its effort to appeal to a certain group of people, has portrayed the violence. The fierce hitting, the wanting to 'kill' people. But it's not really as violent as the television show, 'The Violent World of Sam Huff,' made it out to be. Sure, there are some bumps and bruises, but it's not worse than a good old-fashioned street fight. Football is an aggressive game and demands physical toughness and contact but I have never been associated with a player who tried to deliberately injure an opponent. A lot of people would like to put the war and football together, to make them relate to each other. They do football a disservice. It just isn't the same. If it was, I would get out of it in a hurry."

Joe Paterno's empathy with the New Generation does not endear him to the stubborn authoritarians who still abound in college football coaching, but this awareness and understanding are what set him aside from most of his colleagues. They are what make Joe Paterno someone special among coaches.

11: Down with Little League!

THE GERM OF STUDENT UNREST, Joe Paterno insists, begins to spread long before young people get to college campuses. It is fostered, perhaps unwittingly, by parents' desire to give their children the best of all worlds by involving them in organized sports, like Little League baseball, Pop Warner and other midget football leagues, junior high school football and summer sports camps, that do them far more harm than good.

In many communities, family life revolves around Little League baseball. Mother and Dad live and die with the success or failure of their son. They can tell you what kind of a pitch he hit or how the umpire made a bad call on a third strike. They can come up with the boy's batting average in a flash—unless it's .200 and then it's because of bad calls—and if he is a pitcher Mom can rattle off his earned-run average and won-lost record. And woe to the Little League manager who doesn't play their boy!

Midget football leagues flourish in many places and it's a funny sight to see a bunch of eight-, nine- and ten-year-olds looking like Singer's Midgets dressed up in full football regalia. When they are slightly older, they are put into junior high school programs, often under the direction of an English or shop teacher whose closest contact with football has been an end zone seat at a pro game. The heads of the youngsters are filled with fly patterns, screens, draws and crossover blocking.

Then there are the summer football, baseball, basketball, tennis, golf, wrestling—you name it—camps, where doting parents send their subteens and teenagers to learn from big-name pro and college coaches and star players. The big names are attractions, the tuition rates are high for one- and two-week sessions and nine- and ten-year-olds are thrown into competition with fifteen- and sixteen-year-olds.

"What ever happened to the good old days when, if you felt like playing baseball, you rounded up some of your buddies, got a bat and a ball and went out and played?" asks Paterno. "If you only had four or five guys, you played two-a-cat. Or if you didn't have a bat, you played stickball.

"What do we do now?" Joe adds. "We dress up our kids in uniforms, give them professional equipment, tell them when to practice and when to play, organize their games for them, give them officials and put them in the hands of some guy who doesn't know the first thing about the sport or what's good for an eight-year-old.

"I am unalterably opposed to Little League baseball, midget football leagues and summer camps for boys under fourteen. They should be abolished!"

That's strong talk, but Joe Paterno actually bristles at the mere mention of any kind of organized sports for youngsters of pre-high school age. He feels very keenly that, aside from the unwarranted pressure it puts on young people, it is a contributing factor to the insecurity and problems of the New Generation.

"Kids want the opportunity to do things for themselves," says Joe. "I think they're just sick and tired of having adults organize things for them. They really want to find their own ways of getting games started and to play when *they* feel like it instead of when adults tell them to do it. We destroy their initiative by arranging things for them, whether they like it or not.

"The worst thing about Little League is that kids are asked to produce at too early an age. They are thrown into competition, with all of its pressures, when they aren't ready for it. They get publicity in the newspapers, they're picked up for all-star teams and the public makes heroes out of them. They are made to feel that they've accomplished something. That's just too much for an eleven- or twelve-year-old kid to take in his stride. They're not old enough to appreciate it. They should be having fun playing games, but instead it becomes a serious thing. And what about the boy who isn't good enough to play and has to sit on the bench? Little League can be a traumatic experience for him.

"Parents become so involved in Little League and, while they mean to be doing the right thing, they are actually hurting their kids. I remember a story I heard when I was trying to recruit Lawson Cashdollar, a great high school athlete who went on to become a star end at Princeton. It seems that Lawson's father was a Little League nut and he went to every game when his son played. In one game, Lawson was pitching a no-hitter for a couple of innings. Then, in the third and fourth innings, he walked three or four players in a row, hit a couple of batters and the opposing team got three or four runs. So the coach took him out of the game. Lawson's father ran down on the field, grabbed the coach and screamed, 'You can't take him out. He's got a no-hitter going!'

"Can you imagine what an experience like that does to a twelve-year-old kid? What kind of sense of values can he learn? Parents mean well, I guess, but too often they get carried away in their enthusiasm and, in the end, it's their own youngster who suffers.

"Another thing wrong with Little League is that there is too much of the woman involved in a boy's life. Women have a tendency, especially when it comes to sports, not to appreciate that the great joys are in the effort and even in the disappointments. They try to shield their kids from disappointment, to feel sorry for them when they lose. As a result, kids lose some of the joy that comes out of just playing a game. Parents ought to let them get into a natural situation, to grow into it.

"It's so bad for young kids. Their parents attach too much importance to their playing as Little Leaguers. You go to a game and you hear the parents talk about how some nine-year-old can pitch like a big leaguer or how an eleven-year-old can really hit the ball. They measure these young people by their ability on the baseball field, how they stack up as competitors and whether or not they're winners. How important is that for a ten- or twelve-year-old kid? What happens to him later in life when he doesn't have the talent and the ability to be a star? What it does is make him feel inferior because he was a hero in Little League at the age of ten or twelve and now he feels that he's nothing. And some people wonder why college students dissent and protest against the Establishment."

Paterno feels even more keenly about organized football programs for youngsters of junior high school age. Unlike some college coaches who insist that it is never too early to start training boys to play football, Joe is of the opinion that midget leagues and junior high football are harmful in many ways.

"Kids of junior high school age are just not ready, physically or emotionally, for an organized football program. What's more, it drives them away from football. Consider what usually happens. First, the junior high coach is usually someone who doesn't know the game or some eager beaver who is trying to make a name for himself. The coach plays only so many boys, the rest are cut from the squad or sit on the bench and they never try the sport again. In their minds, they have failed to make the grade in competition. It bothers them emotionally because they can't compete with their friends who may be better athletes at the time. It just isn't right for an eighth grader to be wiped out as a potential player just because he isn't ready to compete at the age of thirteen or fourteen.

"Then take the case of the youngster who is a star in junior high school. Maybe he's the quarterback and everybody raves about him. He thinks he's pretty damn good because everybody tells him he is. All right, he goes on to high school and, suddenly, he finds out that he isn't as good as he thought he was. There can be a fantastic physical and emotional change in a boy between eighth grade and his sophomore year in high school. Now the boy is lost. He can't handle the problem emotionally.

"Seventh and eighth graders aren't mature enough physically, either, and very often they become victims of injuries. It doesn't matter how much protection they have in the way of equipment.

Their bones are soft and they are still growing. They don't know how to protect themselves and they can get hurt so easily in a scrimmage or a game. Frequently they sustain injuries that bother them for the rest of their lives.

"Why not have an intramural program in junior high school with the kids playing just for fun and without any emphasis on winning or losing? What's so important about winning when you're fourteen years old? Let as many youngsters as possible get to play and forget about teaching them to hit and tackle when they're in the seventh and eighth grades. There is plenty of time for that when they get to their freshman year in high school. Then, give them pads and start teaching them how to handle themselves. But, again, the less organized they are, the better I'd like it. The kids get more out of it and they can enjoy playing the game.

"High school football can be part of a boy's development. By the time he reaches his sophomore year he is old enough to appreciate the joy of competing. He is old enough to accept a challenge and, physically, he is better able to handle contact. Coaching has improved tremendously on the high school level and most of the men who are in it these days are dedicated and highly competent.

"I feel very strongly, however, that there have to be some reforms made in high school football. In Pennsylvania, for instance, there are some rules which haven't changed in twenty years. Like the starting date for fall practice, which is sometimes just two-and-a-half or three weeks before a team's opening game. That isn't enough time to get a squad ready physically and, as a result, most Pennsylvania high school coaches cheat. They're having some kind of practice undercover. If they're not cheating according to the letter of the law, they're cheating against the spirit of the law. It doesn't matter that they do it to give their players more time to get in condition physically. What we have, then, is a breakdown in our society. The kids start learning a disrespect for rules, even though the rules are not realistic. Then we wonder why young people have so little regard for law and order. It's our fault. We show them the way.

"I think that the rules ought to be changed to permit some kind

The "Gold Dust Twins": That was what Brooklyn Prep fans called Joe (left) and George Paterno when they were tearing up New York City gridirons in 1944.

A college quarterback: Paterno in his playing days at Brown, 1949, when it was said, "He can't pass. He can't run. He just wins."

Paterno's first—and only—boss:
Snow-covered Charles "Rip"
Engle, shown roaming the sidelines
during a stormy game, persuaded
Joe to give up a potential law
career for coaching.

Collaboration: Paterno and Engle
worked closely at practice while Joe
matured as Engle's right hand man.

"This way": Paterno bends to the task of showing blocking technique during spring practice.

The gambler: Richie Lucas, 1959 All-America quarterback at Penn State, earned the reputation as "a riverboat gambler." Paterno, the quarterback coach then, encouraged the style of play.

"What can we do?": With Penn State trailing Syracuse, Paterno, on sideline, seeks help from assistants, who have better vantage point, in press box high above field.

Final review: Paterno goes over game plan with Frank Patrick (left) and Jim O'Hora, assistant coaches, during flight to Syracuse on a Friday night in 1969.

Someone wins and someone loses: Penn State pulled it out, 15-14, but Syracuse coach, Ben Schwartzwalder, disturbed by officiating of the game, wasn't very happy after the traditional coach's handshake following the battle.

"Try this": Paterno gives instructions to Chuck Burkhart
before the Penn State quarterback goes back into action,
hopeful of turning the tide against Syracuse.

ABOVE:
The Messenger: Paterno give Greg Edmonds, split end, a boost toward the action as he carries the coach's directio to the huddle. Paterno alternates two men at a position for purpose of sending in mos offensive plays.

LEFT:
Lonely in a crowd: That tim when a coach must worry, think, decide, and come up with the right answer in a hurry from the sideline.

RIG
"The world is mine": A 3: lead can move any coach thinking things could ne be bet

"You gotta be kiddin'":
A call by officials has
Paterno upset.

"Oh, joy": Paterno takes
the liberty of indicating
a touchdown by
Penn State.

Two of the best: All-America defensive tackles Steve Smear (left) and Mike Reid, conferring on sidelines during a game, cook up new ways to torment their foe.

An outstanding foe: Paterno congratulates Gary Steele of Army, whose performance as a receiver nearly gave the Cadets victory over highly favored Penn State in 1968. The Lions won, 28–24.

A Menacing Crew: The heart of the
Penn State defense that terrorized oppo-
nents in 1969 waits for the next play.
(Left to right): Linebacker Mike Smith (10);
Tackle Steve Smear (76); End John
Ebersole (89); Linebacker Dennis Onkotz
(35); Linebacker Jim Kates (55); End
Gary Hull (80); Tackle Mike Reid (68);
Linebacker Jack Ham (33).

Press conference: Paterno and Dan Devine,
Missouri coach, relax as they parry
questions by writers before 1970
Orange Bowl game.

Players join in: Dennis Onkotz, Charlie Pittman, and Neal Smith, All-America linebacker, halfback, and safety, respectively, with their coach at pre-Orange Bowl press conference.

The how and why: Paterno at ease during post-game press interview following a triumph at Penn State.

Dressing room happiness: Paterno expresses his feelings to the players after they gained that big one against North Carolina State.

The fans: Paterno is mobbed by youngsters at Harrisburg Airport up his return from 1970 Orange Bowl.

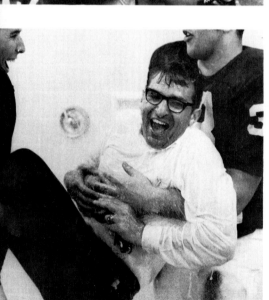

The dunking: Gary Gray (30) and Greg Ducatte (38) toss Paterno into the shower after the second Orange Bowl victory January 1, 1970.

A coach's rewards take many
Victory ride: Paterno is hois
the shoulders of his players foll
major triumph over North Ca
State in 1967. That game estab
Penn State's outstanding defe
a real p

The coach's family: A h
Sue Paterno durin
1969 season sits at
with David, Joe Jr. (
Mary Kathryn
Diana

Governor's blessing: Paterno receives
a pat from Pennsylvania Governor
Raymond Shafer after the 1970
Orange Bowl. The Governor also was
tossed into the shower minutes later
by happy Penn State players.

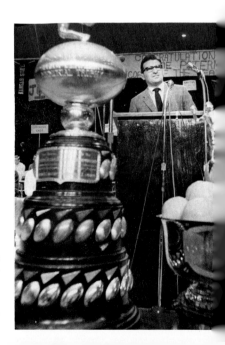

The hero comes home: Paterno at
Penn State celebration following
1968 season and victory in 1969
Orange Bowl game. The coach looks
out over Lambert Trophy and
Orange Bowl award.

The women in his life:
Proud Mama Paterno and
Sue celebrated with Joe
when he was awarded his
second straight Eastern
Coach of the Year trophy in
New York after Penn State's
unbeaten 1969 season.

"Oh I know *him*": A jovial President Nixon welcomes Paterno to the White
House, January, 1970, after their disagreement over which 1969 college
football team was No. 1. Smiling witnesses to this meeting are Bill Murray,
executive director of the American Football Coaches Association and three
former coaches, Jack Curtice of the University of California, Santa Barbara;
Duffy Daugherty of Michigan and Bud Wilkinson of Oklahoma.

Mr. Outside: Lydell Mitchell, who set Penn State season and career records for rushing and scoring touchdowns in 1971, nimbly eludes a would-be tackler.

Mr. Inside: Franco Harris, the other half of the Lions' mighty one-two punch in 1971, bulls his way for big yardage behind solid blocking of teammates.

"Will it work?": A thoughtful Paterno prowls the sidelines as he tries to come up with a brilliant idea to help his team on the field.

The captains: Joe and his four co-captains of the 1972 team (left to right), Safety Gregg Ducatte (now a Penn State assistant coach), Defensive Tackle Jim Heller, Offensive Guard Carl Schaukowitch and Quarterback John Hufnagel.

His just reward: Halfback John Cappelletti poses at a dinner in New York City with the Heisman Trophy, which he won in 1973 as the nation's outstanding college football player, and then-Vice President Gerald R. Ford.

Why he won: Cappelletti, on collision course with Maryland's Randy White, picking up some of the 202 yards he gained that day in Penn State's 42-22 win over the Terps.

Reacting: Paterno shouts instructions to his players during the January 1, 1974 Orange Bowl game in Miami, which the Lions won, 16-9, to complete an undefeated season. Tight End Dan Natale is on the left.

"What went wrong?": That seems to be what Joe is asking George Reihner, an offensive lineman, as he comes off the field in a game in 1974.

A study in concentration: Paterno, away from the crowd
on the sidelines, stares intently at the action, planning
his next move.

A study in frustration: All-America Linebacker Greg _le is alone with his thoughts _ Penn State is upset by North _rolina State, 15-14, in 1975.

_ter of attraction: Linebacker _ Hostetler (38) and Assistant _ch John Rosenberg listen to _terno explain what he wants _s defense to do during 1977 _ory over Rutgers at the new _nts Stadium in New Jersey's Meadowlands. Quarterback Chuck Fusina (14) is on the right.

The 1977 staff: The men who made Penn State a winner.
Front row (left to right): Assistants Jerry Sandusky,
J. T. White, Head Coach Joe Paterno, Assistants Bob
Phillips and Dick Anderson. Back row (left to right):
Assistants Jim Williams, Booker Brooks, Gregg Ducatte,
Fran Ganter and John Rosenberg.

of spring practice period for high schools at a time that wouldn't interfere with other sports. The coaches need more time with their players to teach them fundamentals and how to protect themselves on the football field. This should be on a national basis, similar to the way the NCAA regulates college athletics."

Summer sports camps are another one of Joe Paterno's pet peeves, even though he spent eight years as an instructor at a football camp during his days as an assistant coach. (Because of his experience and disenchantment, Joe now refuses invitations to be on the staffs of summer football camps.) He contends that this is part of the overemphasis on athletics for pre-high schoolers that is so prevalent in today's affluent society.

"Parents feel they *have* to send their kids to football, basketball, baseball or wrestling camps because everybody else is doing it. They think their boy is being deprived if they don't send him to a specialized sports camp, where he can be exposed to people like Joe Namath or Wilt Chamberlain when he was with the Los Angeles Lakers or Willis Reed of the New York Knicks.

"What are they trying to prove? Are they trying to make them better athletes? I don't really think so. Sure, kids need capable instruction and coaching, but not when they're ten or eleven years old. Say the boy starts going to a football or basketball camp when he is ten. He goes every summer and a lot of time, energy, effort and money are spent to make him a football or a basketball player. By the time he reaches his senior year in high school, he must be pretty darn sick of it all and he gets to feel that it's almost a chore. That he has been doing this same thing for seven or eight years. I don't think, psychologically, that's good for any youngster. It deprives him of a chance to perhaps do what he really wanted to do. Like playing the piano or maybe milking cows. I think we ought to let go of our kids. If they get interested in a sport, fine, but let them do it on their own. Don't impose it on them, don't have an organized program.

"Something else that bothers me about summer sports camps is the fact that the range of ages is sometimes from nine to fifteen or sixteen. You take a nine-year-old, put him in a camp with fifteen-year-olds and you ask him to compete and compare himself with the older boys. He lives with and learns from the older

kids for a couple of weeks and I don't think that's a healthy education. He can learn bad habits too easily. It isn't fair to the
youngster. It's too much too soon.

"I say it's time we cut out all this stuff and let kids grow up
naturally. Suppose they don't grow up to be athletic superstars.
That isn't so terrible. Let them find their own interests and their
own levels. Let them be kids instead of forcing them to play at
being adults."

12: The Case for the Black Athlete

ITEM: BLACK FOOTBALL PLAYERS at the University of Washington revolt, charge Coach Jim Owens and his staff with racism.

Item: Indiana University hit by black athlete revolt; football players quit team.

Item: Fourteen black players suspended by University of Wyoming Coach Lloyd Eaton after they announce they would wear black armbands for game against Brigham Young University.

Item: University of Iowa football squad decimated when black players quit, charging Coach Ray Nagle with discrimination.

Item: Eight black athletes at Syracuse University walk out on spring practice, accuse coaches of discrimination, are subsequently suspended by Coach Ben Schwartzwalder, then refuse reinstatement.

Item: Idaho State Coach Ed Cavanaugh suspends seventeen black football players for remainder of season for failing to show up for practice.

Item: Pitt Athletic Director Casimir Myslinski denies charge by Black Action Society that his department discriminates against black athletes.

College football, heretofore almost sacrosanct in a changing world, was suddenly hit full force with a rash of revolts by black athletes in the late 1960's, inspiring newspaper headlines like the ones above. Schools and coaches, whose reputations were considered impeccable in their relations with black athletes, found themselves accused and indicted by their accusers of a wide variety of injustices. The charges ranged from exploitation to unfair treatment, as compared to that received by white athletes, to gross racial discrimination. In some cases, the black athletes were justified; in other cases, some of their charges were without foundation.

There were many reasons for the new attitude of blacks. Some coaches and schools were guilty of exploiting their black athletes. They brought blacks in to play football, to help give them winning teams, and then ignored them socially and academically. In some instances, little or no effort was made to integrate them into the mainstream of campus life. They were given snap courses to take to insure their eligibility, depriving them of equal educational opportunities, and very few were graduated. They were not given the same disciplinary treatment as white athletes by the coaches who recruited them. Of course, not all coaches or colleges were guilty but, unhappily, critics were quick to lump the good ones with the offenders.

Regardless of the merits of the complaints, the fact remains that the revolts by black athletes, and not all of them necessarily militants, swept the country like wildfire. The only section which escaped was the lily-white deep South, where only recently schools had begun to recruit black athletes. Coaches in other areas, whose schools were not hit, sat waiting fearfully for the other shoe to drop. Liberal whites joined the battle in support of the black athlete and national magazines and newspapers ran stories focusing on the problem.

It was apparent that injustices did exist on some football squads and the smart coaches did some readjusting before they were singled out for criticism. They hired black assistant coaches, paid closer attention to complaints, recruited more circumspectly and were more vigilant in supervising their staffs. They consulted with their black players and sought out and settled problems before they became problems. Then they did something about them. But too many college football coaches just sat back and hoped it would all just go away.

While many schools have corrected whatever abuses of black athletes that once may have existed, Joe Paterno agrees that some universities—and coaches—are still guilty of exploiting them. "It's part of the winning-at-any-cost philosophy that some coaches have," he charges.

"A coach shouldn't recruit blacks unless he genuinely respects them as human beings and because the university can do something for them and they can do something for the university," says Paterno. "But some coaches bring blacks in as hired help, just to give them a winning team. They bring in kids who don't belong there academically in the first place, then they isolate them by putting them in an athletic dorm where they're out of the mainstream of campus life and not really part of anything. They put them in easy courses so they can stay eligible. When that happens, they're not getting the same academic advantages that are available to whites and they're being exploited unfairly. They're being used because they can make a team a winner. That's wrong and I don't blame the kids for protesting. They've been misled and the coach and the university are taking advantage of their skills as athletes.

"Some coaches are quick to blame black athletes for all their troubles. They complain about how hard they are to handle, how they don't adhere to the rules and want to be treated better than whites. That's just not true. All they want is to be treated the same as whites, and why shouldn't they be? Although you won't find anyone who will admit it, it's true that some coaches won't recruit blacks any more. A lot of them are even setting up quiet quotas. They say they don't want too many of those 'troublemakers.' Just enough to help them win. It's a shame that it has to happen at all and there are only a few coaches in that category, but it makes it hard to respect some of the men in college football. Maybe they should be taking sensitivity courses."

The pattern of the revolts was pretty much the same all over. At the University of Washington, the black athletes charged, among other things, that Coach Jim Owens and his staff had switched the positions of some players so that the team wouldn't have too many black starters. They also complained that the team trainer often unjustly accused them of "dogging" it and called them "niggers." They demanded the appointment of a black assistant coach to the staff.

Similar charges were levied against Indiana, Iowa and dozens of other colleges and coaches across the country. Syracuse, which had produced a number of black All-Americas through the years —players like Jim Brown, the late Ernie Davis, Floyd Little and Jim Nance—was the focal point of the revolt in 1970. Eight players walked out of spring practice to protest against what they considered to be unfair treatment and they were promptly suspended by Coach Ben Schwartzwalder. The case eventually went to the city and county Human Rights Commission and, sub-sequently, the players were offered reinstatement but refused to report.

Among the charges levied by the black athletes were name-calling by coaches and players, unequal medical treatment, position switches to keep blacks off the traveling squad for away games, harassment, black players were disciplined more severely than whites, a lack of equal tutoring facilities and undue delay in hiring a black assistant coach.

The controversy, which began in the spring of 1970, continued through the season and became a *cause célèbre* among citizens of Syracuse, students, athletes and alumni. Most of the white players on the squad supported the coach, and there was even some talk of canceling Syracuse's first game of the season, against Kansas.

The result was that Chancellor John E. Corbally (who later resigned to become president of the University of Illinois) appointed a special twelve-member committee to study the events surrounding the boycott and Schwartzwalder's suspension of the players. The conclusions of the committee were double-pronged, taking note of the fact that the coach had certain prerogatives and also charging Schwartzwalder, his staff and the athletic di-rector with being "insensitive to changing student concerns."

Generally, the committee found that most of the charges were unfounded, that there was no evidence of lesser medical treat-ment for black players or intended discrimination against blacks in selection of players for road trips, team positions, discipline or tutoring facilities. But, concluded the committee, there was substance in the charge of harassment, based mainly on the tendency of the coaches to regard as "troublemakers" those athletes whose personal values and political beliefs "seemed to conflict with their own."

"The head coach is the boss," admitted the committee. "He and his assistants determine the style of play, the qualifications of players for the various positions and the training and practice rules. While players may express opinions and may be consulted, the final authority is the coaching staff. Insubordination, which includes missing practice without due cause, may result in suspension with no appeal, except to the coaching staff. Some players resent this, some resent but accept this, and some rebel."

Then the committee noted, "The definition of the spring boycott merely as an issue of violating coaching authority, and the penalizing of black athletes without taking into consideration the broader context of their protest was an act of institutional racism unworthy of a great university."

The Athletic Department did not get off easy in a list of recommendations made by the committee. Athletic Director Jim Decker was chastised for a "totally unsatisfactory response" during the nine-month-long crisis and Schwartzwalder and his staff were not exactly held blameless. It was recommended, among other things, that the grievance procedure be changed with a view toward stimulating dialogue and conciliation and that an educative program be instituted to facilitate communication among team members, between coaches and the team and between the head coach and his assistants.

While the situation which developed at Syracuse was deplored, the report concluded that there obviously was some reason for the revolt and the climate it generated on campus. It also suggested that, perhaps, there was a lack of understanding and consultation between the black athletes and the coaching staff.

What happened at Syracuse in 1970 was not unusual. It had occurred at many other schools and is likely to happen again unless coaches become more tolerant and more visionary to the inequalities, some unintentional but nevertheless still prevalent, which have been permitted to exist in college athletics.

The trouble at the University of Wyoming began when fourteen black football players stated that they were going to wear black armbands when playing against Brigham Young—they did not refuse to play the game—in protest of the Mormon religion's exclusion of blacks. Coach Lloyd Eaton reacted predictably. He suspended the fourteen players from the team, refused to speak with them as a group and got ready to play Brigham Young and the rest of Wyoming's opponents that season without them. The school administration backed up Eaton's decision and the players, who unsuccessfully sought to discuss the matter with their coach, were finished for the season.

Joe Paterno reacts predictably, too, to the Wyoming situation. "I'm not sure of all the facts," says Joe, "but if fourteen players on my squad have a common problem, we ought to be able to resolve it. Maybe it's not exactly comparable, but if fourteen Italian players think we're not feeding them enough pizza at the training table, it's a problem and we ought to sit down and discuss it. I don't think it's fair not to talk to them in a group if that's what they want. How else do you resolve problems if you don't talk about them?

"If I thought that what the fourteen black players wanted to do wasn't fair to the rest of the squad or to the university, we would try to work out a compromise. But I also think that problems such as these can be averted if you work at them day in and day out so that you are alert to remove the cause before it becomes an issue. Unfortunately, too many coaches still active are not equipped intellectually to do that kind of job.

"I know this. I'm never going to jeopardize the chances of my team to have a good season by throwing players off the squad just to satisfy a personal whim. I'm going to have a lot of football teams but my players are only going to play on three of them. I don't think it's fair to screw up 33⅓ percent of their college football careers just because I don't like the way a guy looks or what he wears.

"One thing I believe to be very important is that any problems, whether they are with black athletes or white athletes, must be kept on a player-coach relationship. There isn't any problem that can't be solved when the players involved and the coach sit down and consult about it. The trouble is, at some places third parties get involved in something they don't really know anything about, and it's no longer a player-coach relationship. That's what happened at Syracuse, where a vice provost of the university advised the black athletes and the coach was bypassed. From the beginning there wasn't much chance that the situation could be settled amicably because there was a lack of communication.

"The administration wasn't very helpful, either. They pussyfooted back and forth on the subject and then, finally, when an impasse was reached, the chancellor appointed a committee. Now someone had to be right and someone had to be wrong—either Ben Schwartzwalder or his black athletes. If Ben was wrong the university should have fired him. If the black athletes were wrong, Ben should have been supported. Instead, the report handed out a few slaps on the wrist to both sides."

The situation Jim Owens had at Washington was slightly different. The first protest, in 1968, included an allegation that the team trainer was a racist, that he referred to the black athletes as "niggers," called them malingerers and goldbricks and brushed off their injuries as laziness. Owens, who was then both the head football coach and the athletic director, decided to put the accused man on "probation" for a year, hoping that the matter would simmer down. It didn't work. Eventually Owens had to get rid of the trainer and Jim subsequently gave up his duties as athletic director. But that didn't stop his black players from revolting a second and a third time.

Joe Paterno thinks that he would probably have handled that problem differently if he had been faced with it. "You just can't have a racist on your staff, whether he's a white racist or a black racist. And it's a mistake to have anyone on your staff who can't understand and relate to all athletes, black and white. If you have one on your staff, and you know it, you can't hide it. As a coach, you have to get rid of him. I wouldn't give a damn if he was my best friend, I'd send him packing at the first sign of any racism.

"I think Jim Owens was wrong in not settling that part of the problem immediately if the evidence showed that the accusation was true. That may have had a lot to do with the compounding of the other problems."

It was no mere accident that Penn State was not involved in any difficulties with its black athletes in the 1960's although the university, like most other places, did have its problems on campus with militants. One big reason was Joe Paterno, the ultra-modern football coach who was tuned in to the changes in our country. He recognized that all was not sweetness and light for the black student-athlete at Penn State or any other school and he was determined to see that the blacks on his squad got a fair shake.

Over the years, Penn State had not been noted for the number of black athletes on its teams. Oh, there had been a few truly outstanding ones, like Rosey Grier, Jesse Arnell and Lenny Moore in the 1940's and 1950's, but they had been extremely rare. This had not been by design, because an effort had been made to recruit them, but somehow black athletes have not been especially attracted to a college that was a hundred miles from nowhere. They preferred to go to Big Ten and Big Eight schools or, when they couldn't measure up academically, to some colleges in the West, where admissions people were not averse to winking at academic requirements for "student-athletes."

The situation, however, had begun to change at Penn State in the '60s. The success of Rip Engle's team made Penn State more attractive and, suddenly, recruiting quality black athletes became a little easier. There were five blacks on Joe Paterno's first unbeaten squad in 1968 and eight on the second undefeated club in 1969. Three of the four backfield starters, including the quarterback, at the beginning of the 1970 season were black.

Paterno claims no particular credit for the fact that more blacks have been playing football at Penn State in recent years. Indeed, he can't even tell you offhand how many of his players are black and how many are white. He doesn't categorize athletes by color, religion or even skills. To him, they are all human beings worthy of equal consideration. They are either good people or bad people, depending upon their attitude, and he makes a fetish of treating all of his players, including the superstars, alike.

"It's true that sports gave a black man a chance when other fields wouldn't give him one," says Joe Paterno. "At least he could play on a football or basketball team somewhere and have an opportunity to become someone. But let's not kid ourselves. There isn't one black kid on my football squad, or anyone else's squad, who has it as good as a white boy. The black athlete simply doesn't get what he should, if you measure it by what the white athlete gets, on any campus. Socially, the same advantages that are available to the white boy are just not available to the black. I've seen it happen so many times. Take a kid who's a regular on the football team. He isn't necessarily a star, but he's white. After a game, the fraternity people and the alumni knock themselves out trying to please him. If a black player is a superstar, he'll get the same treatment. But, if he's just another boy on the team, there isn't anybody clamoring for his attention.

"It isn't easy to change an attitude held by a majority. I can't tell fraternities whom to invite to their houses after a game, and I can't tell the alumni to make a fuss over our black players. In fact, I would prefer they wouldn't make a fuss over any of our players. But I try to show that we accept our black players as equals, that we respect them and are happy to have them on our squad. They get exactly the same treatment as white players, no better, no worse, and that's all they ever ask for, regardless of what some folks say. And that goes for an All-America, like Charlie Pittman, or a third-string substitute.

"I know some coaches are afraid that their images will suffer with the trustees or the alumni if they don't get tough with their blacks or if they don't have hard and fast rules regulating hair and dress. That's nonsense. A man has to do what he thinks is right or he isn't a man."

Joe Paterno doesn't worry about his image as a football coach. An unbridled liberal when it comes to recognizing the plight of blacks on predominantly white campuses, he does what he thinks is right.

"I think it must be exciting to be a young black kid today," Paterno says. "All of a sudden, they're part of a race that has finally become aware of its great potential. They're on the move, making progress, and every day is kind of a challenge. It isn't like some of us who are just trying to hang on to what we've got. These kids can see the action all around them and they want to go forward.

"What right has a coach, or anyone else, to tell a black athlete not to get involved? That's just not fair to him. They've got to get involved somehow. People have to understand that every single day of their lives blacks are being asked to join in some-

thing that their race has never done before. They're being asked
to get involved in something that they're deeply emotional about.
The pressure is on them every moment.

"All I ask of our players is that they don't do anything that
will embarrass their teammates. That goes for blacks or whites,
Catholics, Protestants or Jews."

Paterno's understanding and commitment to his black athletes
didn't start only recently. One incident that happened in 1962,
while he was an assistant coach, when Penn State traveled south
to play Florida in the Gator Bowl, still sticks in his mind. It involved Dave Robinson, Penn State's All-America end and a black.

The team's chartered plane was scheduled to fly into Jacksonville, but, because of bad weather, was delayed for a considerable
time and finally landed in Orlando. The players were hungry and
they, along with the coaches, crowded into the airport restaurant
and began ordering. But the restaurant manager and waitresses
refused to serve Dave Robinson, the only black man on the Penn
State squad that year.

"I'll never forget the look on Robby's face," says Paterno indignantly. "Here it was 1962 in the land of the free and a
restaurant in Florida refuses to serve an intelligent human being
like Dave Robinson because his skin is a different color."

Coach Rip Engle, Joe Paterno and the other members of the
coaching staff refused to eat in the airport restaurant and they
took Robinson to a nearby coffee shop, where they were served
without question.

"I've never forgotten that incident," says Joe, "and I vowed then
and there I would never permit any of the players I am associated
with to be embarrassed."

The next time Penn State went to the Gator Bowl, in 1967, Joe
Paterno was the head coach and he made certain that his black
players would not be discriminated against in Florida. Athletic
Director Ernie McCoy and his assistant, Ed Czekaj, scouted the
area and selected Daytona Beach as the most likely pre-game
training spot for the Nittany Lions. But Paterno had to have assurance that his black players would not be embarrassed. And
they weren't. Nor have they ever been embarrassed during Paterno's tenure as head coach.

Joe Paterno just happens to believe that all men are created equal, works hard at making it a reality on his own football squad and is repelled by what he sees happening around him. He has demonstrated this on many occasions with his forthrightness in dealing with his black athletes at Penn State.

Perhaps one reason for Joe Paterno's great understanding and empathy for the problems that face blacks is that he grew up as a member of a minority group in a parochial school that was primarily Irish. He was called "Wop" and "Guinea" too many times. Joe knows what it is to be treated as a second-class citizen and he is determined to see that black athletes who come under his wing at Penn State, or anywhere else, are not discriminated against, either on or off the football field.

"There is only one way I know to treat a black athlete," Joe declares, "and that's the way you would treat anyone else, like a human being. What difference does it make what color a man's skin is? White, black, yellow, green, they're all human beings and they deserve to be treated that way.

"Some coaches make a big thing about telling their black athletes not to date white girls. They don't have the right to tell any of their athletes what they should do in their private lives. They, and a lot of other people, have to get over the idea that every time they see a black kid with a white girl that there's sex involved. They don't think that when they see two whites together. A lot of black and white kids have a great deal in common. They're interested in the same things, they like to exchange ideas, they want to be with each other and they have respect for each other. What's wrong with that?

"I tell my black athletes that if they want to date white girls, that's their own private business. But I do point out that, if they want to make it a permanent relationship, to remember that there are a load of problems to overcome and they will have to work them out together. I think I owe them that much interference, if it can be called that.

"I know a lot of people will say, 'Yeah, that's great, but you wouldn't want *your* daughter to date a black.' Well, that's just not true. I once told Charlie Pittman and Jim Kates, two of the finest human beings I have ever known, that if my daughter came home with either of them my wife and I would be very happy. And I meant it."

Idealistic? Maybe. But that is Joe Paterno's attitude and he has made a super-effort to relate to his black players. He wants to know what they're thinking, how they think and what's bothering them so he can help make their world a better one. Joe and his wife, Sue, make it their business to attend the Black Arts Festival at Penn State. They go to other functions held by blacks on campus. Joe has been very active in the Renaissance Fund, an organization formed to help blacks on college campuses.

"I want to know what's going on," Paterno explains. "Maybe it will help me help them."

Despite Paterno's vigilance, there were hints that Penn State had a "black problem" during the 1970 season. Nothing could have been further from the truth and Joe was the first to squelch the rumor publicly.

It all began when Paterno began the 1970 season with a black quarterback. Mike Cooper, an intelligent, unassuming young man whose ambition is to become a coach, had beaten out Bob Parsons and John Hufnagel for the job in spring and pre-season practice and he started at quarterback in the first five games. When Joe made his decision to start Cooper, he realized exactly what the reaction would be. "I knew that if I picked Mike, people would say it was because he was black," said Joe. "And I also knew that if he wasn't the quarterback, people would say it was because he was black. The whole thing was unfair to Coop."

Cooper's reaction was realistic, too. Mike said, "The reason there's a racial thing in people's minds is because people put it there."

Two of Cooper's teammates in the starting backfield were Franco Harris and Lydell Mitchell, both blacks, who had been the second and third leading ground gainers behind All-America Charlie Pittman for the 1969 team. It was a potentially explosive backfield and Paterno adjusted his offense to take advantage of their capabilities. But it didn't quite work that way. Harris and Mitchell were hobbled by injuries, Cooper threw a flock of interceptions and soon found himself alternating with Parsons, whose passing wasn't much better. Penn State lost three of its first five games, to Colorado, Wisconsin and Syracuse.

Paterno had to make a move and he did it, belatedly, some thought, in the sixth game, against Army. He changed his offense to a tighter formation using a power-I and a double wing-T, benched Cooper for John Hufnagel, a sophomore, at quarterback, and kept both Harris and Mitchell, who were still partially ailing, on the sidelines at the start of the game, replacing them with Fran Ganter and Joel Ramich. All three replacements were white. The shakeup worked. Penn State beat Army and, with the same trio starting in almost every other game, didn't lose again for the rest of the season. Harris and Mitchell, however, saw enough action to rank one-two in ground gaining.

Before Paterno made his move, he called in Cooper and discussed it with him. He told Mike he didn't feel it was his fault that the team wasn't winning. The offense was just not productive and he thought that Hufnagel would be more effective in the more conservative attack that he was going to use in the Army game. Cooper, although not happy about the idea of being benched, saw the logic of the move and understood Paterno's motive. There was never a hint that a "racial" problem was involved.

Despite this, a Philadelphia sportswriter dashed off a piece, speculating that Penn State was having a "black problem." Joe Paterno reacted with typical class. He brought the entire matter into the open, airing it on his weekly television show. Joe stated unequivocally that his team did not have a "black problem," admitted that he had made a mistake in going too long with his style of attack, explained exactly why he had benched his black quarterback and praised Cooper, Harris and Mitchell for their cooperation and team spirit. Paterno's frankness nipped the rumor in the bud and there was no more talk of the actually non-existent "black problem" at Penn State.

Joe Paterno isn't at all sure that he will never have a problem with his black athletes at Penn State. No one ever knows what the future holds in store for him. But, if awareness, understanding, frankness, fairness in dealing with all athletes and an intelligent and honest approach to potential inequities can prevent problems from surfacing, then Joe Paterno and his black athletes will live together in harmony.

Joe Paterno has all these qualities.

13: Recruiting Is Football's Greatest Evil

COLLEGE FOOTBALL, for all its popularity and booming success, has its evils and abuses, and no one is more aware of—or more vocal about—them than Joe Paterno, the Don Quixote of the coaching profession, who delights in fighting windmills.

Lest people get the impression that Joe Paterno thinks college football is all bad, he is quick to point out that the game, generally, is good and he doesn't want to be categorized as a chronic critic of the hand that feeds him. But, he wants it to be a better game and he is honest enough to recognize abuses that, if permitted to fester, could bring college football tumbling down like a house of cards. Like the young people he tries to identify himself with, Joe reserves the right to speak out about the sport's excesses and he wants to fight them within the present structure.

"College football is a great game," Paterno insists, "and I'm very happy to be associated with it. If I thought it wasn't good, I'd get out of it tomorrow. Boys can get so much out of football that will help make their lives more meaningful. But, like everything else, there are some things about it that are wrong and I don't think we should stick our heads in the sand like ostriches."

College football is not an evil game but it does have evils which Joe Paterno insists must be corrected, and quickly. He points a finger at recruiting, the unabashed cheating that goes on by some of his colleagues, the trend toward excessive numbers of scholarships at some schools, the lowering of academic and classroom standards for athletes and the practice of red-shirting as some of the major abuses. He takes university presidents and the National Collegiate Athletic Association to task for not doing better policing jobs. Joe also has strong feelings about things like wire service polls and the creeping influence of pro scouts on the game and the players and he doesn't hesitate to let people know about them.

"One of the greatest evils in college football is recruiting," charges Paterno. "It has become a monster that coaches have built and, if it isn't curbed, it will eventually destroy them and the game. The competition for quality high school players has become so intense that some coaches and colleges are guilty of breaking the rules to 'buy' players. Oh, I don't think there is quite as much of that going on these days as people think, but there is enough of it to make me sick to my stomach when I hear about it.

"The coach himself isn't usually directly involved in the illegal offers. What happens is that an alumnus contacts a wanted player and tells him, 'Look, if you go to our school, we'll take care of you. You'll get a full scholarship, room, board, books and tuition, and we'll see that you get some clothes and extra spending money whenever you need it.' It's an arrangement between the alumnus and the boy. But I can't believe that the coach doesn't know about some of this. He may not be aware of all the specifics, but he has told the alumnus that he wants the boy desperately and he has made the original contact. The coach *has* to know there is some hanky-panky going on.

"There is probably more illegal recruiting going on in the Ivy League than anywhere else because they're so dependent on their alumni. They say they don't give athletic scholarships and their coaches aren't permitted to recruit football players. They're so damned hypocritical. They recruit as hard as anyone and sometimes there is a rich alumnus around to take care of a few kids with little extras, like gifts, spending money, high paying summer jobs or a promise of a good job when they get out of school. Then they look down their noses at the rest of us and talk about overemphasizing football."

Then there are the schools that are a little more discreet in their cheating. The way this works is that assistant coaches are usually the bag men. They dole out money, provided by either an Athletic Department slush fund or a friendly alumnus, to some of the players for services rendered. That kind of cheating got the University of Illinois put on probation and cost Coach Pete Elliott his job several years ago. It also cost the University of Tulsa a three-year sentence by the NCAA in 1970. At the same time, Kansas State was placed on probation by the Big Eight Conference for three years for providing two of its athletes with free transportation and expenses to visit a friend the university just happened to want to recruit. Getting caught with their hands in the cookie jar proved to be expensive for Coach Vince Gibson's Wildcats. About $140,000 worth. It cost Kansas State a regional date on television that season.

There are other ways that schools and coaches cheat. One method involves falsification of high school marks so that a recruit can qualify under the NCAA's 1.6 rule, which requires a student-athlete to project a 1.6 average to become eligible for an athletic scholarship. In 1969, Kansas was found guilty on two charges of falsification of high school records of a football and a basketball player and placed on probation by the Big Eight. The action prompted Wayne Duke, the conference commissioner, to issue a stern warning to other league schools to keep their skirts clean.

Most of the time the offenders are never punished because the NCAA usually doesn't take any action unless someone blows the whistle on the offending school. Coaches like to tell people— off the record, of course—that they lost a player because another school broke the rules and paid off under the table but, too frequently, the complaining coach is reluctant to turn in the culprit to the NCAA because he, too, has some dirty linen to hide.

"I don't think the NCAA does enough to seek out the recruiting cheaters," says Joe Paterno. "They've passed too many rules that they can't enforce and half the time the rules are so ambiguous that you don't know what's legal and what's illegal. What the

NCAA should be doing is policing college football instead of waiting for a school to squeal on someone before they start an investigation. It should have dozens of investigators checking up on people and looking into suspicious actions. If the coaches knew that the NCAA was snooping around, they would be more reluctant to cheat. I know the NCAA says it doesn't have the funds to maintain a security staff but all it would take is the income from one national television game. Just one game.

"Pro football has done a much better job of creating the image of being honest. Their security people are alert and the mere fact that people know they are around discourages wrongdoing. Instead of spending his time criticizing football coaches, Walter Byers should be doing some of the things Pete Rozelle has done in pro football."

The buying of players, illegal payoffs and falsification of marks are the worst abuses in recruiting and they go on almost all the time even though few schools are caught and punished. However, Joe Paterno thinks that where the evil in recruiting really lies is in the whole approach to it by coaches.

"Coaches tend to lie to boys," Joe says bluntly. "They go after a high school kid of seventeen or eighteen, who is a good athlete. He gets maybe forty or fifty scholarship offers and then the coaches descend upon him. They build him up, idolize him, kneel at his feet and tell him how great he is, how much they need him and that he's the guy who can win for them. They tell him that if he doesn't come to their school, the entire university is going to collapse. They tell him he's going to be a starter as a sophomore. The coach has lied to him in order to wean him away from a bunch of other schools trying to recruit him. I've been guilty of some of these things myself on occasion and I don't like it one bit. It's demeaning to have to fawn over a teenager like that.

"The youngster immediately gets distorted values about himself and college life in general. We create imaginary utopias and don't prepare a boy for things he ought to be getting ready for when he gets into college. Then he is wined and dined. Kids are pretty smart these days and they get the message in a hurry. The first time you visit a boy, he's delighted to meet you. When you take him out to dinner, he doesn't know what to order.

The second time you take him out, he orders the most expensive steak. The third time, he's really sophisticated. He's trying to decide whether he wants Oysters Rockefeller or Oysters Casino to start with.

"Then the kids begin to play off one school against the other, angling for the best deal they can get. They may visit ten, twelve or fifteen colleges from one end of the country to the other, not because they're really interested in all those schools but just to get some trips to places they've never seen and to be entertained. They're flown in, sometimes in an alumnus' private plane, put up at a fancy motel, given a car to use and some spending money, and I know some places even provide them with dates for the weekend.

"What happens is that the kids get caught in the middle and we, as coaches, are too stupid to realize it. They get us competing against each other for their services and we let them do it.

"Then comes the signing of the letter of intent. The parents usually want it done on TV or in front of a newspaper photographer so that everybody knows their son's important. He's treated like a Hollywood star, but he's still just a seventeen- or eighteen-year-old kid.

"Okay, now a coach gets the boy. The recruiting rat-race is over. He's been lionized, wined, dined, told how great he is and how much he is needed. Then, after the big buildup, he finds out he's just another freshman player on the squad. He isn't a hero or a star any more. He has to make the team just like everybody else. It's a tremendous letdown and not every youngster can adjust to it. So, all of a sudden, the coach has an unhappy player. It's all so wrong."

Partially responsible for this, Paterno says, is the high school coach who oversells his players. Intent on getting athletic scholarships for his boys, the coach very often will overrepresent a player's skills to a college scout. The average halfback becomes a super-runner, the middle linebacker is another Sam Huff and the split receiver has hands like Lance Alworth. In the face of such a glowing recommendation, the college coach, who has seen films of the boy's games and maybe even watched him play, thinks that perhaps he hasn't seen the player at his best. The athlete is recruited but, pretty soon, discovers that he doesn't really have enough ability and is in over his head. The well-meaning but overzealous high school coach has not done the boy a favor. Instead, he has done him a disservice.

"It isn't fair to the boy," says Paterno. "He would have been a lot better off at a smaller school, where his talents would have been more equal to the competition."

Paterno also is bothered by the loose admission standards and the practice of giving football players favored treatment which is prevalent at some schools. He thinks the blame for this must be shared by unscrupulous coaches, college adminis- trators and university presidents.

"A lot of schools are accepting athletes who don't belong there academically because they are being pressured by coaches," says Joe. "The coaches are willing to take the substandard students because they can help win football games and they persuade the admissions people to admit kids who really don't qualify academically. Then the coach has to be sure that he can keep his players in school. So he arranges for him to take easy courses, like maybe archery, basket-weaving and knot- tying, or he is constantly bugging professors to change marks so that his players are eligible. At some places athletes don't even attend classes. The coach and the school aren't interested in seeing the boys get an education or a degree. They're just using them.

"Sure, when this happens, the coach is the culprit and he should be penalized for his actions. But the university president is the one who is really responsible for permitting it to go on. He should make it his business to know what is going on in his Athletic or Admissions Department and in his classrooms. If he doesn't know about things like slush funds, alumni commit- ments to players, falsification of marks, illegal admissions and the other abuses that exist in college football, then he isn't doing his job as a college president. That's as much his baby as knowing what is happening in his English or History Departments."

Happily, the offenders are in the minority but the mere fact that there are still some unconscionable coaches and colleges who indulge in playing the cheating game is abhorrent to a man like Joe Paterno, who believes strongly that a school owes a young man more than just an opportunity to play football. It has a commitment to see that he gets an education and that he graduates.

There are ways that cheating and exploitation of athletes can be prevented. At Penn State, for instance, faculty senate committees control admissions and eligibility. They determine admission standards and make certain that only students—and athletes— who qualify are admitted to the university. The committee on eligibility has standards which demand that every athlete make quantitative and qualitative progress toward a degree. The Athletic Department has a rule which prohibits coaches from calling a professor to discuss a player's marks.

Rules on recruiting at Penn State are also quite unique in the world of high-pressure, big-time college football. When a recruit visits the school, he has to pay his own transportation, except in some cases where a boy cannot afford it, and then Paterno must get special permission from his boss, Bob Scannell, the Dean of the Department of Health, Physical Education and Recreation, to pick up the tab for his trip. If a boy's parents are along, they are put up in the Nittany Lion Inn on campus (at the expense of the Athletic Department) but the recruit stays in a dormitory with a member of the football team, has his meals at the Nittany Lion Inn with the coaches and his parents are usually entertained one evening at the home of Paterno or one of the assistant coaches. No fancy motels, no posh restaurants, no girls.

"A lot of boys have told us that, of all the places they had gone, the worst visit they had was at Penn State," says Paterno. "That's where they got the least attention. But we want them to see exactly what our college is like under normal circumstances. We don't put on the dog to impress them."

Austerity recruiting? Sure it is, but it has proven to be just as effective as the glamorous kind that many other schools indulge in. The quality of Penn State's teams attests to that. That doesn't mean, however, that Joe Paterno and his staff don't hustle the bushes for players. They spend as much time as anyone else in the off-season visiting prospects in Pennsylvania, Ohio, New Jersey, New York and New England, their prime recruiting areas. But they do it on a recruiting budget for travel and entertainment of an average of less than $20,000 a year, as much as, say,

Frank Broyles of Arkansas used to spend on gas for the university planes which flew him all over the Southwest and neighboring states on recruiting missions.

Broyles, on the opening day of the Southwest Conference letter of intent signing season in 1971, in seventeen hours used four planes, touched down in five states—Arkansas, Missouri, Oklahoma, Louisiana and Texas—covered over 3,000 miles and signed more than twenty players. Just an average day's work for fast-moving Frank.

Just as evil as recruiting, Joe Paterno feels, is the excessive number of scholarships that some schools award. It has become a case of the rich getting richer and the poor getting beaten too often. Some schools, like Texas and Arkansas, give fifty grants a year. The Southeastern Conference permits forty; the Big Ten, thirty, and the figure varies from conference to conference. Conversely, others like Penn State, Syracuse, Pitt and Big Ten schools are restricted to twenty-five or so. As a result, the more affluent schools skim off the cream of the crop each year, leaving few blue-chippers available for their competitors in the same area. It's not right, says Paterno.

"Obviously, we can't compete on an equal basis with schools which hand out scholarships in unlimited numbers," Joe admits. "But that isn't the important thing. We don't have to play them if we don't want to. What is important is that the entire system of athletic grants is getting out of hand. It has become a question of keeping up with the Joneses, and that's not an honest way to conduct an intercollegiate athletic program. It encourages cheating to get the super-players. It also is unfair to the high school boy who is recruited and then never gets a chance to play because his school has too many scholarship men on the squad. He gets discouraged and quits. In some places, this is referred to as 'forced attrition.' That's just a way to duck an obligation to a boy and to get rid of him for a better athlete.

"There is only one answer to the problem. The NCAA should adopt a national limit on football scholarships. Twenty-five or thirty would be more than enough for every school competing in big-time football and there are more than enough good football players in the country to go around so that everyone could get his fair share of them. It also would put a greater premium on judgment. The only reason coaches take more than eleven now is that they're not sure which are the best ones. After all, it isn't how many players you take, it's how many good ones you get."

Paterno hasn't been idle in pushing his views on scholarships. As a trustee of the American Football Coaches Association, he has raised the issue, along with his thoughts on a variety of other subjects, in meetings of the group and in conversations with other coaches. His proposals often stir up controversy among some of his more conservative colleagues, who have been content just to mutter that, yeah, something ought to be done, but then do nothing. There have been indications, however, that the AFCA is stirring itself into action in several areas. Joe Paterno doesn't claim any particular credit for this, but it is safe to assume that his rabble-rousing has had some effect on his fellow coaches.

The AFCA, at its meeting in Houston in January, 1970, proposed that the NCAA "limit the overall number of football scholarships at any one time to 120" for the 118 schools with maximum football programs in the major-college division. It also asked for representation on the Executive Council, the law-making body of the NCAA, and proposed that the NCAA divide its membership of 646 active schools into three groups and adopt class legislation for each one compatible with the needs of each group.

Frank Broyles, the outgoing president, explained that the over-all limit of 120 would permit schools to award scholarships to more or less than thirty in any one year just so long as they did not exceed a total of 120 overall. Subsequently, the NCAA's Financial Aid Committee made a similar proposal. Paterno's preaching, it seems, did not fall on deaf ears. Several years later, the NCAA passed legislation limiting football scholarships to thirty a year and ninety-five overall.

One good reason for limiting athletic scholarships, aside from Joe Paterno's feelings about unfair competition, is the increasing worry in college athletic circles about the changing economics of football.

On the face of it, college football has prospered over the years. Total attendance at games continues to rise, seating capacity at many stadiums has been expanded, ticket prices have gone up, the cut from national television networks has increased and coaches' salaries are up. It has become big business. But actually, the picture is not quite what it seems to be. Along with burgeoning attendance and greater income, costs have risen even faster. Recruiting, scholarships, equipment and traveling cost more and feeding a squad of hungry, growing boys enough near-raw meat to keep them mean has become a big item. Consequently, athletic budgets have skyrocketed and many schools are feeling the financial pinch and looking for ways to cut expenses. What hasn't helped the situation, of course, is the fact that, at most colleges, football income supports the entire intercollegiate athletic program, and baseball, wrestling, gymnastics, fencing, soccer, lacrosse, tennis, track and field, golf, all non-income-producing sports, cost more to operate.

Some authorities, like Walter Byers, the executive director of the NCAA, have urged a return to one-platoon football to cut expenses. A school would need fewer players, smaller coaching staffs and less equipment and traveling costs could be shaved, they claim. Others agree with Paterno that limiting scholarships would effect a saving. But Joe goes even further than that.

"There are a lot of things the NCAA can do to help schools cut expenses without changing the rules of the game," Paterno insists. "The first thing would be to place limits on recruiting. High school youngsters should be limited to visits to only three or four schools, there should be a ceiling on recruiting budgets and the length of the recruiting season should be shortened. Make the date for the letter of intent April 1 instead of the first week in May. [Prophetically, some of this happened, too, a few years later.] That would automatically reduce large recruiting budgets at most schools and also serve to eliminate some frantic last-minute under-the-table offers to steal kids away from colleges they have already committed themselves to. One important side effect, too, is that it would make for less opportunities for cheating.

"I blame athletic administrators for some of the financial waste in college football programs. If a school is losing money on its football, maybe it's because the athletic director is a lousy administrator. He has to find ways to tighten up his budget and he has to be able to control his coaches who, by nature, want to spend more and more money on recruiting because they think that's the only way to get a better team. An athletic director has to be a good businessman and, if he isn't, then he should be fired."

Paterno reacts like an angry cobra on the subject of athletic directors. Although he respected Ernie McCoy, his former athletic director at Penn State, and enjoys a pleasant working relationship with Ed Czekaj, his present A.D., Joe says quite openly that many athletic directors are simply not doing their jobs. He deplores the fact that some A.D.'s can't or won't control their coaches and the free spending that goes on for recruiting. He is critical of them for not policing their schools' recruiting practices and for the current vogue of filling football schedules ten years or more in advance when they have no way of knowing the future strength of their opponents.

"They say they have to book games that far in advance because everybody else does," Paterno says. "That's ridiculous. Teams and schools change and it's stupid to get tied down that far in advance. That's why there are so many mismatches in college football. If the athletic directors can't get together and decide that they're making a mistake with their long-range scheduling, then the NCAA ought to step in and legislate against it. They ought to limit scheduling to four years in advance. That's plenty long enough and it would give schools that have improved their football programs an opportunity to play tougher schedules. It would make for better games."

Most college football coaches think that they have the best of all worlds when they can be both the athletic director and the coach but, characteristically, Paterno disagrees. He insists that there is a conflict of interest in the two jobs. "How can you be a good athletic director when you've got to be concerned first with your artistic success as a coach rather than your business success?" he asks.

How many college football coaches do you suppose agree with *that*?

14: Red-Shirting, Polls and Eastern Football

JOE PATERNO'S DEFINITION OF ABUSES and evils in college football is not limited to recruiting and scholarships. To a somewhat lesser degree, he deplores such things as excessive red-shirting and the weekly wire service polls which rank the top twenty teams in the nation. Joe doesn't stop there, either. While he confesses that it really doesn't affect college football generally, he is annoyed by the lack of appreciation by the rest of the country for Eastern football and the reluctance of the Ivy League to mix it up with the big fellows. Although his position on all these subjects may not be popular with everyone, he tackles them with typical volubility.

"What's the use of being against something if you don't talk about it," Joe says honestly.

Red-shirting is the ploy by which a boy is kept in school for five years, although NCAA regulations limit a player's varsity eligibility to four seasons since freshmen became eligible. Except for the Ivy League, Army, Navy, Air Force and a few others, red-shirting is a common practice in most of the rest of the country. Even worse, it is now possible under the rules to red-shirt freshmen before they have attended a single class at their schools.

The way it works is that a coach will decide that he has plenty of quarterbacks, tackles, defensive backs or, maybe, pass receivers returning in one particular year. He really doesn't need some of the incoming sophomores, or maybe the coach thinks that a few of his freshmen haven't come along as quickly as he likes, so he will red-shirt them—hold them out of action for an entire season—to make them eligible to play in their fifth year in school. At some schools, where they used to award forty or fifty scholarships a year, as many as twenty or twenty-five players have been red-shirted at one time. Some coaches will give their players a choice, to warm the bench and waste a year of eligibility or sit out a season so they can play in their fifth year.

Coaches who espouse red-shirting argue that a large percentage of college students take five years to graduate anyway, for a variety of reasons. Some are in five-year courses of study, others spread their credits out so they can carry a lighter load each semester or they just aren't able to finish in the normal four years. What difference does it make if you ask a football player— or twenty-five of them—to do the same thing, they say.

Joe Paterno is sympathetic to a point, but he is opposed to *complete* red-shirting. Aside from the fact that it gives schools an unfair advantage over those which prohibit the practice, Joe believes it just isn't right to deliberately hold back boys who want to play football and still graduate with their class.

"There have been some instances of entire classes of players being held back a year in order to insure a better football team," Paterno points out. "The coaches who do that are strictly within their rights because the NCAA permits it. But I question whether the rule is a good one. Like anything else, excesses are bad."

Paterno is in favor of limited red-shirting, which would permit no more than six or eight players to be held out in any single year. But he would give the players the choice. "It all goes back to what a boy should get out of playing football," Joe says. "If he can get something out of it personally—satisfaction, enjoyment, character qualities—by playing in his fifth year, then he should be permitted to do it. The boy I'm talking about, of course, is the one who just isn't good enough to play when he's a freshman or a sophomore. Perhaps he is young and hasn't matured enough, or maybe he's just taking a little longer to reach his full potential.

"However, he should be permitted to make the decision about the fifth year when he is a senior, even though he has played only three varsity seasons. If he decides that he wants to graduate with his class, he should be able to do it. Then, if he wants to continue in school for a fifth year so he can use up his last season of eligibility, he should be able to do that, too. But, in any case, I don't think that more than six or eight players in any one year should be red-shirted. This practice of red-shirting a couple of dozen players every year is an abuse of the rules and shouldn't be permitted."

Paterno also feels very keenly about the increasing influence that pro football scouts have on college players. Their scouting systems have become so thorough that they start working on college players when they are sophomores and juniors and they make demands on their time. It isn't unusual to see a dozen or more pro scouts crowded along the sidelines during spring practice sessions at almost every big-time football college in the country. They compare notes, lie to one another about their opinion of a prospect but rarely fail to make their presence known. Paterno doesn't permit them to talk to his players in the locker room at Penn State, but the scouts manage to contact them on campus and in their dormitory rooms. The influx begins in the spring and continues throughout the season.

"Those pro scouts are like ants, they're all over," Joe complains. "They put a lot of pressure on the kids. They want the players to run sprints so they can time their speed, they get the boys' phone numbers, call them constantly, get friendly with them and start giving them advice. Some scouts will tell a kid that he isn't being played enough or he isn't playing the right position. I put players in positions where I think that they will help the team and not where they might have a better chance of making it as pros. If I convert a 195-pound running back into a linebacker, I do it because that's the best spot for him to play on my team and I don't want a pro scout telling that boy he should be a running back if he wants a chance to make it in pro football.

"College coaches are not in the business of developing players for the pros. Our job is to see that a boy gets the most out of his football experience in college. After all, that's what he's there for. The pressures from the pro scouts have too many kids thinking about their pro careers when they should be thinking about their college careers. Sure, we let the scouts look at films of our players, and I have no objection to giving a pro scout my opinion on a boy's ability or whether or not I think he will make a pro. I'm happy to do it. But sometimes it works against you. Why, one year I had an irate father of one of my players complain that I told a pro scout his son didn't have the mental toughness to be a pro. He was indignant and told me I had no business trying to ruin his son's chances for professional football. You can imagine what my relations were with that' boy and his dad for the rest of the season! All I did was give an honest opinion to a pro scout in confidence and he should have respected it.

"Pro football is a great game and I respect most of the men who are in it, but the scouts are invading our domain when they try to influence our players. It has to stop."

One other thing that bugs this outspoken coach is football polls. Joe Paterno's criticism of the polls reached a crescendo after the 1969 season when President Nixon, taking his cue from the weekly wire service rankers—some suspect he actually took it from Bud Wilkinson—decided to make his the official word on which team was the best in the nation. Paterno screamed loudly over the Presidential decree that Texas was No. 1. His Penn State team that season, for the second straight year, had gone unbeaten and, yet, the Nittany Lions were never higher than No. 2 in the weekly Associated Press and United Press International polls. Sportswriters vote in the AP poll while a select group of coaches casts ballots in the UPI version.

There were some people who' called Paterno's gripe sour grapes, but Joe's feeling that the polls are an evil in college football antedates his skirmish with President Nixon. He criticized the polls when he was an assistant coach and he continued to blast them when he was a head coach, even when his teams' didn't deserve to be ranked in Centre County, Pennsylvania.

Joe's position is that polls don't belong in college football, that they are an artificial way to build up interest and they lead to a situation that is "inconsistent with good sportsmanship." He decries the fact that newspapers and magazine help to foster the myth by picking pre-season top twenty teams.

"I don't think polls should be a part of college football," Paterno says pointedly. "Maybe there should be a consensus vote at the end of the season, but these week-by-week polls only sell a few more seats and maybe a few more newspapers."

What Joe would prefer to see is a national championship play-off at the end of each season involving conference champions and the best of the independents. This view is supported by Michigan State's Duffy Daugherty and many other coaches but it isn't likely ever to come about because of pressure by the people who run the post-season bowls.

Paterno is in the minority on the question of polls. The fans like it and most of his colleagues think they are just fine and that they add another dimension to college football—the incentive to be No. 1. Notre Dame's Ara Parseghian was frank to admit that he was all for the polls. "I like them," Ara said. "Notre Dame isn't in a conference and we can't look forward to winning a championship, so our goal every year is to be No. 1 in the polls, to be the national champion."

"If you win all your games, what's the difference whether you're ranked No. 1, 10 or 20," Paterno argues. "You did what you're supposed to do, You had a goal, an objective, and you achieved it. That's the joy of being a coach!"

Paterno, however, admits that his players are interested in where they rank and they do get a bang out of being rated high. They were sorely hurt and frustrated when the voters in the 1969 polls ignored them in favor of Texas despite their unbeaten record. That was the major reason that Paterno made so much noise about a No. 1 ranking in a poll that he doesn't believe in.

Joe was just as annoyed a year later, when the National Football Foundation and Hall of Fame voted its MacArthur Bowl, symbolic of the national championship, to both Texas and Ohio State, who were unbeaten in 1970 prior to the post-season bowl games. Paterno's anger this time was not public. It simmered until he happened to bump into Jimmie McDowell, the Hall of Fame's irrepressible public relations director, at a function in New York.

Paterno buttonholed the unsuspecting McDowell, who had had nothing to do with the selection, which was made by a committee, and asked heatedly, "Why did the Hall of Fame vote co-champions this year and ignore Penn State in 1969 when we had gone through two undefeated seasons and our record was the same as Texas'? I'll tell you why, they didn't have the guts to go against the President!"

Paterno charges that, because teams play for the rankings, there is a tendency for some coaches to run up the score against weak opponents to influence the pollsters. "If you have to go out and beat someone real big to get a high ranking," Joe says, "that is inconsistent with good sportsmanship. That's not what college football is supposed to be all about."

Although few college coaches will admit that they actually *do* run up the score on weak opponents, there is mounting evidence that Paterno's charge is valid. Tom Harp, when he was the coach at Duke, was a victim of having the score run up on him on more than one occasion. Tom's reaction was, "Top teams have to be impressive to hold their high ratings, which is the one really bad thing about weekly polls. Naturally, all coaches deny they run up the score, but they try to be impressive in the first half. Then they put in the second team but the second team usually does all right, particularly if the opposition is broken in the first half. Even if the opposition isn't broken, it has to play catch-up, with the usual result that it falls further and further behind."

Texas and Notre Dame, among others, have often been accused of running up the score to protect or enhance their rankings and, while Darrell Royal and Ara Parseghian denied the charge, their teams were involved in some lopsided games in recent years.

After his Longhorns, who ranked No. 1 at the time, crushed Texas Christian University 58-0 in 1970, Darrell shed a few crocodile tears for the poor Horned Frogs. "I hated to see those points climb up like they did. Good golly, somebody just asked me didn't I leave the first team in longer than usual. I had them in there when we led 30-0 in the third quarter. TCU would have the wind in the fourth quarter and nowadays 30 points can go like zap. It's awfully embarrassing when you take your first team out of a game and then have to put it back in. It makes you feel ridiculous."

Maybe so, Joe Paterno says, but not half so ridiculous as TCU felt against Royal's Longhorns that afternoon in 1970.

Jim Bertelsen, one of Royal's halfbacks in that game, was more honest. "We always listen for the scores. We know it's all up to the pollsters," admitted Jim. "It's a bad deal, I know, but that's the way they vote a national champion, how many points you score against people. So I always have it in mind. Guys will tell you that we're just out there to win, but you've got to be a realist."

There is still another facet to the polls that helps to bolster Joe Paterno's position. Some coaches who vote in the UPI poll have been known to use it to further their own ends. Bob Devaney of Nebraska, whose team was ranked No. 1 for the 1970 season after the post-season bowl games and after the MacArthur Bowl was voted to Texas and Ohio State as national co-champions (both were rudely upset by Notre Dame and Stanford, respectively, in the Cotton and Rose Bowls), very frankly admitted that he voted for his own team. Just think of all the interesting possibilities that presents. Suppose *all* the coaches voted their own teams No. 1. Some year, there could be a thirty-five-way tie for the national championship!

Several years ago, when Pete Elliott was coaching at the University of Illinois, he voted for his own team, not as No. 1 but further down on the list, and his ballot was enough to rank the Illini No. 20 one week, even though they had not won a game all season. That really threw the UPI into a tizzy, but it didn't change anything. Coaches have also been known to vote a high ranking for teams they are going to play, on the theory that they can get more credit—and a boost in the rankings—if they should happen to beat the No. 1 team.

While Joe Paterno's objections to the polls may just be a small voice in the wilderness, there is some substance to his views, however unpopular they are. Obviously, if a poll can be manipulated by self-serving coaches, it is not good for college football.

A discussion of the pros and cons of polls usually leads Joe Paterno into another one of his pet peeves—the lack of appreciation for Eastern football. Although Joe doesn't regard it as an evil or an abuse of the game, he deeply resents the fact that the rest of the country looks with disdain on the so-called effete East.

"If an Eastern team beats a club from another section of the country, it's regarded as a fluke because your opponent didn't take you seriously," Paterno complains, with some justification. "If we lose, it's because we're lousy."

Paterno places part of the blame for this attitude on some Eastern sportswriters who, he claims, tend to downgrade their own teams and are more impressed with the accomplishments of the Texases, Notre Dames, Southern Californias and Nebraskas. When Syracuse, Penn State, Pitt and, less recently, Army and Navy, the Eastern colleges which play bigtime intersectional schedules, come up with a good team, it is considered to be a phenomenon by the media in the East and suspect by folks in other sections of the country. There is the usual cry of "Who have they beaten?" That was particularly true during the three seasons that Penn State was accumulating its thirty-one game winning streak. Yet the Nittany Lions had beaten teams like UCLA, North Carolina State, Kansas State, Kansas, Colorado and Missouri in addition to their perennial Eastern rivals.

However, the drums were beating for Texas when the Longhorns compiled their winning streak, mostly against weak Southwest Conference teams—Rice, Baylor, SMU, TCU, Texas A & M. Aside from Oklahoma, Arkansas, California, UCLA and Notre Dame in the 1970 Cotton Bowl, Texas' opponents were no more formidable than Penn State's.

The undefeated 1959 Syracuse team which won the national championship and beat Texas in the Cotton Bowl may have been one of the best of all time but the Orange is rarely mentioned in the same breath with the Oklahoma elevens of Bud Wilkinson's time or the great Michigan State, Notre Dame, Alabama, Ohio State and Texas teams of more recent vintage.

What the East needs, Paterno contends, is more chauvinism on the part of its media and a better public relations image. "We suffer in comparison to the rest of the country," Paterno says, "because we don't have the glamour of a conference like the Big Eight, the Big Ten, the SEC or the SWC. As independents, Penn State used to belong to the Eastern College Athletic Conference, which represents some 200 colleges with different interests and goals in college football. We had a commissioner and a public relations man but they didn't spend their time building up the image of Eastern football and selling it to our own Eastern sportswriters and sportscasters and the rest of the country. Our independents play intersectional schedules and we beat teams from other sections of the country regularly but we rarely get credit for our accomplishments."

Former Ivy Leaguer Paterno also feels that the Ivy League is partly responsible for the low esteem in which Eastern football is held in other sections of the nation. The Ivies are content to play one another and steer clear of entanglements outside of their own little group, although a few are planning to spread their wings soon. Their teams are well coached by dedicated, knowledgeable men like Carmen Cozza at Yale and others in the past and present and, frequently, they produce undefeated clubs which gain national ranking. Joe Paterno's quarrel with the Ivy League is that its good teams should be playing intersectional rivals to enhance the prestige of Eastern football.

"It would help the Eastern image if the Ivy League got away from its incestuous relationship," Joe insists. "They won't venture out of their own league, yet they want to be considered the equals of the independents who play tougher schedules. How in the world can anyone know if an unbeaten Dartmouth, Yale, Princeton or Harvard team is better than a Penn State or a Syracuse which may lose a game or two to strong teams outside the East? I would be happy to play them so we can all find out. Why shouldn't they be playing Army and Navy? They say they can't compete with us because they don't have spring practice and we do. Well, why don't they have spring practice? Their coaches want it and it wouldn't affect their amateur standing one bit.

"Ivy League schools get some great athletes every year and I know because they are the toughest to recruit against. They should be playing schools like Stanford, Michigan, Georgia Tech, Tulane, Vanderbilt, UCLA, California, Northwestern and some others in the Big Ten with high academic standards. They talk about competition and how their good teams can play with anybody in the country, but they sit in their ivory towers and never give their teams a chance to prove it. They should put up or shut up!"

Such words are not likely to endear Brown alumnus Joe Paterno to his friends—if he has any left—in the Ivy League, but Joe believes in speaking his mind regardless of where the chips may fall. He is vehemently opposed to what he calls the "hypo-critical" athletic policies of the Ivies and rarely resists the op-portunity to make known his feelings on the subject. Whether or not they are partly responsible for Eastern football's lack of stature in the rest of the country is open to argument, but not in Joe Paterno's active mind.

"It's no fun beating someone who isn't very good," Joe says. "You can fulfill yourself completely only by competing against the best."

15: The Year of the Bluebird

THE 1967 PENN STATE SEASON actually began after the 1966 victory over Pittsburgh and evolved out of a summer of hard work, during which the Paterno family—Sue and the three children—were almost ignored. It developed also from the talents of some outstanding athletes who ultimately put together the finest defense in the history of college football. Goal-line stands, blocked punts, intercepted passes and recovered fumbles became the trademark of this Penn State defense, which was probably the most exciting creation of football in the late 1960's.

These men of Joe Paterno's never quite made it to No.1 during their college careers, partly because of the President of the United States. But they had a pride in what they achieved that was unusual for college players, and Paterno, a quarterback by action and offensive coach by career, oddly enough was the man who put together this amazing defense. Statistics don't say this. But statistics are only reasons to win bets and are not necessarily proof of on-the-field action. Any team that ever got the ball to the Penn State 30-yard line found it rather difficult to budge an inch more.

Dan Devine, whose Missouri team lost to Penn State in the Orange Bowl on January 1, 1970, said, "Texas may have been No. 1 but Texas would never have scored against Penn State." It was the 1970 Orange Bowl defense that was developing in the summer and fall of 1967 through the work of Paterno and his athletes.

Paterno wasn't satisfied with the defense he had produced in 1966. A 5-5 season wasn't something to brag about and, if his ideas of Penn State football were to be achieved and his own goals gained, something had to be done. He probably did it by himself, insofar as the planning goes, and then the likes of Dennis Onkotz, Jim Kates, Mike Smith, Steve Smear and, later, Mike Reid and Jack Ham would fill in the physical achievement, though the greatest attribute of this Penn State defense was its intelligence. These were not rinky-dink football players saying "Yeh, Coach. What, Coach? Now, Coach? Who he, Coach?" These were men who executed a most difficult assignment, one that may carry on at Penn State but one that requires students, not witless athletes interested only in hitting people.

The summer of 1967 was a difficult time for the Paternos. Joe got up regularly as early as 5:30 A.M. and went into the den of his split-level house to work. He closed the door against intruders and was oblivious to his family. Sue Paterno had to get the children up, feed them, explain that Daddy was working and then take the family swimming for four or five hours. She rarely saw her coach-husband during the summer of 1967. And Joe and Sue hadn't had a real vacation together since they became Mr. and Mrs. Head Coach of Penn State football.

There, in the hermit-like existence Joe Paterno set for himself, the boss man of the Nittany Lions came up with his plans for defense. What came out of it wasn't considered the greatest invention in football by historians. It never received the attention, for instance, of the T formation or the forward pass. But team after team began using Paterno's style of what is known in the trade as a 4-4-3 defense.

Simply stated, this means four men in the line on defense, four linebackers directly behind them and three defensive backs. But it never looks that way, so what a Penn State 4-4-3 really

means is mobility. That is what Paterno achieved. He put together the most mobile defense in college football history and
team after team that faced it couldn't believe what hit them until
coaches of the many losers looked at films. Even then some did
not credit Penn State with doing something unusual. But the
brilliant bunch of athletes involved did do something—they
stopped everyone for quite awhile.

The most misunderstood part of football is defense. Television
reporters, including former football stars, can easily tell you
about the offense. After all, the offense is required to set in a
formation for long enough to describe it. It can't move forward
or jump around. But defense is different. The guys who have
to outguess the ones with the ball can move all over the field
at will. And Paterno took full advantage of that, dreaming up
some great things while secluded in his den in State College in
that summer of 1967.

Sue remembers, "He worked after dinner, even. A lot of times
he went to the office just to catch up on stuff there and then returned and worked on his other thing." The other thing was that
damned defense. It had to work. Paterno was bugged with the
idea that defense was the key to success. He just turned the old
idea around to say, "A good defense is the best offense."

Joe was so concerned with his work in the den that Sue imagined, "I could have left with the kids and he would not have
known we were gone except that when he wanted dinner it
might not be ready. Or his lunch might not be ready. And I was
confused because sometimes he skipped lunch and just worked
on through. I could have really left town and it would have been
nothing to him. Deep down, you wonder, is it worth it?

"But then he'd have periods of success in that den, or he'd hit
upon something, and for about two days we'd have a human
being with us again. He was relieved that all of a sudden things
fit together. Then he'd try to figure out names for his plays on
defense and we'd play these games of naming them. He'd try to
explain these plays related to something we both knew. We tried
to think up names and, really, that was the most fun we had all
that summer."

As the summer ended, things began falling into place. Even

the Paterno home had more of a father than a coach again. Sue's suggestions for the names of defensive formations usually were the names of places where Joe had said they would go that summer before he decided to seclude himself to find a new defense. Joe Paterno had promised, but never fulfilled, many trips for Sue and the kids. He was so intent on the problem of bettering a 5-5 record that his family suffered. Joe is the first to admit this, but Sue understood. "You know, he hadn't quite done it in 1966," she points out. "He felt he let the school down and that he would have to do a better job. He felt he let the team down. Joe is stubborn that way."

While his family sat through that hot summer, Joe dreamed defenses more than offenses and the result was great once he added another element—the right players. All the thinking in secluded rooms can be worthless unless you have the men to do the work. That's where Paterno learned another lesson in the second game of 1967. It was a Friday night in the Orange Bowl, where the University of Miami played its home games and where Paterno later sent two great defensive teams to extend the undefeated streak of the Nittany Lions.

The 1967 season opened with an unnecessary loss to Navy, a game described by Paterno as "one of the two most disappointing games I've ever been connected with." The other was the loss the year before to Army, when Paterno admitted he was outcoached. Oddly enough, both games were against service academy teams.

"We had hoped to be able to handle Navy," he says. "We thought he had a pretty good football team going into the ball game. We were young but we just had a good pre-season practice and we were quite optimistic. But we lost the game because we didn't coach well."

Navy won, 23-22, on a touchdown pass in the last minute of the game at Annapolis, Maryland. Once again the head coach learned through this defeat. Despite all his summer work on defense, he learned at Navy not to sit back on defense. "We ran a prevent defense late in the game and we didn't play it well because we hadn't coached it well," he said. A prevent defense is thrown in late in the game by a team in the lead which knows full well the trailing team is going to pass in order to catch up.

Usually one or two linemen or linebackers are replaced with faster defensive backs and the strength of the defense is back where the receivers go. But from that Navy game came one thing—a totally aggressive defense for Penn State for the next three seasons.

"That game taught me one lesson," Paterno said in naming his umpteenth lesson as head coach. "From that game on I made up my mind that I'd never sit in what they call a prevent defense. We are going to attack right up to the end. If we get licked because somebody's able to complete a pass with a lot of pressure on them, that's fine. But I'm not going to sit back and just give people passes."

Joe also learned again never to underestimate the ingenuity and determination of the little pixy he married.

The Navy game was the start of a new season and the first road opener for Paterno and his team since he became head coach. Sue Paterno felt somewhat left out when the team took off on Friday afternoon for the bus trip to Annapolis. It had just never occurred to anyone that wives of coaches should be invited to the Navy game. In his concern for his new start, Joe had not given a thought to having Sue in the stands at the Navy-Marine Corps Memorial Stadium.

As Friday afternoon came to an end and evening settled on University Park, Sue began to get itchy about wanting to see the game. Joe had worked so hard all summer and taken himself away from the family so often in order to produce a new Nittany Lion team, that Sue felt she had a right to be there when the labor of the summer was put to the initial test.

"It was almost like fear. There were so many apprehensions about that game," Sue says. "I just had to go. So I called Bets O'Hora and asked her if she'd go with me. Her answer was no and she said we'd get killed driving down there. None of us could even read a road map."

Then Sue turned to Sandra Welsh, wife of the former Navy quarterback and Penn State assistant coach. After all, Sandra should know the way to Annapolis. But Sandra, it turned out, was not too good at reading road maps, either.

Sandra, however, had the adventurous soul that was kin to Sue's driving spirit. All they needed, then, was someone else to drive and—oh yes, a couple of tickets to the game. The tickets weren't really too important since they probably could buy a pair at the gate but the girls figured they would make it a package deal.

As night wore on that Friday, Sue got desperate. She ended up, after finding no easy transportation, calling the local radio station and asking for help. Would the radio station please announce a plea for someone to drive a couple of persons to Annapolis Saturday morning, and preferably someone with a couple of tickets to the game?

"But make sure you don't use my name or Sandra's," were Sue's instructions. "Just give my telephone number. O.K.? Thanks."

About 10 P.M., Sue was in the basement of her home, putting a load of diapers in the washing machine, when the kindly radio announcer gave Sue's want ad time on the station. It went like this:

"Ho, ho, ho. Joe Paterno took his football team to Navy and now his wife wants to go. He thinks she's staying home. Now, if anyone has a ride for her, call her at her home (and he gave the phone number). This is for her and another woman and they would like to buy two tickets to the game."

Sue dropped the diapers on the floor—a floor she wished she could fall through at that moment, never to be seen again.

But it all turned out well. Sue and Sandra got a lift from two male undergraduates who had extra tickets because each had expected to have a date for the game. Their dates had cancelled out, however, so Sue and Sandra got their transportation and tickets.

Toward the end of the game, Penn State was leading and Sue was happy enough to let Joe see her. She and Sandra jumped down on the field from the 5-foot wall that fronts the stands at Navy and stationed themselves near the exit that the Penn State team would use after their "victory."

The trouble was, though, that Navy scored in the final seconds to win the game and there was Sue, wishing she could get back into her seat. But jumping down from a 5-foot wall was one thing. Climbing back up was another. So, all Sue and Sandra could do was stand right where they were.

As Joe, disconsolate over the defeat, trotted by on his way to the exit, he looked up, saw Sue and asked, "What are you doing here?"

"I came to see the game."

"Oh, I thought something happened at home last night. Is that why you're here?"

"No, I wouldn't have come down if anything was wrong."

Joe finished this short dialogue: "Oh, fine. I'll see you at home."

Paterno didn't learn about the radio want ad until three years later. But Sue and Sandra, in their own way, did succeed in getting some recognition from the wives of members of the coaching staff. Now, an effort is made each season to see to it that the wives get some trips to road games, those games not too far away. Sue also gets an occasional extra trip with the university president and once in a while from a thoughtful Pennsylvania governor, such as the journey to Colorado in 1970, when Governor Raymond Shafer invited her to be his guest on his private plane.

But, when Navy beat Penn State in 1967, Joe had little time to worry about Sue's surprise trip to Annapolis. He was more concerned about his football team.

"After that game I felt, for the first time, concerned about my future as a coach," says Paterno. "I wondered whether I really had it. There were doubts in my mind. I had coached eleven games at Penn State as the head coach and I was five and six. It just had never dawned on me prior to that game that I wasn't going to be a good football coach or that I couldn't be a good football coach. But now, out of a clear blue sky, I'm in trouble."

Joe's father-in-law, Augie Pohland, an architect in Latrobe, Pennsylvania, also got in trouble with his daughter, Sue, after the game. Trying to lessen the disappointment of the loss, Augie said, "It's only a football game." Sue retorted, "Now, Dad, if one of your houses fell down, how would you like it if I said, 'It's only a house'?"

The bus trip back to Penn State from Navy was a time of searching for Paterno. Where was all the summer work? Wasted? What about this defense that looked so good on paper and what about needing constant pressure on the opponent? Another of those lessons for Paterno developed as the losers made that long trip home.

Another problem was that Penn State had lost for the season its finest defensive player, Linebacker Mike Reid. The future star of the Nittany Lions' defense reinjured his knee, which had been hurt in the National Collegiate Athletic Association wrestling championships the previous March. Reid was out for the season. He was to return to a well-established defense the next year as a tackle and, along with Steve Smear, give Penn State one of the finest tackle tandems a defense has ever had.

But on that journey home, Paterno realized he had gone too long with some players from the previous 1966 team. He had some fine athletes who were sophomores who spent the Navy game mostly on the bench.

"I resolved in my mind on that bus trip that we had some excellent young players whom I hadn't played enough in the Navy game. These were people we were going to stake our future upon—Onkotz, Smear, Kates and Pete and Paul Johnson and Neal Smith. And Charlie Pittman, also."

There wasn't too much time. The next game was the following Friday night in the Orange Bowl against a good Miami team. It could be hot there in September, even after dark. Paterno decided it was time to change personnel and go with good young athletes instead of the ones who had worked with him for only five victories in eleven games. The coach was ready to go all out with his new and more aggressive defenses.

During the week of practice, Paterno didn't let his sophomores know it was going to be their turn. He didn't mention heat and he scheduled a trip that is unusual in this day and age of college football when teams arrive a day ahead of a game and sit around doing little to keep their mind off the game. Penn State traveled to Pittsburgh Thursday night after practice, stayed in the Allegheny County Airport Motel and flew to Miami Friday morning. That afternoon, the team was put up in rooms at the Miami airport where air-conditioning kept their minds off the heat. The pre-game meal was served in the airport and the team was bused to the Orange Bowl.

"Until they hit that stadium, I don't think our kids knew how hot or how humid it was down there," Paterno recalls.

Paterno started practically the same group that had opened against Navy the week before—the group that had experience but not the talent of the eager young sophomores, particularly on defense. Of course, there were such performers as Tommy

Sherman at quarterback, Bob Campbell at halfback, Jack Curry at split end and Ted Kwalick at tight end, players no one would displace. These were the stars of the offense and the men who played through much of the long streak.

After one play in the Orange Bowl that Friday night, Paterno sent Jim Kates in at linebacker. Then, one by one, in went Pete Johnson, Neal Smith, Dennis Onkotz and so on until there were seven or eight sophomores playing, mostly on defense. Onkotz became one of the finest linebackers in the nation, as did Kates. Smith became an excellent safety man in his senior year though he played corner back to start with.

Paterno said, "I'm sure it wasn't until midway through the third quarter that those kids realized the big changes that had been made in the lineup. By then they had played so well that they held Miami—and it was a good Miami team—scoreless."

Miami didn't score until there were forty seconds to go and Penn State won, 17-8, the beginning of the many heroics by this attacking defense for Penn State. Actually, the offense came away from that game with the biggest praises as Campbell executed a fantastic run to set up Penn State's first touchdown. Kwalick caught nine passes and Sherman "came of age," according to his coach.

Campbell's run was a classic during which he went 50 yards, broke tackles a half-dozen times and forced Andy Gustafson, the Miami coach, to admit, "That was the greatest run I've ever seen in a game in the Orange Bowl."

Paterno was grateful to his outstanding halfback despite the fact that Campbell and Paterno had their differences during Bob's career at Penn State, one that was hampered by injuries. "I've always felt obligated to Bobby as a result of that run. I felt he and Kwalick turned our season around in that game," Joe says.

The game in Miami was just a bit too far for even Sue Paterno and Sandra Welsh to get to on their own. But the Friday night before the game was not a time for loneliness for any of the coaches' wives. Betty McCoy, the wife of the athletic director, saw to that.

Betty decided to have a radio dinner party for the staff wives so they could be together and listen to the game. She invited them all to her home for an affair that was possibly intended as one where the wives could console each other. After all, Penn State was supposed to lose to Miami.

The dinner party was just perfect, especially since it was accompanied by the radio report of Penn State's surprising upset victory over Miami. What a night together for the wives! It was just great—so great that the next day Sandra Welsh sent Betty McCoy a thank-you note in which she enclosed a feather from a bluebird.

Two weeks later, Betty McCoy had another gathering at her home while Penn State battled at Boston College on Saturday afternoon. This time, the athletic director's gracious wife had a bird cage adorned with the names of Penn State's remaining opponents. Inside the cage was a toy bird with blue feathers. Each feather represented the wife of a Penn State coach.

Victory came Penn State's way at Boston College. It was the start of the long unbeaten streak and the wives became known as the Bluebirds of Happiness. Even Ernie McCoy started wearing a blue feather for good luck. It was truly the Year of the Bluebird.

The victory at Miami started the bluebirds winging for the coaches' wives at Penn State but the football team wasn't quite ready to begin its flight to victory.

First came the 17-15 loss to UCLA the next week, a loss that didn't seem to hurt a new mode of Penn State football that was destined for big things under Joe Paterno. UCLA had Gary Beban, the winner of the Heisman Trophy that year, as quarterback. But the game was won largely because of a blocked punt that gave the Bruins of Coach Tommy Prothro a touchdown in the early going for a 10-7 lead and gave Paterno living proof of the need for the big play or gamble.

The primary thing about the loss at Penn State was that the Nittany Lions' defense proved its worth. Beban, a scrambling, running quarterback who tore teams apart single-handed, was held to less than 10 yards on the ground by the Penn State sophomore-strong defenses, and it was evidence that the Nittany Lions were on the way defensively.

Some of the coaches were afraid that the victory over Miami might have been a bit of a fluke. Penn State inserted new faces, put up the summer-made defenses more than against Navy and presented Miami with a new-look Penn State, which might have caught the Hurricanes by surprise. But the manner in which Paterno's men held UCLA, despite a lack of offense, warmed the heart of the coach, who was considerably more confident than he had been after losing to Navy.

One of the things that Paterno remembers most about the 1967 UCLA game was the way the Penn State fans cheered and cheered the Nittany Lions at the end despite the loss.

Paterno looks back, saying, "I remember those cheers so well. In a sense it was great to hear it. But in another sense I just hoped the day would come when our fans will want us to win and expect us to win. I think just being close is not good enough for us. We had to begin thinking about winning all the time and I felt very strongly then that we had to turn this kind of situation around. We had to begin beating the UCLA's. We had to expect to win.

"People told me later how lucky they were to win on the blocked punt. But I always said 'no' to that. I never felt that way because a great team expects to win and it expects to do something somewhere during a game that will turn it around. Every great team goes on the field expecting to win every game and possessing the confidence that it'll come up with the really big play necessary to win a tough game."

That's what UCLA did against Penn State, and from the next week on Penn State did just that almost every week for three years. People who lost to Penn State grumbled that it was "luck" on the part of the Lions. But those who followed Penn State during its long streak got to the point where they sat back confident the defense or offense would make one big play to turn things around when the going got rough. It always happened during the remainder of the 1967 season, the 1968 and 1969 seasons and in two Orange Bowl games. The one exception was the 1967 Gator Bowl game.

As lessons kept piling up for the coach and his team, the UCLA affair proved to Paterno and the squad "that we were sound defensively, that we could play with anyone in the country and that we were sound in what we were doing. I think it also gave me a chance to illustrate that a great team is going to make the play that is necessary to win—which UCLA, a great team, did that day."

Penn State lost Campbell for the season during the UCLA game when he injured a knee and underwent surgery the next day. But the team was together and ready for the surge. A victory at Boston College, 50-28, on a relatively easy afternoon of football the next week began the streak that didn't end until Penn State had gone through thirty-one straight games without a loss. Only that Gator Bowl affair kept it from being a thirty-one-game all-winning streak.

Coming into their own now were Don Abbey, the fullback; Charlie Pittman, the halfback, and others as Penn State moved past West Virginia, 21-14, beat Syracuse in one of the most physically tough games of the year, 29-20, and romped over Maryland, 38-3, in what Paterno called "not really a good football game." Kates, who was outstanding against Maryland, was just warming up for one of the biggest plays an athlete could imagine. It came the next week against North Carolina State.

Suddenly Penn State and Paterno had the football world paying some attention to a radical change out there in the middle of the Keystone State. Could these Nittany Lions have a chance against the team ranked No. 3 in the nation, an unbeaten North Carolina State team, whose defense was the best in the country by statistical ratings? Hardly. N.C. was coached by Earl Edwards, a 1931 graduate of Penn State, former member of Penn State's football staff and a man edged out for the head coaching job at Penn State a year before Rip Engle took over.

North Carolina State went up to Beaver Stadium set for the kill that would put Edwards' team into a bowl game of stature. The proud defense of this southern team wore white shoes to distinguish itself from its offensive partners in running up eight victories in eight games that season. Penn State would be tough, yes, but hardly the team to stop N.C. State.

But Joe Paterno was thinking again. He had developed a knack for coming up with an early twist in a game, a maneuver that would throw the opponent off balance just enough to gain a slight edge for Penn State. Penn State had used a twist to get started against Syracuse a couple of weeks earlier and it hadn't panned out to any great advantage. Penn State went back to basics on offense to win that game.

But Paterno was not going to let that discourage him. A new twist would help against N.C. State. So it was developed. Ted Kwalick, the big tight end, was a known threat to any team. His strength to run once he had the ball and his ability to make fantastic catches caught the eye of any scout and certainly the North Carolina State scouts. So N.C. State, like most teams, would double-team this man—put a couple of fine defenders from the white-shoe corps to cover him and prevent Tom Sherman from throwing to him.

Over on the other side of the Penn State offensive line was Jack Curry, a fine split end. Could N.C. State handle both Curry and Kwalick? The Wolfpack from Raleigh, North Carolina, certainly imagined it could because N.C. State had the No. 1 defense in the land. But Paterno had a simpler gimmick.

Joe mapped a switch for the first few plays by Penn State's offense. Instead of having Kwalick at tight end to one side and Curry at split end on the other, Paterno moved Kwalick over to a slot-back position between Curry and the split-side tackle. This put Penn State's two fine receivers on the same side of the offense, a problem of surprise for the N.C. State defense. Then Paterno called for a short punt formation which put Tom Sherman, the quarterback, 5 yards back of the line of scrimmage for the center snap. He could pass more quickly from that set and try to hit Curry or Kwalick, who were flooding the one side.

It worked and got the Lions off to a quick touchdown as Kwalick caught a scoring pass. Then Onkotz intercepted a pass and ran it back for another touchdown before seven minutes had gone by. N.C. State was stunned, but Edwards' forces rallied and adjusted to the Kwalick switch so Joe Paterno sent Ted back to his normal tight-end position opposite Curry and Penn State called upon its defense for the most important stand in its young career.

The night before the Penn State-N.C. game, Edwards might just have learned of the Kwalick switch if he had decided to take his team to State College's Holiday Inn, where most visiting teams now stay when playing at Penn State. But the N.C. State coach, as is the case with some other coaches, housed his team in a motel in Altoona, Pennsylvania, Friday night and bused the squad to the game Saturday afternoon. It's a ride of about forty-five miles from Altoona to Beaver Stadium.

Paterno has followed a close relationship with a number of reporters who cover Penn State regularly. Friendships gained are honored on the basis that "we both have a job to do and anything that makes it easier and more productive is worthwhile." Following this theory, Paterno will inform some of his most trusted friends among reporters of any twist he plans for a game. He gives the plan to those sports reporters Friday on the idea that a reporter can better cover a game if he understands what surprises to expect.

But that Friday night before the Penn State-N.C. game, the word leaked out beyond the group of trusted reporters. It has never been determined who let it slip, but the mishap never hurt Penn State, though it could well have been harmful. Sitting around the Holiday Inn bar late Friday night, it became clear to a group of reporters that they weren't the only ones who knew of the Kwalick switch. Some fans also knew what was in the offing. Had N.C. State decided to stay at the Holiday Inn, only three miles from Beaver Stadium, the word would obviously have been heard by someone from Carolina.

But the Paterno gimmick of the week worked and Penn State was ahead by just enough when its defense faced the test that was to whip N.C. State and send the Lions into the Gator Bowl. Penn State didn't score after those first 13 points but N.C. State did, though it didn't make a touchdown. A couple of field goals and N.C. State was ready for the big charge. Late in the game, Penn State had its back to the wall. With a minute to go, the North Carolinians were at Penn State's 1-yard line on fourth down.

A touchdown would almost certainly mean defeat because Penn State had missed its second extra point and N.C. State would surely go for two extra points with a run or pass. That 13-6 looked as if it would suddenly be 14-13 for the Carolina team. Earl Edwards called time out to speak to his quarterback. Tim Montgomery, the Penn State safety, went over to speak to

Paterno then. Joe remembered this as one of his times of "genius" in coaching. "I told Tim I thought they'd fake inside and go outside. We had a goal-line in and a goal-line out defense. To show you what a great coach I am, Timmie said, 'You know, we've been working all week on that fake that they make and I think they'll probably go to that.'

"This was a fake to the fullback, who led to the left and then the quarterback handed off to the tailback, Tony Barchuck, who went inside. I said, 'Gee, Tim, I don't know.' But I finally said, 'O.K.' and we went with the inside defense. Sure enough, they came with the inside play and we stacked it up."

That play was amazing. Jim Kates hit low under the pileup and Dennis Onkotz stood high to slam back any attempt to dive over the pile. Both Kates and Onkotz had Barchuck and threw him back in a play that made college football recognize Penn State's defense as worth worrying about. The screaming fans in Beaver Stadium didn't shut up for hours. Penn State took a deliberate safety for 2 points in order to free-kick the ball out of trouble and, with less than a minute to go, a 13-8 victory was assured.

Paterno remembers the goal-line defense against N.C. State as "one of the greatest plays in Penn State history. Most people didn't realize that Tim Montgomery was really the guy who stopped them by calling the inside defense. I sure as hell would have screwed it up."

So the road to the Gator Bowl was cleared by Montgomery, Onkotz and Kates and the other Penn State defenders late in the game and by Kwalick, Sherman and Curry in the early stages of the victory that ended N.C. State's winning streak. Penn State met and beat Ohio University and Pittsburgh rather handily to finish the regular season 8-2. The invitation to play Florida State in the Gator Bowl was made official and the Nittany Lions, who had started the season so poorly, ended it in a blaze of glory.

There was more to come, though, in Jacksonville in late December. This was the game that ended in a tie, something no team really wants and least of all a Penn State team coached by Joe Paterno. But it was in the Gator Bowl that Paterno enhanced his reputation as a go-for-broke man, a fellow who would never sit on a 10-10 tie, as some coaches do, or a 17-17 tie, for that matter. It was Paterno's penchant for gambling that gave Florida State the opportunity to go for a 17-17 tie.

Major adjustments took place in the Penn State offense and defense as the squad prepared at Daytona Beach for a meeting with pass-happy Florida State. In secrecy, Paterno worked his team into a new-look group of Lions to prepare for that game he and the players had worked so hard to achieve in their first real year of working together.

Paterno moved offensive players to defense, put his team into a new offensive formation and defensive alignment and practically threw out the book which had brought him success during the 1967 season because he wanted to give Florida State something new to look at. It all worked to a point—about midway in the third quarter when the Lions were ahead of Florida State, 17-0. All the changes had worked and, as Paterno said, "We were playing a fine game, a real strong game. But the defense was tired."

Penn State had the ball on a 4th-and-1 situation deep in its own territory, with a comfortable lead. Joe thought to himself, "All right, Paterno, here's where you put up or shut up since you're always talking about taking a chance." All the reasons that were involved included the fact that the offense wanted to try for the first down with less than a yard to go. Paterno and the players felt they could make it.

Also, the coaches knew Penn State's defense was so tired that maybe, if the Lions punted here, Florida State would come barreling down the field in a hurry and take away control of the game. So Penn State went for it, with Tom Sherman trying a quarterback sneak. But the Lions didn't make it, according to the officials. Onkotz, standing on the sidelines, remembers, "One of the Florida State guys pulled Tom back by his pants after he'd made it with something to spare. The films show this too. But . . ."

Ernie McCoy, the athletic director, was in the press box at the Gator Bowl, watching as Paterno was talking to his players before giving the O.K. on going for the first down on that play. McCoy kept saying, "Paterno wouldn't go for it. He just wouldn't. No, he wouldn't go for it. . . . My God, he's going for it!"

From that missed first down, Florida State got two touchdowns within seconds, since Charlie Pittman fumbled the kickoff after the first Florida State score. Then came a tying field goal and Penn State went home a team in a deadlock.

Jack Curry had always been a player Paterno considered close to the coach. The two had a fine relationship and an understanding. Occasionally Curry would speak to Paterno about some team problems or of some gripes the players might have and Joe always listened.

The day after the Gator Bowl, the team flew home not too happy, but not too upset. They had tried. The players had insisted they could make the first down and Paterno had felt they could. During the flight, Curry, who was sitting in the back of the plane with a number of the players, got up and went forward to where Paterno was sitting with the coaches.

Jack said, "Coach, the players would like you to know something." Paterno was pleased with this, since he was down in the dumps about the fourth-down failure if anyone was. Joe said, "Sure, Jack, what is it?"

Curry, with straight face, said, "Coach, we feel that you blew it."

This broke what tension there was, and the remainder of the ride home was not so bad. From then on Paterno has made light of the 4th-and-1 at the Gator Bowl and jokes about it during speeches and clinics.

His favorite story of the incident is to tell of one reporter in the dressing room after the Gator Bowl game who kept insisting on knowing from Paterno, "What went through your mind when you didn't make that first down?"

Paterno relates, "I looked at him and thought he was kidding but he kept at it. So I said, 'Look, Mac, all I can tell you is the story they tell about the nun and the Marine who were stranded on a raft and in order to pass the time of day they were doing crossword puzzles. The nun asked the Marine, 'Sergeant, what's a four-letter word for bird droppings?'

"The sergeant thought it over and said, 'Sister, I believe it's grit.'

"'Oh,' she said. 'Do you have an eraser?'

"Mac, what the hell do you think I felt? I turned to my assistant coach and said, 'Grit'!"

Paterno believes that going for the first down got his name before the public. The Gator Bowl, like other bowl games, was televised that day between Christmas and New Year's Day in 1967. Paterno claims, "When we went for it and didn't make it there were 50-million people watching who jumped up from their easy chairs and said, 'Who the hell is coaching Penn State?' Now they know!"

Later in the Gator Bowl game, Florida State had a chance to win. Coach Bill Peterson's team was at the Penn State 20-yard line with about 3 yards to go. It was a fourth-down situation and Peterson ordered the field goal attempt that was good and tied the game.

Frank Spaziani, one of Penn State's fine defensive ends, came running off the field after that kick, storming like a bull. "God damn, I'd rather lose than get tied. Why the hell didn't they go for the win? Why the hell didn't they try for the touchdown?"

Paterno said, "Right then and there I knew for sure that these kids would always play to win."

16: The Twelfth Man

JOE PATERNO CHECKED INTO a small room at the Los Angeles headquarters hotel of the National Collegiate Athletic Association convention on January 7 in 1969. That was just six days after Penn State beat Kansas in one of the most unusual and exciting finishes ever seen in the Orange Bowl or any other bowl game for that matter. Paterno was obviously the man to be named Coach of the Year by his colleagues in the collegiate coaching profession that week during the concurrent convention of the American Football Coaches Association in Los Angeles. But Paterno was also a man struggling with the problem of whether or not to accept an unusually lucrative offer to coach the Pittsburgh Steelers of the National Football League.

Now a highly successful coach, Paterno had just taken Penn State through its first undefeated and untied season since 1947 and topped it off with an Orange Bowl victory. The 1947 team got only a tie with Southern Methodist in the Cotton Bowl. Joe was wanted by many who desired winning teams. His friend, Art Rooney, president of the Steelers, kept raising the ante in an attempt to induce Paterno to give up college football and coach the professional team that had never, in four decades of existence, been able to come up a champion.

The popular owner-president of the Steelers offered just about everything short of the Golden Triangle in downtown Pittsburgh to get Paterno. Dan Rooney, Art's eldest son and vice president of the family-owned club, had also been dealing with Joe in the attempt to move the new hero of Pennsylvania.

Sue Paterno kept insisting she would go wherever Joe decided was best for the family. To add to the temptation, if Joe accepted the Rooney offer it would mean no more financial problems for the Paternos and their children for the remainder of their lives. The length of the contract and the money and fringe benefits involved would have insured that.

Shortly after the Orange Bowl victory, Joe left Penn State and went on the recruiting trail alone for a few days before flying to the West Coast. He wanted to be alone on that search for talent primarily so he could think out the Pittsburgh offer by himself, an offer 99 percent of the coaches in the nation would have jumped at without thoughts of what they left behind, finished or unfinished. But, when Paterno arrived in Los Angeles late Tuesday afternoon, he was still somewhat undecided, though on the verge of a final decision.

A few minutes after he arrived in his room, Jim Tarman and Joe's brother, George, joined him and the discussion went directly to the point. Pittsburgh or Penn State? Both Tarman and George Paterno had more than a passing interest in what happened. Joe had gotten the Rooneys to agree that if he went to the Steelers he would be, if not necessarily the general manager in name, the boss and would run the show his way. This would mean that Tarman would go along as, probably, the assistant general manager and that Joe would be able to hire George Paterno as one of his primary assistants. George was then head coach at the United States Merchant Marine Academy and was debating an offer from Duffy Daugherty to move to Michigan State as offensive backfield coach.

Within an hour after Tarman and George Paterno joined Joe the room became crowded as one of this book's co-authors, on assignment covering the NCAA convention, joined the group, followed by Tom Cahill, Army's coach and by then a close friend of Joe Paterno's. Cahill entered the room with Dick Lyon, his first assistant coach, and the late Ron Lanthier, Tom's traveling companion and good friend, who owned a Pontiac dealership in Newburgh, New York.

Joe asked each one what he thought he should do—go to Pittsburgh or stay at Penn State. Maybe, because everyone felt Joe didn't really want to leave Penn State, or maybe, because everyone there was more for college than pro football, each indicated he would like to see Joe stay where he was.

Paterno offered all six who were squeezed into the little room a drink of bourbon from the lone bottle he had, ordered a huge antipasto brought to the room and turned to call Sue on the phone. When he got his wife on the phone, Joe asked about the kids and then said, "Pack your things and get ready to move. We're going to Pittsburgh."

This sudden decision shocked the six crowded in the room as much as it obviously shocked Sue on the other end of the phone 3,000 miles away. A long pause followed and Joe said into the phone, "Why didn't you tell me? That's all I want to know."

When Joe hung up he explained to those sitting on the radiator, the dresser and the luggage bench, "She began crying when I told her we were going to Pittsburgh. I guess I wanted that sudden reaction to find out exactly what I should do."

The next day Paterno released a statement for the press in which he explained why he was turning down the Pittsburgh offer:

"Today, I have informed Dan Rooney, vice president of the Pittsburgh Steelers, that I have decided to remain at Penn State. The Steelers made me an extremely generous offer to become their head coach—an offer which not only would have afforded a great personal challenge but would have assured lifetime financial security for my family. Previously, professional football has held very little attraction for me, but in this instance the opportunity to help make the Steelers a championship contender, made me seriously consider leaving college fooball.

"But, in the final analysis, my decision at this time has to be to remain at Penn State. This decision is based on many factors—my genuine love for a great university and the community in which we live, the relationship of a college coach with fine young men at such a vital stage in their lives, my personal goal of giving Penn State the best of big-time football within the framework of sound academic and financial policies, and my deep belief that football can and should be fun and make a strong contribution to higher education. To leave Penn State at this time would be to leave with the feeling of a job undone and a great challenge still unfulfilled. And, most important, I have too strong a feeling of obligation and friendship to the players on our squad and to the loyal friends, coaches, university officials and colleagues who have contributed so much to our success."

Though this sounded much like being too idealistic in this age of cynics when most persons jump at the buck, it was a public way of telling the truth. And Paterno has described himself as sometimes too much of an idealist.

Sue explained her reaction to that phone call by saying that she "broke down because he wouldn't have been fair to himself."

Sue really didn't mind moving because her family is from Latrobe, a short distance from Pittsburgh. She revealed, "Talks with the Steelers started before the 1968 season was over. Joe kept giving the Steelers impossible things that they couldn't come up with. But then they came up with everything, which unnerved us both. But the point that kept basically going through his mind was that he'd made a commitment to Penn State. He'd waited all his life for this job and why would he suddenly chuck it? He'd waited fifteen years and he'd turned down other coaching jobs. He wanted to make Penn State a unique spot and a place from where to build up state pride and see if he could make things work that way at Penn State.

"Also, there was his feeling toward this group of kids, who were his first complete team. He didn't see how he could leave them. He'd become very attached to them, naturally." That was the group of juniors and seniors of 1968 who started their varsity careers in 1966 or 1967.

With typical honesty and integrity, Paterno didn't even turn to Ernie McCoy, the athletic director, and hold the Pittsburgh offer over his head to demand more money for himself. He got a raise after the 1968 season but, more important to the coach, he did insist on some future changes pertaining to football in the Department of Athletics. These included some personnel changes which Joe wanted to insure the proper direction and growth of the football program. He also wanted assurance that future football schedules would be beefed up. A new coaches' office was built, one that was more attractive, less crowded and a show spot when ushering recruits around Penn State.

Paterno had already made his decision to stay when he had a talk with McCoy in Los Angeles, and following conversations between McCoy and Dr. Eric Walker, president of Penn State, things were settled to the satisfaction of those concerned and Paterno went back to planning for another undefeated and untied season in 1969.

The flush of surprising victory in the Orange Bowl remained strong with Penn Staters at the time of Paterno's plan to remain put. This must have helped him gain some of his programs for Penn State. For, what team ever won as Penn State did over Kansas?

Kansas suffered only one loss in the 1968 season, Penn State none. But just who were these Nittany Lions? Everyone knows Big Eight Conference football (Kansas' league) produces better than the East can muster. Kansas was favored despite eighteen straight games without defeat for Penn State. And Kansas had a fine quarterback in Bobby Douglass compared to just a routine Chuck Burkhart for Penn State, despite the fact Burkhart had never lost a game he started in high school or college.

Burkhart had succeeded Tom Sherman, the quarterback who graduated after the Gator Bowl tie. Burkhart's great claim to fame was his ability to not make mistakes and his charm as just a winner. But that great fame hadn't gone far beyond the Penn State campus.

Kansas got a 14-7 lead in the fourth quarter of a none-too-thrilling contest that remained that way for almost fifty-nine minutes. Morning paper reporters were beginning their leads on this night game well before the conclusion. They had deadlines to meet and wanted a good hunk of their stories ready to go the instant the final gun sounded.

Mike Reid did his usual thing and slammed Douglass for two straight losses deep in Kansas area. But there was only a minute and a half to go when Kansas punted to give Penn State one last chance. But that chance was of little concern to most. Even some

Penn State fans had left the big arena to beat the rush back to hotels and motels in Miami or Miami Beach.

With a minute and sixteen seconds remaining, Penn State received the punt at the 50, called time and Paterno did another of his fine sideline coaching jobs with two of his stars. Calling Burkhart and Bobby Campbell to the sidelines, Paterno said, "Bobby, I want you to run a deep post pattern and Chuck, you just throw it way out there. I don't expect you to try to complete it but, whatever you do, don't underthrow the ball so they intercept. I want you just to loosen them up so on the next play we can throw short to Kwalick who can run 20 or 30 yards and get us close. We have time, so just don't underthrow, Chuck."

Penn State did have plenty of time in a sense, with two times out remaining and the ability to stop the clock on incompleted passes such as the one Paterno expected on the ensuing play from Burkhart to Campbell.

As the quarterback and tailback left Paterno to return to the team on the field, Campbell yelled to Burkhart, "Now look, I'm going to be at that post and you make sure the ball is there."

Burkhart replied, "Don't worry, it'll be there."

Paterno, now really worried, hollered out to them, "Never mind putting it there. Just throw it deep and don't let them intercept. I don't give a damn about completing it. Just don't let them intercept."

Burkhart's word was good. Just as he got whacked by a Kansas defensive player, he let fly with one of the longest good passes of his career. Campbell caught it and ran to the Kansas 3-yard line. Paterno had said, "You know, we could practice that play twenty times without any defenders to bother the practice team and we'd only complete it three times."

From the 3-yard line, it took Penn State three plays to score. Burkhart got the touchdown when he ran to his left after keeping the ball on an improvised play. It was supposed to be a buck by Charlie Pittman. But, when the ball was snapped, Burkhart saw it wouldn't work so he kept the ball. Out on the left flank was Campbell as a pass decoy and Bobby was obviously surprised to see Burkhart coming toward him with the ball. He hesitated a second or so and then went ahead to block anyone in Burkhart's way. There was no one to worry about, as most of the Kansas players, anticipating Pittman as the ball carrier, went gunning for Charlie.

Burkhart just followed the tactic used by Y. A. Tittle of the Giants, when he quarterbacked the New York pro team. Tittle would call for a run and at the last second keep the ball and throw a pass. Receivers were always out on pro plays, so Tittle had someone to throw to. His theory was, "If I fool my own runners, think of how I fool the defense."

The Burkhart touchdown came as the final gun sounded, so all that remained was the try for the extra point, and Paterno didn't hesitate a second. He went for 2 points and a victory rather than settle for a tie. On a pass right to Campbell, Penn State missed connections and the game was over—or was it? The Kansas fans were storming the field to crowd around their winning heroes. But wait a minute. There was a flag on the field, and an indication that Kansas had committed a foul.

Foster Gross, an Eastern College Athletic Conference official, was the umpire. He threw the flag when Penn State tried for the extra 2 points. The signal was for an illegal formation by Kansas. The Jayhawks had twelve men on the field, a slightly illegal type of defense. Maybe there had been a mistake in the Kansas substitution arrangement and someone didn't leave when another player was sent in. Kansas Coach Pepper Rodgers said later that had indeed been the case.

Penn State got a second chance to try for 2 points and the victory and made it when Burkhart handed off the ball to Campbell, who smashed over for a 15-14 win and the greatest triumph in Penn State football history. When the final gun sounded, Kansas fans were all around the end zone and Penn Staters, who had been resigned to a certain defeat, became delirious with joy. They had seen another big play pulled off by their team and their coach had succeeded on a gamble for victory.

The following night, at the Orange Bowl celebration ball, Paterno made a point of thanking Foster Gross for his alertness in catching the twelfth man. Gross said, "Joe, I count players on every play. I spotted it immediately."

A coach has to be grateful for such a call since, in the confusion of goal-line stands, with subs running in and out and quick plays running off without a huddle, officials, as well as players and coaches, can miss important items that tell the story of a game. So Gross was alert, he said, and Penn State was saved.

But a couple of days later, after the films were seen by coaches of Kansas and Penn State, a Kansas assistant coach let the world know the truth. He saw on the films that Kansas didn't have twelve men on only the first 2-point conversion play. He saw that Kansas had twelve men on the field from the time the Nittany Lions reached the 3-yard line. That is, the Jayhawks had 12 men on the field for four straight plays, with Gross, who counts on every play, spotting the twelfth man after Kansas had actually gone three plays with an extra man.

At least Gross finally got around to counting. But why didn't the other officials ever count and then, what about Penn State and Kansas coaches watching from above, those men who direct by phone to the sidelines, suggesting plays or changes during a game?

When Paterno learned that Kansas had twelve men for four plays he wondered, "What the hell were my fellows doing up-stairs? I had George Welsh, Joe McMullen, Bobby Phillips and Frank Patrick working up there on the phones in the press box."

Joe got his four "upstairs" men and asked, "What in God's name were you guys doing up there when there were twelve men on the Kansas team for four plays?"

To a man they answered, "Joe, we were cheering."

Paterno observed, "We sure as hell had an expensive, cheerlead-ing group at the end, didn't we?"

But it was over, Penn State had won in a thriller and "this Orange Bowl game put us on the map," according to Paterno. Believers began cropping up here and there. Penn State was a team of destiny, a team of near-great defenses and a team that had more guts than any team in the nation—college or profes-sional. Paterno's gambling had paid off, even if he instilled it so strongly that his players, especially Burkhart and Campbell, wanted to gamble even more than the coach. This was a team coached to have fun and the fun produced victory.

The trip to the Orange Bowl of 1969 was easy when you look back at it. But week by week it had not been all that simple. Penn State put together a string of ten victories against Navy, Kansas

State, West Virginia, UCLA, Boston College, Army, Miami, Maryland, Pittsburgh and Syracuse. It was the first Penn State team to win ten games in a regular season and Paterno was finally becoming satisfied that his way was the winning way and his program a good one for Penn State football. He didn't have doubts anymore and he knew what was happening came about because of what he did—gamble, go for broke and enjoy football after working hard in practice.

Despite the success, Sue Paterno didn't enjoy the entire season. Her troubles started when Beano Cook, the former Pittsburgh sports information director who had moved to ABC-TV as college football press director, sent out a tongue-in-cheek release explaining why the date of the Penn State-Syracuse game had been switched from October 19 to December 7. "Television can't be blamed for everything," began the release. "The main reason the game is now scheduled for December 7 is that Sue Paterno, wife of the Penn State coach, is going to have a baby some time in October."

The release went on to say that Sue had called Roone Arledge, president of ABC sports, and asked him to change the game to December 7 because doctors predicted the baby would be born on October 19 and she didn't want to miss the Penn State-Syracuse game.

Arledge reportedly agreed and the release quoted Sue as saying, "You see, sportswriters can't blame television for the switch."

It was a fun release by Beano Cook and newspapers and magazines used it as such. But some irate Penn State and Syracuse fans swallowed the gag as the gospel truth and Sue Paterno was bombarded by letters and phone calls, some of them really vicious. They took her to task for requesting the switch in dates, and one "fan" even asked how she would like it if there was a blizzard on December 7 and "dozens" of people were killed in automobile accidents on their way to the game.

It was a bad time for Sue Paterno, who pointed out that the date of the game had actually been changed by the network before anyone knew she was pregnant.

"It was all a joke," she said forlornly.

It was in the 1968 season when the defense became a proud and powerful unit, with Reid back at tackle and Kates, Onkotz, Pete Johnson, Paul Johnson, Neal Smith, Mike Smith, John Ebersole, Jack Ham, Gary Hull and the others contributing the big defensive plays. But the offense had one of the best games in the year of Penn State fine defense when the Nittany Lions rolled over a Miami team, 22-7. The second half of that game was declared by Paterno as "probably the best half we have ever played at Penn State."

The big problem was a guy with the nickname of "the Wild Stork." He was Jim Hendricks, a tall, lanky All-America defensive end who specialized in wrapping his long arms around runners going to his side of the line. He now plays good defense for the Baltimore Colts. But that day at Penn State, Paterno's offense wisely ran away from him and Charlie Pittman and Bobby Campbell picked up 208 yards between them in the second half, with Pittman scoring three touchdowns in the last thirty minutes to give the Lions a win.

The defense did its share, as usual, blocking punts, intercepting passes and recovering fumbles. But, by now, this was becoming routine and standard operating procedure for Penn State.

The week before Miami, Penn State beat Army in one of the finest games played by the cadets under Tom Cahill. Quarterback Steve Lindell and End Gary Steele combined to almost drag down the Nittany Lions in a wild second half. But an onsides, or short, kickoff by Army late in the game settled the issue as the ball was pounced on by twenty-one of the twenty-two players on the field. However, the ball was squirted out of the pack and Ted Kwalick, who for some reason was not in the pile, easily took it to his chest and romped 53 yards for the touchdown that clinched a 28-24 Penn State triumph.

Paterno explained that victory quite easily. With tongue in cheek and a sly grin on his face, he told people, "We worked on that onsides kick all week, knowing Army was good at it. We had it set so that all hands would fall on the ball, which would squirt out to Kwalick waiting on the right. It was hard work to get it that way, but a week's work at it made it happen. Then we used the practiced play, Kwalick was ready and we scored the easy touchdown because we had coached for that play. And if you believe that one, you'll believe anything."

But it all added up to a great year of success for Penn State under the coaching genius of Joe Paterno. And he was justly rewarded in Los Angeles in January of 1969 when his colleagues voted him Coach of the Year for 1968. This is an honor reserved only for the top man in college football.

Joe Paterno was the top man.

17: Who's No. 1?

ONCE A TEAM HAS GONE through an undefeated and untied season, won a bowl game and gotten its boss named Coach of the Year, it has created a situation than can pile extreme pressure upon itself for the coming campaign. Winning streaks in any sport make the winning team a target of all opponents. Anyone who knocks the mighty off the perch will be recognized as somebody special.

College athletes are growing men, not necessarily fully matured, and human young men who can feel the load of such pressures more than a more mature group of athletes. For the college players, it marks the first time they are going through the trials of national recognition. The publicity and build-up for each game on a streak can become unbearable. The coach must tone this down if he is to get the same efficiency out of his players that got them to that point.

Penn State entered the 1969 season riding the biggest streak in the nation—nineteen games without a loss—and the Lions had won their last eleven games. Pressure was there.

Penn State's fifth game of 1969 was against that enemy again—

Syracuse. Paterno's forces were a bit sluggish in the first half and Syracuse was dynamic. The Orange led, 14-0, at halftime and Penn State was obviously in grave danger of having its streak (now twenty-three games) broken by the one team, if any, that Penn State would not want to lose to.

The pressure was there, yet Paterno talked quietly to his players in the dressing room at halftime. Joe recalls, "I said to the kids at halftime, when we were getting our rumps kicked in, 'I don't know whether we can win. But I tell you what, I know you have the kind of pride that you're going out there and you're going to give it all you have. I know you won't quit and that's all I want you to prove to the world in the second half. You won't quit in the face of adversity. If we walk off this field a loser after this ball game, we're going to walk off as men who have given everything we have. If we don't win, O.K., but we'll find out what we're made of this half.'"

Penn State found out what it was made of, and so did a lot of other people, as the Lions rallied to win, 15-14. There was that score again—15-14—a score that was so important in Penn State football during the long streak. Penn State beat Kansas, 15-14, in the previous Orange Bowl and Texas was to beat Arkansas, 15-14, later in 1969 to get the Presidential blessing as No. 1.

But Paterno proved he didn't panic at Syracuse and his players proved the same as they won. The post-game controversy, however, was the loudest off-field hassle in recent years in Eastern college football. Ben Schwartzwalder was fit to be tied. He sat on the problem over the weekend and traveled to New York on Monday, after the loss to Penn State, to let loose publicity against Penn State, Paterno, his players and the officials. Ben felt his team had been done in by poor officiating and unfair play by Penn State players.

A number of penalties late in the game contributed to Schwartzwalder's feelings. The Syracuse coach let it all out and accused "that Penn State No. 73" of holding "75 percent of the time during the game and no one called it." His forum was the New York Football Writers Association weekly luncheon at the New York University Club.

"That No. 73" was Tom Jackson, offensive tackle and one of the three players sharing captain's roles for the Penn State team

in 1969. But Schwartzwalder hadn't done his homework on this
one too well and, as a result, his complaints after the game lost
plenty of their punch.

Paterno has always had a messenger service. Joe alternates a
couple of players at one position on offense so they can keep taking in the next play that he wants used. During the 1969 season,
Jackson and Vic Surma alternated at one of the offensive tackle
spots, since they were Paterno's chosen messengers. Joe used
offensive split ends the year before. They didn't switch on every
play, but they went in and out about 70 percent of the time.
Thus, Jackson or Surma might be in the game for two or three
straight plays if Paterno sent in a series.

As it turned out in the Syracuse game, Surma spent more time
in action than Jackson. "That No. 73" was in the game only about
40 percent of the time Penn State was on offense. So Ben
Schwartzwalder was incorrect when he accused Jackson of holding 75 percent of the time—it was impossible.

That was the closest Penn State came to defeat during the 1969
season or in the January 1, 1970, Orange Bowl. Maybe any worry
about pressure was unjustified. The athletes lived up to any
added problems from national fame like the troopers that Paterno
hopes he raises at Penn State.

Maybe it was because Paterno had the attitude—"to hell with
the streak." He never talked about it to his players during the
1969 season and never tried to show concern about it. Of
course, everyone knew about the streak and knew what it
would mean to lose. But Joe kept telling his players, "Don't worry
about losing a football game."

Obviously the Lions didn't "worry" too much as they sailed
into a weak Navy team to open the season with a 45-22 triumph.
A corps of running backs, the likes of which is rarely seen on
one college team, tore the Middies apart easily and made the
score easy. The game marked the sophomore debut of Lydell
Mitchell and Franco Harris, who were to become outstanding
runners for the Lions. But Charlie Pittman led the attack with
his running and Navy didn't have a chance.

After the game, Paterno's primary comment was, "They should
be ashamed to play a big-league game on a cow pasture like
this." The turf at the Navy-Marine Corps Memorial Stadium in

Annapolis, Maryland, was not of the best quality that warm September afternoon in 1969.

Penn State went on to beat Colorado, Kansas State, West Virginia, Syracuse, Ohio University, Boston College, Maryland, Pittsburgh and North Carolina State. Great defense once again enabled Penn State to hold on to a 17-14 victory over Kansas State as Paul Johnson and Jack Ham made important interceptions and when Lynn Dickey, the Kansas State quarterback of All-America stature, was nailed for a loss trying to pass on a late 4th-and-2 situation.

It was all there again, that strong defense with the offense that just took its time to wait for the big play to break open games week after week. As this season kept moving along, it became obvious to all that Penn State would never be No. 1 because Ohio State, riding a two-season unbeaten string of its own, was voted on top in the polls each week. No one would ever dislodge Ohio State and Paterno didn't mind too much being rated behind the Buckeyes, Texas and Arkansas as the season progressed.

And as Penn State kept moving along undefeated, it became apparent the Lions were going to another bowl game. Which one this time? Well, there were Texas and Arkansas standing above Penn State and just behind Ohio State in the weekly polls most of the season. All four were also riding undefeated streaks.

On the afternoon of November 15, Penn State trounced Maryland, 48-0, and returned home to decide which bowl bid to accept. Monday, November 19, was invitation day in 1969 for the bowls, which are not permitted to extend bids until a certain date each year. Within a few days, many critics of Penn State said, "Why in hell didn't they take the Cotton Bowl? Are they afraid to play Texas, the No. 1 team?"

Far from it. Penn State would have liked nothing better than to play the No. 1 team to prove the Lions were really worthy of No. 1. But fate was scrambling the whole bowl picture so that Penn State could get little more than a Presidential offer of an undefeated and untied plaque.

Ohio State, undefeated and untied on the day the bowl invitations were issued, was No. 1 and preparing for its expected victory over Michigan on November 22. Neither Penn State nor anyone else could meet Ohio State in a bowl game on January 1,

1970. As a member of the Big Ten, Ohio State was bound by that league's contract with the Rose Bowl and with the conference rule. Ohio State had won in the Rose Bowl the previous year and under Big Ten rules, Coach Woody Hayes' Buckeyes could not return to Pasadena, nor could they play in any other bowl game.

So, Michigan, which everybody was sure would lose to Ohio State, would be the Big Ten representative in the Rose Bowl. Michigan didn't even have to beat the Buckeyes to get that berth. And Ohio State was going to win, right? Right.

This was the thinking of the Penn State players, along with everyone else in the nation. Ohio State would beat Michigan, finish the season No. 1, couldn't be challenged in a bowl game, so no team could dislodge the Buckeyes of Woody Hayes from that lofty spot—bowl victory or not.

The choice for the Penn State team on November 17 then was—Do you want to play the No. 2 team, Texas, or do you want to return to the Orange Bowl where players enjoy more fun and games than at any other of the major bowl games? It was hardly a contest. Coaches and players at Penn State felt they couldn't prove anything by meeting and beating Texas, so they opted for the Orange Bowl once again.

Then the impossible happened—Michigan whipped Ohio State. But that was six days after Penn State had accepted the Orange Bowl bid against Missouri, a team that lost only one game during the season. Now Texas was No. 1, and looking ahead to the big meeting with Arkansas on December 6.

Darrell Royal's Longhorns beat Arkansas by that now familiar score of 15-14 before President Nixon and got the President's blessing as the nation's No. 1 team. Penn State was No. 2 and Orange Bowl-bound and Texas was No. 1 and Cotton Bowl-bound against Notre Dame. The Irish were making their first appearance in a bowl game since 1925 because Notre Dame needed the money.

It was then that the furor over No. 1 broke out. Joe Paterno wasn't at all bashful in his criticism of President Nixon and the wire service polls and he picked up vocal allies all over the state of Pennsylvania, among them Governor Raymond Shafer.

Some fans scorned the Nittany Lions for their choice. The truth was, they had no choice when you consider the attitude of

Paterno and the attitude he instills in his players and coaches. "Why not have fun at a bowl game and why play the No. 2 team [Texas at the time of choice] when you know you're better anyway? You don't prove anything, and a bowl game should be some reward in the way of enjoyment."

So, off to Florida, Miami Beach and fun, preceded by hard work at practice in Fort Lauderdale. Penn State was to defend its feeling that it was really No. 1 for weeks and maybe forever. The 1969 Penn State team *was* the best team in the nation. As Dan Devine said, "Texas would never have scored against Penn State."

That journey to Miami for Penn State was a double excursion, a bowl trip unique in college football annals. But Paterno is one who believes, "If you go—go first class."

Penn State was taking a team to a bowl that had a group of seniors who hadn't been home for Christmas in 1967 and 1968. These seniors on the team had practiced for the Gator Bowl and the Orange Bowl the previous two years without returning to their families for Christmas. Some could become bitter over this fact and Paterno knew it. The answer was simple—take the team to Fort Lauderdale for pre-Orange Bowl practice for a week or ten days, fly it back home on December 23 and then return to Florida on December 26 for the last few days of practice.

This meant two round-trip charter flights on a jet, a rather expensive proposition, but actually no more costly than remaining in Florida. But Paterno got his athletic director, Ernie McCoy, and the university president, Dr. Eric Walker, to go along with the plan. Penn State spent more than $200,000 to earn $411,000 from the Orange Bowl. It was worth it, since the team enjoyed the experience more than the Christmas away from home during the previous two seasons.

There was one Penn State football buff who saved the university considerable money each time it traveled to the Orange Bowl after those unbeaten seasons of 1968 and 1969. This was the late Skip Rowland, bachelor, truck driver and son of a former chairman of the Penn State Board of Trustees.

Skip, a large, bluff man with a resounding voice, owned his own big trailer-truck rig and commuted with cargo between New York and Chicago, Boston and Detroit, Pittsburgh and Cleveland and any other towns where there's a buck to be made on freight. He always found time, however, to be at the Penn State football games, home or away. When those games were at University Park, Skip worked on the chain gang, the group that handles the down stakes on the sidelines.

Skip came to the aid of the Nittany Lions when he offered to truck all the football equipment for the team to Florida prior to the '69 and '70 Orange Bowl games. One of the most expensive items for a traveling football team is the cost of air freight for the heavy equipment—uniforms, helmets, shoulder pads, etc. When a team goes to a bowl game training site it's even more expensive, since a team takes along tackling dummies, numerous sets of uniforms, a fully equipped training room, etc. Thus the air-freight cost for a bowl appearance is much higher than a regular season away-game cost for moving equipment.

So, in mid-December, Skip Rowland packed up his truck with a load of football gear and headed south along Interstate 95. But on that first trip in late 1968, there was an extra item of interest —a half-dozen cases of Rolling Rock beer.

George Olsen, executive director of the Gator Bowl in Jacksonville, loves his beer and his favorite brand is Rolling Rock, which is brewed in Latrobe, Pennsylvania. Skip loved his beer, too, but wasn't too particular about the brand, just so long as it was cold and there was a lot of it. Following the 1967 Gator Bowl, Skip promised George Olsen, "If we get down here again I'll bring plenty of Rolling Rock for you."

So, one night in December of 1968, a big truck stopped in front of Olsen's home, which faces the Atlantic Ocean a few miles east of Jacksonville. Skip got out and deposited six cases of Rolling Rock in Olsen's garage and went on his way to Palm Beach, just north of Miami, where Penn State had its pre-bowl training site.

Skip Rowland had been known to arrive on the Penn State football scene in surprising fashion. When the Nittany Lions played at Maryland in 1968, Skip took a slight detour from a job he had going from New York to Chicago. He went west by way of College Park, Maryland, to see his favorites play in that university town just outside of Washington.

While the team was having its Friday night meal in a motel, the big truck pulled into the parking lot and Skip came bouncing into the dining room to announce his presence. His cargo on that journey was a full load of bananas. Skip, no small man, had eaten a hand of bananas for his lunch on the way from New York to College Park.

The only thing that disrupted the Orange Bowl experience was a police action in Fort Lauderdale against Paterno's mild-mannered quarterback, Chuck Burkhart, just before the trip back home for Christmas.

Burkhart and Dave Radakovich, a sub linebacker and nephew of Dan Radakovich, Penn State linebacker coach, drove to a hamburger stand in Fort Lauderdale one evening after practice, dinner and team meetings. Well within curfew regulations set by Paterno during practice, the two players were driving a courtesy car given to the team by Orange Bowl officials. A young man from New York City, who didn't like college football players or Penn State players in particular, began to call Burkhart and Radakovich names and even went to the point of punching Burkhart when the quarterback was outside the car.

Paterno has always instructed his players that if such a situation happens, "Don't hit back. Just get away." Burkhart tried to. He got into the car but the persistent tormentor reached in and slugged the quarterback again, and by this time Burkhart had blood over his clothes and the police were arriving on the scene.

Burkhart and his troublesome new critic were both arrested and Chuck got out on $80 bail. Penn State's solution to the problem was to ignore the summons for an appearance in court the week between Christmas and New Year's Day and Burkhart forfeited $80 bail he had to pay himself. This cut down on publicity about the incident and Burkhart seemed to forget the issue as much as possible, though it was brought up at the one press conference prior to the Orange Bowl.

In fact, Paterno was the one who brought it up. When he introduced Burkhart to the press in Miami, Joe cracked, "Show them your boxing stance, Chuck."

Burkhart must have ignored his off-field battle during the Orange Bowl game against Missouri as this quarterback, still rated a poor passer by many, completed eleven of twenty-six passes for 187 yards in the Penn State 10-3 victory over Dan Devine's forces.

What made this so astounding was that Missouri's big threat was supposed to be its passing attack and Burkhart outpassed the Tigers by 187 yards to 117 in the game. But then, Penn State was supposed to have a good running attack and Missouri outgained the Nittany Lions, 189 yards to 55, on the ground.

The one thing that held up according to past performance was that ever-pesky Penn State defense. Dennis Onkotz, Jim Kates, Mike Reid, Steve Smear, John Ebersole, Paul Johnson, Pete Johnson and Neal Smith were playing their final game for Penn State. These eight, along with George Landis, Jack Ham and Gary Hull, were virtually unmovable when it counted—down near Penn State's goal line.

With twenty-two seconds remaining in the game, Landis made his second interception of the game to protect Penn State's 10-3 lead. That was the seventh interception by Penn State as Onkotz and Smith each had two and Hull had one. Never before in a major college bowl game had a team stolen seven passes. It was the same old story—Joe Paterno, who earned his wings as a young offensive genius, had produced the strongest defense in college football history.

So ended the real body of one of the longest streaks in college football history—thirty games without defeat and twenty-two straight victories against strong teams and weak teams, as is always the case. The major triumphs against strong teams in the long streak were over Syracuse and North Carolina State in 1967; Kansas, UCLA, Army and Miami in 1968; Kansas in the 1969 Orange Bowl; Colorado, Kansas State, West Virginia and Syracuse in 1969, and then over Missouri in the 1970 Orange Bowl.

No wonder Joe Paterno felt his team was the best and deserving of being ranked No. 1. He repeated for many to hear, "Just whom did Texas beat in 1969? When you're in a conference like they are, you're in a two-team conference—Texas and Arkansas—and everyone else is easy pickings. They didn't play the schedule we did and all they beat were a couple of strong teams."

Later, Paterno was able to joke about the controversy over No. 1. When he was asked if his team would have beaten Texas, Joe quipped, "I never said we could beat Texas. All I said was that I didn't think Texas could beat us."

The Coach of the Year for 1968 had proved his worth and his

team's strength and ability again in 1969 despite the President and Texas.

The streak had one more game to go—another easy victory over an outmanned Navy team to open the 1970 season. Then the bubble burst at the base of the Rocky Mountains in a shocking defeat by Colorado when, maybe more than at any time in Penn State history, the players coached by Paterno and the coach himself proved to be the true men they were.

But when Paterno was named Coach of the Year in January, 1969, for his 1968 work with Penn State, such games as Colorado in 1970 were far from his mind. Joe's job was to prepare a team for the 1969 season, tone down the streak that was building up pressure and do it all despite the heavy load of demands on a man named Coach of the Year. Speaking engagements, other public appearances and general public attention from the media had to interrupt Paterno's preparations for the 1969 campaign. Any man who is Coach of the Year is lucky to come out of the off-season demands and keep his mind on the big job at hand—coaching his team that spring and the next season.

But even a Coach of the Year can find those light moments to look back on.

There was that wonderful gal, Sue Paterno, who again injected her two cents just about where it was least welcome. Joe nearly went through the floor of an Atlanta, Georgia, hotel one evening when Sue thought she was being helpful again.

The American Football Coaches Association places demands on the man it names as Coach of the Year by vote of its members. Among the demands is the assignment to coach either the East or West team in the AFCA all-star game in June, the first major game of what has now become a much too long football season. Paterno, therefore, was the man picked to head the staff for the East team in the June, 1969, all-star game, then played in Atlanta and since moved to Lubbock, Texas.

Pepper Rodgers of Kansas, who was the losing coach to Penn State in the 1969 Orange Bowl, was assigned to coach the West team. He earned this by being the top vote-getter for Coach of the Year honors in his district. Rodgers was also the national runner-up to Paterno.

The same old problem haunted the coaches in preparing for

this all-star game. They had a bunch of great football players from college senior ranks of 1968 who were to meet one another on a field for the first time less than a week before playing the all-star game. How do you mold a team in such short notice no matter how good they are as individuals?

Before going to Atlanta for the game, Joe sat Sue down and said, "Now, remember, Pepper Rodgers is the coach of the other team in this game. Remember, he was the man who coached Kansas in the Orange Bowl and he lost to us and he had twelve men on the field. Whatever you do, don't mention that. Don't say a word. Drop it. It's ancient history."

Sue agreed, and Joe thought he'd have no problems with Mrs. Paterno.

But a couple of nights prior to the all-star game, Pepper Rodgers and his wife invited the Paternos to their hotel room for drinks before dinner. Maybe the problem is that Sue drinks only Pepsi-Cola—bottle after bottle of it every day, even at breakfast—and never touches that hard stuff.

Anyhow, Pepper and Joe got to talking about the game ahead and Pepper asked Joe, "How are you going to get plays to those guys we have coached together for only a couple of days so far? They'll never get what you want them to do."

Sue felt it was was time to make a suggestion. She said, "Well, you know, Pepper, you might try a transistor in the helmet. You know, we played UCLA back in 1965 and they used a transistor in Gary Beban's helmet to give him the plays each time."

Pepper answered, "Well, you know, I hear it was done."

At this moment, Joe was sliding down in his chair trying to give Sue a high sign to just plain "shut up." It didn't work.

Sue said, "Joe, I'm talking about UCLA, not Kansas," as she remembered Joe's warning not to bring up Pepper's troubles earlier in the year.

Pepper turned to Sue as Joe slipped lower and lower in his chair, and said, "Sue, I was the quarterback coach that year at UCLA."

"You were not," Sue said, believing Joe and Pepper were putting her on.

Pepper insisted he was at UCLA in 1965 and Sue turned to Judy Rodgers. "Was he?"

"Yes."

Then the Rodgers' son walked into the room and Sue asked him if he had ever lived in Los Angeles. He said, "No, we lived in a suburb outside Los Angeles when Dad was at UCLA."

That did it. Sue got the word and Joe kept insisting to Pepper, "I swear, she didn't know."

Sue reflects on that, saying, "You know, I put my foot in my mouth and twisted it. But that won't be the last time. It's mainly because I don't follow any other college particularly except us. I don't watch any other games but ours."

After such experiences, and in between off-season engagements, it's always back to the drawing board, where Paterno and his colleagues at other colleges never quite feel they have anything settled, regardless of the talent around. But Joe did, for once, express confidence in the 1969 season when fall practice ended and the second undefeated season was about to begin.

He couldn't predict victory every Saturday but he could be sure that there was hope. As it turned out, there was more than hope in 1969.

18: 1970–A Year of Trial and Error

JOE PATERNO WAS DAMNED IF HE DID and damned if he didn't when he entered the 1970 season. This was the general tone of fan reaction, and especially the alumni, when Paterno was about to send his undefeated team against Navy in the 1970 season opener.

Perhaps the Penn State alumni and fans had been spoiled by success. Although the Nittany Lions had lost many of the stars—men like Mike Reid, Dennis Onkotz, Steve Smear, John Ebersole, Charlie Pittman, Neal Smith, Jim Kates, Paul Johnson, Pete Johnson, Don Abbey, Tom Jackson and Chuck Burkhart—who had made Penn State the talk of the nation, everyone expected that Paterno, the miracle worker, would pull players out of a hat, wind them up and, presto, produce a third straight unbeaten team. Even though the defense had suffered most from graduation losses, Joe knew that his biggest problem was to find a quarterback.

Chuck Burkhart had led these amazing Nittany Lions through undefeated and untied seasons, through two Orange Bowl victories and extended an unbeaten streak to thirty games since that last loss to UCLA back in 1967. He was the baby-faced quarterback in 1968 and 1969, when everyone said he couldn't pass and couldn't run. All he did was think—and win. Paterno loved him, maybe because Joe remembered his own days as a quarterback at Brown. As far as Paterno was concerned, Burkhart was the perfect quarterback—a winner.

Burkhart and Mike Reid had accepted the big Orange Bowl trophy at the January 2, 1970, celebration in Miami. Both men had been winners in the same place the year before, but they were humble enough to be happy over getting this second big award. Maybe both men, about to leave Penn State, knew what was in store for their coach. The coach knew it, and so did some others. But fans wanted more victories added to the streak and they wanted to know who was to be the quarterback.

That was Joe Paterno's biggest problem going into spring practice. He had Mike Cooper, a bright young black man from Harrisburg, Pennsylvania, who had been Burkhart's back-up during the two unbeaten seasons. A pretty good passer and runner, Mike was planning to be a football coach when he was graduated from the university. There was also Bob Parsons, a 6-foot-3 junior from Wind Gap, Pennsylvania, who threw a pass like Johnny Unitas—in practice. Parsons, who also did the team's punting, looked great Monday through Friday when football was not fun at Penn State. His big problem was that, when it was fun on Saturday, his passes looked more like Chuck Burkhart's. Then there was John Hufnagel, a sophomore who came from the same high school as Ted Kwalick and Chuck Burkhart—Montour in McKees Rocks, Pennsylvania. But Hufnagel, from the beginning, was just the No. 3 quarterback who also became a part-time defensive back when the 1970 season opened.

What complicated matters was that Mike Cooper was black. Penn State had never had a black quarterback, and people were watching Paterno to see what his decision would be. Joe knew that if Cooper got the No. 1 job, some folks would say he had gotten it only because he was black. He also knew that if Cooper didn't get it, there were others who would be quick to say that he had been sidetracked because he was a black. For many coaches, it would have been a dilemma. But not for Joe Paterno. He was interested in only one thing: he wanted the best man to be his starting quarterback.

The combination of circumstances led to a confusion that

Paterno now admits was his mistake. "I've always been a one-quarterback man," he explains. "Parsons was so close to Cooper with his good arm in spring practice but Mike was, after all, our back-up quarterback when we won."

Mike Cooper, the senior, won the job on his merit and not because he was black. In Paterno's considered judgment at the time, he was simply the best man for the job. Cooper had the experience, he was smart and Joe thought he was the man to move his offense, which was built around Franco Harris and Lydell Mitchell, a pair of black backs who had been sophomore sensations in 1969.

So Cooper got the call when Penn State went against Navy in the first game of 1970. He won—and big. He won so big—55-7—that there was no doubt among Paterno and his coaches that he should be the man to quarterback the team when Penn State went against Colorado the next week at Boulder in the second game of the season.

The trip to Colorado was a trip to defeat—the end of the great road of victory. Snow fell two nights before the game, but it was warm and pleasant on the afternoon of the kickoff. Coach Eddie Crowder had his Colorado team ready. It wanted to beat Penn State, especially on national television. Crowder's team knew it had a chance to end Penn State's unbeaten streak—the longest on the current football scene.

Joe Paterno and his wife, Sue, sat quietly in the restaurant of a Denver motel that Saturday morning with a thirty-one game unbeaten streak hanging over them. They acted like kids on a honeymoon. Joe was happy and Sue was goggle-eyed by the mountains that push themselves toward the true giants of the Rockies. She had never been in Denver before. But the real business was at the University of Colorado in nearby Boulder.

Prior to that morning, little things had happened to the team that might just have been unheeded signs that this wasn't going to be another glorious year. A week and a half before the Navy game, Gary Hayman, a sophomore whiz, broke his ankle. He hadn't played a game for the Penn State varsity but he was to be the wide receiver in a much wider offensive attack than during the recent big winning seasons. He could fly and catch about anything thrown, so that Cooper—or perhaps Parsons— should be able to work well enough with such a catcher at the other end. But Hayman was out and Gary Deuel, a senior with experience, moved in. Deuel could move, but could he catch?

Then, on the flight to Denver Friday night before the Colorado game, Charlie Zapiec complained of a stomach ache. By midnight, Charlie underwent an emergency appendectomy at Swedish Hospital in Denver. Zapiec had made a big switch, uncomplaining, during the previous spring, moving from offensive tackle, where he had been a star, to linebacker. But, despite the unexpected loss of Zapiec, there was no gloom nagging around the Penn State team as it boarded the bus for the late morning trip from Denver to Boulder, where the University of Colorado meets its football opponents at the base of the big, beautiful mountains—mountains that make Nittany Mountain in Pennsylvania look like a mere bump in the road.

All went well for awhile, with Penn State winning the toss and electing to receive the opening kickoff. That is, all went well until the first play from scrimmage. Then the undefeated streak collapsed with a loud boom and Penn State crashed down to join the world of mere mortals, those many other teams in college football who win some and lose some and don't have the glamour of a long unbeaten streak.

That first play of the game was a Cooper-to-somebody pass that never had a chance. The ball was intercepted by an alert Colorado player and the Buffs had their first touchdown within two minutes and thirty seconds of the start of the game. That was only the beginning of Penn State's troubles. The Buffs smashed and humiliated the once-proud Nittany Lions, 41-13, in full view of millions of viewers who watched the game televised by ABC-TV. The defeat was the headline news as Penn State's streak of thirty-one games without a loss ended and the demise of the Nittany Lions tumbled all over the nation's sports pages.

The gory details aren't too important. Penn State was soundly beaten by a team ready to win. The after-effects are important, though, in judging men from all parts of the game.

In defeat, Joe Paterno and his team were gallant. They were so humble and faithful to what sportsmanship is supposed to

mean that, in the age in which we live, it was almost unbelievable. But proof of their excellence in defeat was given in
Colorado newspaper reports that Sunday morning.

Eastern teams walk into a hornet's nest when they travel away
from home. To most folks in other sections of the country, they
are the snobs from the effete East, arrogant and pompous. At
least that is the way they are categorized and they have a difficult time proving differently. But Joe Paterno and his players
won over the Western press in the few minutes of a post-game
dressing room interview.

Joe sat in the Penn State dressing room listening to the cheering from the Colorado players in their quarters nearby and told
newspapermen, "They deserve to enjoy it. We've won and now
they've won. We were outcoached all around today and they
deserve it all."

The newspapermen were dumbfounded as Joe then went over
to the Colorado dressing room and, with a big smile, congratu-
lated Eddie Crowder and patted him on the back. But the
newspapermen weren't the only ones who were dumbfounded.
Two Colorado players watched Joe smilingly congratulate their
coach and some players. One of the Colorado players asked,
"How can that man smile after what has happened to him? How
can he show any stiff upper lip?"

Joe Paterno is special, that's why. He knows how to lose graciously. He doesn't like to lose, but his philosophy has always
been, "If we lose, it's not the end of the world. We'll be back to
play again next Saturday and the Saturday after that."

Joe Paterno was praised in defeat. So was his team, which took
its disappointment like the men Paterno taught them to be. Penn
State students also took the loss in stride. Some 2,000 of them
were on hand to greet Joe and his players when they returned
to University Park on Sunday at 3 A.M.

What thrilled Joe even more than the loyal reception committee, though, was a note he and his wife found when they
reached their home. It was from his four sleeping children,
Diana Lynn, Mary Kathryn, David and Jay, and it said:

"Dear Mother and Father: We are sorry we lost. We love you
and we're glad you're home safe."

There were some fans, however, who were not as kind, and

Sue Paterno spent an uncomfortable day Sunday after the game answering the phone and being abused by people who had been magnanimous in their praise when Penn State was winning. Some were even outright vicious in their condemnation of Joe Paterno.

"People called all day, telling me how to run the team," Sue says. "They didn't give their names, of course, but I recognized some fair-weather friends. They charged Joe with misguiding the team in the game and demanded to talk to him. They didn't believe me when I told them Joe wasn't home. They called me a liar. But he *wasn't* home. He was with the other coaches getting ready for the next game with Wisconsin."

Things didn't improve after Colorado. Indeed, they got worse as Penn State went to Madison, Wisconsin, to meet the University of Wisconsin Badgers in a game even the previously defeated Nittany Lions should have taken. But they didn't and Wisconsin had a 29-16 Lion skin to hang on its trophy wall. That was even a bigger surprise than the Colorado loss. But it was swallowed as before—with a smile.

Then came a 28-3 victory over Boston College and a 24-7 defeat by old rival Syracuse, which chose to ram the ball right at Penn State in what Paterno called "the worst Penn State-Syracuse game I've ever seen." But it was Syracuse's victory and Paterno learned from it. Joe realized that it was time to make changes, to pull in the horns—those wide flankers, pass receivers and wide-open offensive formations that had really gotten Penn State nowhere during the year. And it was time to make a change in quarterback. Cooper and Parsons, who by this time were dividing the time underneath the center, were simply not moving the offense. The next opponent was Army, a team having more than its share of problems. But Penn State was no world-beater either, when they met at West Point.

The Army game was proof of a coach's full-range plan for a whole season. It was a time when some things solidified and others luckily fell into place for victory—not just that day but for the remainder of the year. Army was a testing ground that left Cooper and Parsons on the sidelines, produced a new and capable quarterback and put the Penn State offense back where it worked best—tight and strong.

"We just had to change," Paterno said. He sat on the sidelines at Army's Michie Stadium that Saturday afternoon before the game, talking to the officials, coaches, Tom Cahill of Army and others as he pondered the future. After going thirty-one games without a defeat, this team had two victories and three losses and it was already the middle of the season. Of course, one must realize that a college football team's personnel changes with the seasons and isn't able to count on the same men returning each year as is the case with a professional team.

Joe Paterno pictured the approach to the 1970 season and the mid-season developments as a change and then another change. First of all, he says, "We didn't have the defense we had the two years before 1970. So, we had to score and score more than in the past year in order to buy time while our defense matured and strengthened to the point where we had another fine defense. That's why we planned a wide attack with wide receivers and so on. We thought we had the offense to score."

But it hadn't worked too well, to put it mildly, and Penn State was there at West Point with more losses than victories—a highly unusual situation for Joe Paterno's Nittany Lions, who had become so used to winning the three previous years.

So, in came the wide receivers. They moved back in tight and once again, like in the days of Rip Engle, the offense was based on powering the ball at or around the other fellow. But who was going to run this attack?

Cooper and Parsons hadn't managed too well for too long. Paterno was ready to make his move. He decided to go with Hufnagel, the sophomore quarterback who had been warming the bench all season, against Army. Joe had been impressed with the way John ran the offense in practice. He handed off well, passed respectably and had confidence in himself. He didn't pass like a Parsons or have the experience of a Cooper. But he had Coach Paterno on his side against Army. That's like having your boss in your corner when he tells you that you are to replace a corporation vice president.

Paterno explains what happened in the formation change at Army by saying, "We made blocking assignment changes. It wasn't a difficult thing, but we just had to bring things in tighter. We had to get down to being a precise team again. We just went back to doing nothing more than we could handle. And, besides, we felt now that our defense had grown up and could handle things."

Actually, Joe had made the decision to go with Hufnagel at quarterback the day after the loss to Syracuse. He called in Hufnagel and told the happy young man, "You're going to start against Army and I'm not going to take you out. It's your game."

However, Paterno, unlike many a boss, informed the deposed men of the plan. Cooper and Parsons were told that Hufnagel would be the quarterback against Army. They had to go along with the decision. After all, their performance in the first five games had not been exactly spectacular. For the good of the team, they accepted the decision the coach had made.

More important, the team had worked better the week before the Army game. A final decision had been made on the quarterback and there was no unsettled feeling. Paterno had resolved the issue. Joe may have made a mistake earlier, staying too long with both the quarterback and his offense, but there isn't a coach in college football who doesn't go with what he knows best, even if that is not the most potent weapon he may have. There is safety in working with known quantities.

So, the Hufnagel-led Penn State team whipped Army, 38-14, and the Nittany Lions never lost another game the rest of the season. They romped over West Virginia, 42-8, Maryland, 34-0, Ohio U., 32-22, and Pitt, 35-15, to end the year with a five-game winning streak.

"I thought Hufnagel ran the team well against Army," Paterno said, "though I was well aware that one game doesn't make a quarterback. But I felt after the Army game that he would make it for us."

The coach saw other things after the Army game that gave him hope. "I always felt that we had a good offensive line," Paterno confided, "but we needed momentum. Once we started to do things well there was that old swagger even during practice. The seniors could have said, 'We had our glory, so the hell with it.' But they began showing more pride again."

Whatever happened under Hufnagel or at Army, it all turned out well for the remainder of the season for Penn State except for one thing—Joe Paterno made what some at Penn State considered a tactical error. Paterno is usually one of the most public relations-minded men in his business. He doesn't watch every word, but he guides his listeners through a tour of tactics and humor that leaves most reporters with the impression that "this man is great." Joe can charm the face mask off a Dick Butkus. But many thought he made a boo-boo after his team trounced Pitt to end the 1970 season, which had loss, recovery and victory. Joe won't ever admit it and he bristles at criticism of what he did, but the fact remains that even some of his closest friends thought he was wrong.

Within an hour after Penn State had beaten Pitt to end a 7-3 season, mediocre for the Nittany Lions by recent standards but more than adequate for most teams, Paterno challenged unbeaten and untied Dartmouth to a post-season bowl game in New York to play for the right to claim Eastern supremacy. To some, it was a grandstand play.

As always, Dartmouth had played seven of its nine games in the Ivy League, the conference Paterno played for but has criticized for its reluctance to take on some of the nation's better teams. Dartmouth had won the Lambert Trophy as the outstanding major college team in the East. Penn State, which had won the Lambert Trophy the three previous years, had a mark of seven victories and three defeats against tougher competition, to be sure, but its record was no match for the Hanover Indians' undefeated season.

The problem was many-headed. First, Paterno knew that Dartmouth, as a member of the Ivy League, was unable to play in a post-season game. This has been an Ivy regulation for years and years. No Ivy member has played in a post-season bowl game since 1934, when Columbia surprised Stanford, 7-0. The Ivies weren't about to change their rules merely to accommodate Joe Paterno.

Also, it sounded as if Paterno were bitter about losing the Lambert Trophy. His teams had won it three of the four years he had been head coach at Penn State. So, Joe challenged Dartmouth for the Eastern championship. Then he got himself into a scramble of denials, saying, "I don't want the Lambert Trophy. They can have it. But they should play someone else to decide who is *really* the Eastern champion."

It all went back to Paterno's charge that the Ivy League won't come out of its shell and play other schools to prove its teams are as good as anyone else's. The challenge was probably ill-advised, and it may have been a mistake by a man who had the outstanding class to smile at his first loss in some time at Colorado and then realized his error in time to reform his team for an attack on the season that produced a 7-3 record. Penn State was invited to a couple of lesser bowl games toward the end of the 1970 season—the Liberty and Peach Bowls. The coach and his players turned them down, yet here was the coach challenging the Dartmouth team to a post-season game.

Bob Blackman, the Dartmouth coach, had a field day. He is no man to reject the chance at such publicity. But Blackman, who left to be the Illinois head coach a few weeks later, had all the ammunition. His pet statement was, "It's fine for a guy to challenge you to a fight when you have one hand tied behind your back."

Blackman referred to the Ivy rule prohibiting post-season football games for its teams. Joe Paterno knew about this rule and he also knew there wasn't a chance in the world that Dartmouth could play his team, yet he threw out a challenge to Blackman and Dartmouth on the day his team beat Pitt.

Blackman also became the New York Football Writers Association's Eastern Coach of the Year, something Joe Paterno had been for the previous seasons. Paterno, however, was big enough to make a point to attend the awards ceremony in New York in December of 1970 when Blackman was honored, and the two coaches chatted amiably during the evening. All was well again between Penn State and the Ivy League. But then, Blackman already knew that he was heading to Illinois, since his coaching change was publicly announced within days after the awards night.

Paterno justifies his flip challenge by saying, "I had a reason to offer Dartmouth a bid for a post-season game. I've talked privately with Ivy coaches who want spring practice and want to play more teams like ours. This was an opportunity to bring this out in the open. If someone challenges the Ivy League, there is the chance to bring it about—a game between their best and the other best in the East."

There was another team, however, that old enemy Syracuse,

sitting up there in New York State with all its racial problems, and boiling over Paterno's presumption in challenging Dartmouth. Syrause had beaten Penn State, for a change, in 1970 and had done it by stuffing the ball down the Nittany Lions' collective throat. The Orange had gone on to have a 6-4 season after having survived more problems than any team in the East ever had. Blacks revolted. The Syracuse coaching staff and Athletic Department were in grave jeopardy of being on the unemployment rolls, overloaded enough in upstate New York. Syracuse was annoyed because it felt that, since it had beaten Penn State, if any team was privileged to play Dartmouth for Eastern supremacy, it was the Orange and not the Nittany Lions.

Perhaps, as many insist, the whole idea of issuing a challenge to Dartmouth was a grievous error on the part of Joe Paterno. Eventually, Joe may create a game between the Ivy League champion and the best of the Eastern independents, but he obviously picked the wrong time and the wrong place to make his pitch. Penn State's overall record in 1970, despite its five straight victories at the end of the season, was hardly comparable to Dartmouth's fine undefeated and untied record.

Besides, Penn State—and Joe Paterno—wouldn't have given Dartmouth even passing notice if 1970 had been a third straight unbeaten season. The Nittany Lions would have been in the Cotton Bowl against undefeated Texas, playing for No. 1 in the nation.

But that's Joe Paterno. He speaks out, regardless of the consequences, when he has something on his mind.

19: "More Bowls and a Graduation"

LYDELL MITCHELL AND FRANCO HARRIS were that rare combination of two running backs that gives a team amazing offensive punch in the middle, around the ends and all places in between. Joe Paterno came to feel that his pair of backs in 1971 were the best such double offensive threat since Army had Doc Blanchard (Mr. Inside) and Glenn Davis (Mr. Outside), the All-America duo who finished their Cadet careers in 1946. But a couple of things got in the way of near perfection that season and both had to do with Harris, the big Mr. Inside of the twosome.

Although the 1971 season ended on one of the highest notes of success for Penn State under Paterno coaching with the big upset triumph over Texas in the Cotton Bowl, 30-6, there was just a tinge of regret on Paterno's part as he said, "Now that I look back, I think I made a mistake in the way I handled the situation" with Franco Harris.

Since his very successful career began with the Pittsburgh Steelers, Harris has been a close friend of Paterno's. The big fullback has helped Penn State recruit football players. He has enjoyed long fat-chewing sessions with his former college coach when their paths have crossed since 1971. But they were not on the best of terms in that big year of 1971.

Harris suffered from a series of nasty, not-so-serious but very annoying injuries that kept him out of action quite a bit. Then, four or five days before the Cotton Bowl game with Texas, Harris showed up late for a practice.

Paterno said, "I chewed him out and told him that I just wouldn't stand for it. Franco was just a great kid but I guess I got to him and he wanted to test me or something. Anyway, the next day he showed up three minutes late." The result was that in the big Cotton Bowl game against a highly favored Texas team, Paterno did not start Franco.

"I guess Franco understood later because we always have been good friends and we talk a lot."

Obviously, Penn State could have beaten Texas without Harris. Penn State could have beaten Texas without Paterno on the sidelines the way this amazing, one-sided affair turned out. It was a runaway in the second half that demolished a myth—the strength of the wishbone.

Mitchell had started the 1971 season with five touchdowns in a 56-3 route of Navy. Harris had four touchdowns the next week against Iowa in a 44-14 easy one. Alberto Vitiello was needed to win the third game in the fourth quarter with a field goal that edged a surprising Air Force team, 16-14. Then Mitchell scored three times against Army, John Hufnagel scored twice in a victory over Syracuse and from then on Mitchell ran to records with four touchdowns against Texas Christian and four against Maryland.

Everything was moving along so smoothly that when the Lions lost to Tennessee in the final game of the regular season down in Knoxville, it was a shock—not so much that the strong Vols won the game but the way they won. Penn State made enough mistakes in that game to turn Paterno's hair gray in one afternoon.

That loss set up Penn State for the underdog spot in the Cotton Bowl at Dallas, January 1. After all, who could imagine these Easterners daring to threaten Darrell Royal's mighty Longhorns who had a wishbone attack well developed and working like a steamroller over all opposition.

Paterno had a defense, though, to go along with the Mitchell-Harris attack that had been so well directed by John Hufnagel at quarterback all season. Mitchell, in setting most Penn State running and scoring records, made people overlook the defense. Yet four of Penn State's 1971 opponents failed to score a touchdown. This was forgotten. After all, Texas had not failed to score a touchdown at least once in every game for many years. And this Cotton Bowl game would help settle that battle of words over who really was No. 1 in 1969.

The No. 1 spot in the nation was not at stake in this game. But a lot was on the line—particularly for Penn State. It was a game of pride.

The first half was an unimpressive affair with Texas gaining a 6-3 edge at halftime on two field goals to one. Then the contest became all Penn State's and it was Charlie Zapiec, linebacker and co-captain, who made one of those big breaks Paterno always has his team look for and jump on. Zapiec recovered a Texas fumble at the Longhorns' 41-yard line and Mitchell went over for the first and winning touchdown four plays later.

The game became a rout after that. But when all was finished and even though Mitchell was named Most Valuable Player of this Cotton Bowl game, it was the defense that had done the job on the wishbone. The wishbone is designed to decoy defenses so that they overcommit and then the option aspect of the wishbone is brought into play whereby the quarterback can flip to someone else or keep. Penn State contained the Texas wishbone because Paterno coached well in preparation and never had his defense make that commitment to a ball carrier until it was certain the man with the ball was the one to tackle.

Paterno had done his homework in getting his team ready. And Harris did, after all, play a part in the victory and go on to a lasting friendship with Paterno, who still has football played his way at Penn State.

Joe Paterno said of this Cotton Bowl victory, "It is one of the greatest victories in Penn State history. I don't think we've ever had a game that we had to win more than this one."

During that 1971 season Paterno had a big, strong defensive back who was a mere sophomore. He was John Cappelletti, who looked more like a big, strong offensive back as he led the team in punt returns and kickoff returns when serving on the special teams. He did not, however, get too much notice during the '71 campaign as all eyes were on Mitchell who was Penn State's well-publicized candidate for the Heisman Trophy. (The publicity did not work as Auburn's Pat Sullivan, a quarterback, edged out Cornell's Ed Marinaro for the big prize in college football.)

With both Mitchell and Harris gone, Paterno quietly moved Cappelletti into the offensive backfield for the 1972 season. The switch hardly created a murmur because, after all, wouldn't it take a long time for anyone to come along and make Penn Staters forget Mitchell and Harris? Well, they have not really ever forgotten Mitchell and Harris, but Cappy made them think a little less about the Nittany Lions' version of Mr. Inside and Mr. Outside.

Cappy quickly became a one-man package of Mr. Inside and Mr. Outside. Powerful, fast, intelligent and a very popular young man of calm dedication, Cappy was the perfect All-America football player—the one movies are made about.

Cappy had been a high school quarterback in Upper Darby, Pennsylvania. He was an offensive running back in his freshman year at Penn State and then the coach moved him to defensive back as a sophomore in 1971 where he started five games. After all, there was little room for a newcomer in the 1971 Penn State backfield with Mitchell and Harris there.

It was the 1972 season that brought out what John Cappelletti was really made of. He was made of everything a college head coach wants from a running back. He did it all from the I tailback.

Following an opening-game loss to Tennessee, again, Penn State, with Cappelletti and Quarterback John Hufnagel, who set a bunch of school records for total offense and passing yardage, leading the way, ran off ten straight victories before going to the Sugar Bowl to meet the favored Oklahoma team. As always, Penn State was the underdog in its bowl game. And shortly before the kickoff, Penn State learned that Cappelletti was sick with a virus and would be unable to play. Without any offensive punch and despite a defense that did its utmost, Oklahoma won the Sugar Bowl, 14-0. This was Paterno's first loss as head coach in a bowl game and only Penn State's third loss in eleven bowl games.

But this did not stop the 1973 graduating class at Penn State from inviting Joe Paterno to be its speaker at commencement exercises. The man who made coaching more than just X's and O's and grunts and groans and who would talk on almost any subject at any time donned a cap and gown and spoke to the 1973 graduates of Penn State.

He was addressing the Penn State class of '73 at the height of the Nixon-Watergate troubles. From coast to coast universities were inviting "experts" on the Washington scene to make commencement addresses. All Paterno had done of note within recent months had been to take a team through a bowl season again and turn down another big money offer to coach in professional football—this time the Boston Patriots. After all, he had been doing this sort of thing for years. What was special? It seems just the fact that Paterno appeared to the graduating class to be a calm man in stormy days—a man with an unusual set of values. These values were old-fashioned.

In speaking to that class, Paterno may have set down for the first time in such a talk his real thoughts of his life work. He said, in part:

"Some of you [in this graduating class] have every right to feel let down that after four years of hard work you have to listen to a coach at your graduation. Furthermore, what would outsiders think of this great university having such an unlettered individual represent its academic community? But, in spite of these and other misgivings, I accepted [the invitation to address you]. I accepted because I realize that in a day when materialism is rampant, many of you felt that my interest in doing other things besides making money has in some way helped you to reaffirm your ideal of a life of service, of dignity, and a life of meaning which goes beyond financial success.

"Again, the fact that there has been generous praise from many places for my decision to remain at Penn State made me wonder just how strong, at any price, has become our commitment to materialism and made me think that perhaps I could say something to you which would put things in perspective. However, I assure you that in stepping outside of my role as a football coach, I do it with great trepidation and humility. Who knows, I may be the only commencement speaker this year who doesn't give his opinion on Watergate. Although I do want to make one comment on President Nixon's role in the affair. I'd like to know, How could the President know so little about Watergate in 1973 and so much about college football in 1969?"

Later in the speech, Paterno said, "Success without honor is an unseasoned dish; it will satisfy your hunger but it won't taste good. This is why I enjoy coaching at Penn State so much. We set high goals for our people. We strive to be No. 1. We work hard to achieve our goals. We aren't afraid to lose. It is being involved in a common cause which brings us joy and memories which endure in teammates."

But the most significant thing this outspoken coach told the graduates of 1973 in relating football and coaching to the future for the young folks about to get their degrees was:

"I chuckle at people who blame the 'system' for our problems, just as I laugh at those who claim that we should have blind faith in our government and our institutions. What is this notorious 'system'? In my game, people talk about offensive formations as the cure-all. After we lost to Oklahoma in the Sugar Bowl, many people asked, 'Are you going to switch to the wishbone formation?' Believe me, it isn't the plays or the offensive system which gets the job done, it is the quality of the players which makes the formation effective. And it is you who will make the organization work for you and you will become victims of this system if you fail to execute your responsibilities to yourself and to your fellow human beings. You have a part to play and, if you loaf or quit, don't sit back and complain that our method is no good. The system, the organization, the method, the government —is you. If each of us is easily seduced by expediency, by selfishness, by ambition regardless of the cost of our principles, then the spectacle of Watergate will surely mark the end of this grand experiment in democracy. One of the tragedies of Watergate is to see so many bright young men, barely over thirty, who have so quickly prostituted their honor and decency in order to get ahead, to be admired, to stay on the 'team.'

"These same young people within the short period of the last ten years sat in convocations such as this. They were ready to change the world. They didn't trust the over-thirty generation. I warn you—don't underestimate the world—it can corrupt quickly and completely."

With his words ringing in their ears, the young degree winners at Penn State must have headed out into the big world to straighten it up and remain honest for the remainder of their days. Paterno, on the other hand, went back to the drawing board. He had proved the honesty of his belief in college athletics by turning down millions of dollars as a pro coach in order to coach the best type of college football in the big-time often cut-throat intercollegiate football system.

Of course, going into the 1973 season, Paterno had little need for too many fancy drawing-board innovations. He had Cappy. This successful season, Paterno's third undefeated and untied campaign as head man for the Nittany Lions, was possibly Penn State's strongest one under the man from Brooklyn. Each game started with Cappy off tackle and each game ended with Penn State in front. From start to finish Cappy carried. He carried forty-one times in one game. Penn State thus went to the Orange Bowl and beat Louisiana State, 16-9, on a slippery artificial turf with Cappelletti somewhat limited that night of January 1, 1974, because of a mild ankle sprain.

Paterno describes 1973 by saying, "Everything fell into place just right for us. We had John Cappelletti back and maybe our best offensive team. That defense wasn't bad, either, with guys like Randy Crowder, Ed O'Neil and Mike Hartenstine. Cappelletti, of course, was just tremendous.

"John was just one of those young men who come along once in a coach's lifetime—full of talent and a joy to coach."

This time the world recognized the talents of Penn State's fine offensive back as the big fellow won the Heisman Trophy to become Penn State's first player to win the major individual award in college football.

Then the world learned what a really fine person Cappy was, the person his teammates and coach had recognized for four years at Penn State. In an emotional acceptance speech at the New York Hilton Hotel where the Downtown Athletic Club presented him with the Heisman Trophy, John Cappelletti graciously accepted the prized award and then dedicated it to his young brother, Joey, who was dying of leukemia. Although persons close to the Penn State football team had known for years about John's brother, it was not really public knowledge until that night.

Rarely in the history of sports has an athlete made such an impression upon his fellow man as Cappy did that night when, choked with tears, he got through his acceptance speech while his kid brother sat in the audience.

Gerald Ford, then Vice President of the United States, who was the featured speaker at the banquet, led the audience in giving John a standing ovation, one which he so richly deserved.

The 1974 and 1975 seasons were not as successful as the 1973 season but only by a slim margin. After all, when you run out of Mitchells, Harrises and Cappellettis, what do you do for an encore?

The Nittany Lions went to a bowl at the conclusion of each of these seasons, as usual, beating Baylor, 41-20, in the Cotton Bowl and then losing to Alabama, 13-6, in the Sugar Bowl. Coach Paul "Bear" Bryant's entire football team broke strict Bryant curfew hours two nights before that game in New Orleans. Richard Todd, the quarterback for Alabama who was to become the successor to another Alabama grad, Joe Namath, as New York Jets quarterback, was the leader of the late-hours Crimson Tide players found to be in Fat City, an area of music nightclubs just outside New Orleans.

Paterno has always insisted on letting his players have some fun at bowl games, where they can enjoy the rewards of a successful season. Bryant had long insisted upon hard-and-fast curfew rules although he was beginning to relax them somewhat after years of not winning a bowl game. But this relaxation by the Alabama players less than 48 hours before the big game was even more than Paterno or Bryant would ever allow. However, Bryant could not punish his players or else he would have had to penalize all and there would have been no one to play in the Sugar Bowl.

The 1976 season was something new for Penn State. Even Paterno did not claim his 7-4 Lions were real bowl material. But there were the Nittany Lions in the Gator Bowl on a cold December night in Jacksonville, Florida, going against the Fightin' Irish of Notre Dame. Why? It seems Penn State got the invitation to the Gator Bowl because Notre Dame wanted Penn State. Put another way, Notre Dame refused to play in the Gator Bowl against any of the other teams that were possible opponents for the Irish in the fifth largest bowl of post-season football.

Penn State did not belong there and the Irish, with a young defense that was to become much better, whipped the Lions, 20-9. Penn State's arch rival, Pittsburgh, was over at the Sugar Bowl about to beat Georgia and finish undefeated and untied and get the vote as the No. 1 college team in the nation for the 1976 season. That Sugar Bowl was Tony Dorsett's final college game and Coach Johnny Major's last game at Pitt before he moved on to Tennessee.

Paterno said of 1976, "It wasn't a question of whether or not I felt we deserved to be in a bowl game after a 7-4 season. You have to remember that we lost two games by 6 points, 12-7 to Ohio State and 7-6 to Iowa. Then, after Kentucky beat us, we won six in a row before Pitt beat us in the last game of the year. When the chance came to play in the Gator Bowl, our kids welcomed it and I did, too, especially since it was a chance to play Notre Dame."

But success of a bigger kind was just around the corner for Penn State once again. The 1977 season proved to be the kind a coach such as Paterno enjoys most—the success of satisfaction in a job well done.

"Sure, this team of 1977 had to be one of my most satisfying ones," said Joe. "Coming after the 1976 season, we felt that we had to prove some things. We had some pretty good players—Jimmy Cefalo, Matt Suhey, Steve Geise, Mike Guman, Mickey Shuler and many more. We also knew that Chuck Fusina, our quarterback, was probably the best we ever had at Penn State in my time. He could throw the ball as well as or better than anyone. We also knew that we had to come back after a poor season, poor at least for Penn State."

Referring to 1977, Paterno put it differently. He said, "We worked real hard, the coaches and the players and everyone associated with the team. I knew we were going to be pretty good but it was hard to tell how good."

Following easy victories over Rutgers, Houston and Maryland, Penn State suffered its only loss of the season to Kentucky. But maybe Penn State's worst defeat was an off-the-field controversy when it came time for naming teams to the bowl games. Following one of the most confusing and heated bowl selection days in memory, Penn State lost a chance at the Orange Bowl and went to the Fiesta Bowl where it beat Arizona State and Paterno voiced his complaints about journalists who influence bowl bids.

The whole situation came to a head the week of November 19,

which was the Saturday that the bowl committees were permitted to extend invitations to teams. Penn State had just the one loss to Kentucky against its record. Pittsburgh had just the one loss to Notre Dame marring its record. Penn State and Pittsburgh were still to meet in their final game of the season on November 26. Both teams were idle on November 19, the bowl selection day, because they had moved their game back a week in order to be nationally televised. This had become standard practice for the Penn State-Pitt game in recent years as they met in a TV game on Thanksgiving Day weekend.

It was clear that Notre Dame was going to meet Texas in the Cotton Bowl and Alabama would meet the loser of the Ohio State-Michigan game on November 19, in the Sugar Bowl. Penn State, ranked a bit higher than Pitt in the weekly polls, was the apparent choice for the Orange Bowl to go against Oklahoma, champs of the Big Eight Conference. But, just wait a minute, suppose the Orange Bowl picked Penn State on November 19 and then Pitt beat the Nittany Lions a week later in the TV game? If that happened, shouldn't Pitt be going into the Orange Bowl against Oklahoma?

Wait just another minute, please. Paterno decided he wanted nothing to do with that playoff idea for the Pitt-Penn State game. The Orange Bowl Committee obviously did want to wait and see. Then Paterno changed his mind, as he admits, and said, "O.K., we'll wait and see." He said it too late, apparently, because the Orange Bowl committee, fed up with a week-long battle of words across the nation in the media, selected Arkansas, the Southwest Conference runner-up, to meet Oklahoma. Seems Barry Switzer, Oklahoma's coach and a onetime Arkansas player, strongly suggested Arkansas to the Orange Bowl Committee.

Before the whole thing ended, Paterno even criticized Herschel Nissenson, the Associated Press's prime college football reporter, who is stationed in New York City. During an exchange on a public address system phone hookup at the New York Football Writers Association Monday luncheon, Paterno blamed Nissenson for causing Penn State to lose its chance at the Orange Bowl, indicating he thought the AP man was prejudiced in favor of other areas of the country.

No matter, the Orange Bowl Committee selected Arkansas on

November 19 and Penn State and Pitt had to fend for themselves with what bowls remained. The Fiesta Bowl selected Penn State and the Gator Bowl took Pitt. Each pick was a good one as Penn State and Pitt each won its game and the Nittany Lions, in a demonstration of fine offense behind Chuck Fusina, whipped Arizona State, 42-30. Meanwhile, Arkansas upset Oklahoma in the Orange Bowl and, when Notre Dame beat Texas in the Cotton Bowl, the Irish were voted the national championship in the final AP and UPI polls.

Paterno, speaking after the season about the bowl scene, said, "After our Temple game, which was a week before the date for official bowl invitations, I was told by one of the Orange Bowl people that Penn State was their choice. So, after discussing it with the squad, we decided that we would not wait until after the Pitt game to announce we would go. Then, as I heard it, there was an enormous amount of pressure put on the Orange Bowl Committee by Pitt people.

"I've been told the Pitt people told the Orange Bowl folks that they were going to annihilate Penn State and the bowl would be embarrassed by having a loser if they didn't wait until after we played each other. Pitt didn't annihilate us."

Penn State beat Pitt, 15-13, in another good game between these old rivals, in the snow at Pitt Stadium.

There was a resulting clamor to have the bowl wait until all teams finish their season before selections are made for these post-season football games. Unless something drastic such as common sense is brought into action, the bowls will continue to pick before all teams are finished.

But, regardless of the confused ending of the 1977 season, it was another 11-1 year for Joe Paterno and his Nittany Lions. There was satisfaction enough in that accomplishment. And there was 1978 and subsequent years to look forward to for another shot at that elusive national championship.

20: The Mystique of Coaching

JOE PATERNO LEARNED a great deal from both success and adversity in his first five years as a head football coach. Although he was an "oldtimer" in years of service as an assistant to Rip Engle at Penn State, it wasn't until he became the head man himself that he had to assume full responsibility for the organizing, planning and evolving a method of bringing his team to the proper peak in time for Saturday's games. But, putting his own philosophy to practical use, and learning from experience during that first difficult year in 1966, Joe has devised his own system of doing things.

Joe Paterno's system differs in many ways from the usual procedures followed by many of his coaching colleagues. For instance, he doesn't believe in emotional pep talks, nor does he feel that it is necessary for his team to have daily group meetings with the coaches to discuss strategy and game plans. Joe also doesn't want his squad to be on the scene for a traveling game a full day or more before the kickoff. To him, all football fields are alike.

"We play every game with the same kind of football," Joe says.

Most coaches will deny that there is a mystique to football coaching, but not Joe Paterno. Part of the mystique, he insists, is convincing your players that they can win every time they step out on a football field, that they should never be afraid to lose and that they should enjoy playing the game on Saturdays. The rest of it is in knowing how much work your players need and to pace your team so that it is ready to play at the opening kickoff, not the day before or the day after the game.

Penn State teams, during the long string of success prior to 1970, followed a general pattern. Defense was the key to victory. At least, it was until the Colorado game of 1970. When defeat finally came Penn State's way for the first time in many a moon, Paterno had to admit that he went against his usual ideas, those plans which had produced so much victory and enjoyment for the players and coaches.

"We had always won the big games on defense and I thought we'd win the Colorado game on offense," Joe confesses. "I went against my philosophy."

Paterno's philosophy is simple, stated too loosely, maybe, by the boss of Penn State football fortunes. There is a lot more to football philosophy, game plan ideas and attitudes between coach and players. There is a delicate balance involved and, if either player or coach oversteps the bounds, one or the other can upset the entire team. For week-to-week problems change and players change and the coach has to be able to feel out his squad, putting all he knows within the framework of hard but fair labor during the preparation for Saturday's game.

When necessary, the coach sometimes has to break from routine, though a set routine is usually the best way to work each week. A schedule that is somewhat flexible, but not sloppy, is the best or, at least, that is the Joe Paterno approach.

Penn State's coach broke from routine following the third loss in 1970. When Penn State lost to Syracuse, the Nittany Lions reached a new low from their once high standing. This was the time to make some changes, using it as a way to move back up again.

Normally the team watches films of each game it plays on Sunday evening. That has been one of Paterno's rules as the new week starts for another game. He shows and discusses the film with the entire squad. But the Syracuse films were not shown to the whole group after that third loss in five games. It was shown to various segments of the team separately, such as linebackers, offensive backs, etc.

Paterno told the team, "What's the use of looking at these films and berating ourselves. I'm embarrassed and we played a horrible game. The people around here take it all right. But that's not good enough for us. We can't take it like that. We have to be proud and we have to think back to last August when we felt pride. Regain that pride and don't look back."

Army was coming up after the Syracuse debacle. Army really wasn't too good a team at that time. The Cadets were a bunch that Penn State should beat 99 out of 100 times with the particular matchup of personnel that week. But Paterno was having none of that. He was not only embarrassed by Syracuse, he was also getting that anger thing running through his system.

He has said, "When you lose, you get that sick feeling in your stomach. Then, before Sunday, it turns to anger and the anger gets you to work harder and gets you to show some real pride. Damn it all, there's nothing in this world as bad as losing, really. You have to take it like a man. But it hurts."

With Army in the offing and no Syracuse films for the whole team, Paterno began cracking the whip. At the Sunday night squad meeting after dinner, Paterno set down some new rules for the week of practice ahead. He told the team:

"First, respect Army and every Army player. Respect them as if they were the best team you ever had to play in your life. We won't see Syracuse films as a group, but during the week, at every possible moment, you get over to the office and look at films of Army. Look at the films over and over to get to know the Army team and your assigned man inside out."

Then, for the first time since he became head coach, Paterno told the squad that he had given specific orders to each coach that he could throw any player off the practice field at any time during the week for backsliding in the least. One thing that had been getting to Paterno was the talking on the field. While one group of offensive players run through a play, the waiting players were talking and not paying enough attention. It was obvious that even whispering might cost a player to be set down. Once off the practice field, a man might just not make it back to play against Army on the following Saturday.

This wasn't exactly like the old days in a grammar school classroom where the teacher tolerated no unnecessary talking. It was worse. Paterno was stiffening. He wanted his team to do the same.

As that unhappy early part of the 1970 season progressed, Paterno was becoming more and more annoyed at written reports in newspapers, particularly in the *Collegian*, the Penn State campus paper. He had no use for player quotes which blamed someone or something specifically for the wrongs that took place on the field. Though Paterno had not, in the past, been too restrictive on players who talked to reporters, he clamped down and told the team to shut up.

Earlier in the year, Paterno had become upset when Bob Parsons' broken nose became public knowledge. The quarterback had suffered a broken nose during the Monday practice before the Colorado game. It was not a big problem and a nose break is not too serious five days before a game. But Paterno felt, "That broken nose was no one's business but the team's."

That report and other written words made Paterno order a halt to talk with persons who write such quotes and report such nosebleeds. Years of coaching experience go into decisions like telling a team to stop talking. Some coaches just outlaw reporters. But Paterno's philosophy didn't include putting his players in quarantine until the time he felt it was important to do so. Attention and pride had to be restored. This was just one step in the plan to bring back a losing squad. It broke from the general rules. Yet Paterno can change like anyone else.

One thing that bothered Joe about the quotes blaming specifics for the losses was that "if we lose, we lose together because we sure as hell were winning together when we were winning." There just was no reason to put the blame anywhere but on the whole team.

Prior to that Army game in 1970, Paterno used his built-in flexible regulations and lengthened practices during the week by a few minutes. He worked the team harder than he had been doing. But even here he didn't want to overstep those bounds that had proved the source of success before. He didn't want to "leave the game on the practice field."

"Bud Wilkinson once told me that if a single one of his coaches mentioned that practice was getting too long he would cut it down. That's generally a good rule," Joe insists.

But between the Syracuse and Army games, the whole coaching staff went along with the boss on lengthening practice. Nothing else had been working too well during the season, so why not make that change along with some others? There were player personnel changes in store for the Army game and, in talking to the squad before the week's work began, Paterno said, "We're going to make switches. We're going to start over again and you'll win a job by working for it. Those who step down will have to take it the way it is meant. Have the pride to accept it for the team's good. If you can't accept it that's your problem and you can do what you will. But I'm sure this team has enough total pride that each man will take what happens and go along."

No player walked off the team when Paterno made those switches.

Paterno usually talks in that manner to his team. He isn't emotional or a "one for the Gipper" type of talker. Coaches don't really talk that way too much these days. It doesn't pay. Frankness and a touch of the realistic outlook are part of Joe Paterno's football style. Tell it as it is.

Like any sound approach to work based on a strong philosophy, Penn State's football wouldn't get off the ground without an equally strong practical application. That's where the weekly work program, that time when football is not fun, comes in. Paterno and his players don't have a fun and games time between the Saturday games. Work starts early Sunday morning and ends at kickoff. That's when the fun is supposed to start.

Joe is about the first to get to work as he drags himself out of bed at 7:30 A.M. Sunday and after church gets with it in a football way. Following a breakfast chat with Ridge Riley, who gets Joe's thoughts on the previous day's game for his weekly football letter, Paterno's first stop is the training room out near Beaver Stadium around 10 A.M. There, the good or bad news is learned as bumps and bruises from the day before are found to be either minor or serious. Most of the players report in for some steamroom sitting to boil out the aches.

Paterno feels the pulse of his team while chewing the fat in the Sunday morning get-together over training tables and locker benches. Is the attitude right for what's ahead? Is there over-confidence or some unnecessary worry about the next opponent, still six days away? Hoping he gets the proper pulse reading, Paterno then moves to his office about a mile away on the other side of the campus.

Paterno wants to get a feeling of his team's next opponent. So, Sunday morning office work is a matter of looking at films of that team in previous action during the season. Films are exchanged between most opponents and a coach likes to have those films of yesterday's games by the opposing team in his projection room Sunday morning. The projection room is that office space where Paterno wishes to put up the screen.

During the screening, Joe gets an overall picture of what's ahead. Nothing really specific comes out of it. Specifics begin to emerge during the next forty-eight hours. There's time for that after the right feel is gained. Sometimes Paterno or any other coach misses that feeling. But experience, again, gets a coach closer and closer to the true look of the opposition as each week and each year comes along.

After Sunday lunch back home with the family, Penn State's coach sits down in his den and begins to "doodle" out some basic ideas about offense and defense for his Nittany Lions on the next Saturday. Then, a walk or short drive back to the office and the team work begins. This is the team work within the coaching staff, not the work of the team on the field. A 2 P.M. meeting on Sunday can turn into a rough session. It is there that the coaches become "super-critical of ourselves" at times.

"We criticize each other," Paterno explains. "We find out if we were sound the day before in that game. This is not so much a talk about the kids' actions on the field. It is our talk about ourselves."

This session can go on for two to three hours before the scout who saw this week's opponent gives his report. However, Paterno's staff does not meet as much, as a group, as do football staffs at other colleges. Joe believes much more work can be done individually in planning as coaches work alone or in groups of offense or defense or two and threes. He has veto powers but he doesn't get a final game plan from the various coaches or groups of coaches for some time.

Sunday evening is the film festival time when, normally, the boys who played the day before see the films of the previous day's game as a group. The Sunday after the Syracuse game in 1970 was the noted exception.

Paterno said, "I believe the public thinks that at such meetings with the players we really chew them out. They think we give 'em a real going over. Nothing could be more wrong."

Joe believes, "Screaming doesn't do anything. Reality tells a lot more. The coaches tell the players that we won because we were good yesterday if that's the reason we won. If we won because the other guy was lousy we tell the players that. This simply means that if we play mediocre ball but win then we're just heading for trouble when the first decent team comes along.

"Also, if the coaching erred then we tell the team Sunday night. After all, they know. For example, I misjudged the Wisconsin quarterback in 1970. That was a coaching error. Basically, we're critical, and remember, a critic can praise as well as punish."

That Sunday night team skull session lasts only until about 8 P.M. There is studying to do, you know. Classroom studying, that is.

"Now the coaches meet in earnest," Paterno says as he explains getting down to the nitty gritty for the week's work. The whole staff listens to the scouting report and some plans begin to develop, such as whether Penn State is going to stick to its basic 4-4 defense or maybe a pass rush is more appropriate than pass coverage for this Saturday's enemy.

Home with a beer and sandwich, Paterno begins what he calls his "doodling" again so that before he gets to bed Sunday night or early Monday morning he has scratched some plans. It's at this time at night, while putting things on paper, that Joe enjoys the background of operatic music. His favorite is *La Bohème*.

"Something to work by, I guess," Joe laughs.

Monday the real hard work begins, and it starts at 5:30 A.M., a time when Joe can look forward to two hours alone in his home. Sue and the kids are still sleeping and this, he says, "is when I start to get particular, adding something here and there to the general ideas. If I can't find just what I want, then that missing link becomes the first item on the agenda for the next staff meeting."

Paterno puts an emphasis on Monday and Tuesday work. "This is the tough time for the staff. If, by noon on Tuesday, you don't know exactly what you're going to do when facing the 'foreign' team, the reserves who emulate next Saturday's players, then you're in trouble. Remember what I said about getting things into that game plan Friday for Michigan State in 1966. That's bad. You just have to be set by midday Tuesday. You see, the Monday workout of the team isn't very extensive as last Saturday's players only go out in sweat clothes to run through some things for timing. It's in Tuesday and Wednesday field practices that it all shapes up for Saturday."

On Monday morning, the staff goes over its substitutes or even its freshmen to find the players to act out the part of the opposing team for the week's practices. Paterno's defense has to get a look at something resembling the foe's offense during the week. If the upcoming opponent has a good rollout quarterback, for instance, the coaches go down the list for the best man to imitate him in front of the Penn State defensive players. (For the 1970 Orange Bowl game with Missouri, Richie Lucas, the old Penn State All-America quarterback, was drafted to simulate Missouri's Terry McMillan.) If the opposition has a fast wide receiver, Paterno's brain trust looks for that on the list of subs. And so it goes, even to big, quick linebackers or short, slow tight ends. The problem is that big, fast linebackers are usually on Penn State's first defense already so subs can only try to mimic the opponents.

Monday morning is also time to go over the computer report on next Saturday's rival. Most major college and pro teams have computerized their scouting reports to add to the direct report from the man who scouted the team last week. Basically, the computer report tells probabilities. It is not personal. It can't give talent evaluation as the scout can. But the computer shows that if the team is on its right hash marks between its own 20- and

40-yard lines with third and short yardage it usually employs certain plays. This probability system also works for defenses. The scout has returned to Penn State to feed the hungry machine, and out come the long sheets of "odds."

As Paterno says, "We have to work on what they have done. We can't work on anything they haven't done." Maybe that's why Joe loves to use something he hasn't used before. It's the coach's dream to get away with a sleeper play no one ever saw his team use before. The probabilities all go into the game plan. It's just a matter of what to do when you are at a given spot on the field, both on offense and defense. Odds dictate what you do.

Paterno meets later Monday morning with the defensive coaching staff headed by Jim O'Hora. Joe will always ask, "Can your people do the job we have sketched out? If not, find another way." Then it is time to work some particulars out with the offense. "Does their linebacker make it impossible for our tackle to trap him easily? Well, then, maybe we should go to an unbalanced line so the tackle gets a better shot at the linebacker."

How long does all this take? "Well," Joe says, "sometimes we come up with the answers by noon. But usually we stick at it through lunch in the office. Then I return to the defense group and we can have that part of the plan pretty well ironed out by 3 P.M. Monday. The offense takes a little longer."

Paterno wants to see the ideas for the offense working on the field Monday afternoon in the light workout. Going through the motions, the players give him a better idea of the sound moves and the not so practical ones.

Prior to the Monday workout at about 4:15 P.M., Paterno may give his team a short talk. This isn't a pep talk. It's just a few words of what one can possibly expect Saturday. Joe is honest with his squad. "I won't tell them that the Saturday opponent is a superman team if, actually, it is a bunch of ordinary players."

Then to work. Paterno contends, "I have a very strong feeling that if you practice well you will win. And a team just can't remain the same week after week; otherwise you go backwards on Saturdays. You just have to practice better and better each week and then the results will be what you want."

But the coach warns about practice overconfidence. "The minute during the week of practice that you feel sure you're going to win Saturday without a doubt," Paterno insists, "that's the moment when you've lost the game."

Unlike many other coaches, Paterno has only two total team group meetings per week. There's that post-game film festival Sunday night and the pre-game meeting Monday night. Other teams meet every night through Thursday.

Tuesday involves another 5 A.M. rising and some more doodling. Here the doodling becomes quite specific as Paterno sets down exact practice schedules for the workouts on Tuesday and Wednesday afternoons. This is where Paterno says: "Seven minutes on this. Four minutes on this. Eight minutes on this and maybe we don't have to bother with this for this week. So many minutes on the kicking game."

On that kicking game—Paterno and most coaches put plenty of work into it. Few persons realize how much of a football game is involved with kicking. It can amount to 20 percent of the plays, so maybe a coach will devote 20 percent of his practice to it. Prior to Tuesday's workout Paterno and his staff have watched the films to determine what the other team's kicker can do. Does he get the ball off too quickly for a rush to stop him? Then he might overkick his own team's coverage of the punt and Penn State can concentrate on runbacks with a good start.

By Tuesday afternoon most of the plays are set for Saturday. What may happen is there are too many plays. Paterno says, "One of the hardest things to do is to eliminate plays from your offense. We meet during the week to do some paring. That's difficult, and my coaches will argue me out of some of my own pet ideas at times. You can't have a bag of tricks that's too heavy a load for the team."

Wednesday, or any time possible, players drop into the coaching office to look at films of their opponents. Offensive linemen look at films to see what their defensive forward wall does. For example, a coach may say to Vic Surma, a tackle, "Now, look, Vic, see that linebacker's move there just before he stunts. O.K. Now see what I mean. It's that little move right—there."

Such a tipoff of moves has cost many a team a victory. There have been quarterbacks who set their feet just so for a pass play or another way for a run. There are receivers who look over their shoulder when they are to go out for the pass and not at any other time. Penn State's eagle-eyed coaches look for these things and impress their players with little tips on film studied between classes each week.

Things ease up a bit on Thursday and the practice is quite a light workout. Paterno recalls, "I have seen many teams play great football Saturday and then the next week play poorly and the third week play great again. That's probably because it was a good team that worked or practiced too much. Yes, work hard while at it. But don't spend too much time at it. I imposed just enough more practice time that week before Army in 1970 because it was needed to get them back into things. But I didn't work them real hard except Tuesday and Wednesday."

Thursday night is get-together night for the coaches and their wives. That's when, following a couple of cocktails at one of the coach's homes, they all go over to the Tavern in downtown State College. Football is discussed over dinner.

Joe Paterno has a strong feeling about family ties. "I feel the wives get involved with things then," he says. "They should be part of it. This is a whole program not one where wives are left out in the cold."

Friday is the only day Paterno can sleep in. That's when all the work and planning should be done as well as possible and it's too late to make major changes. Minor adjustments are made at a morning meeting, but rarely are major steps taken to change the attack or the defense.

The Friday workout is just a matter of running a bit and, if the weather is bad, the team doesn't even go on the practice field. Paterno differs from most coaches in that he holds all Friday workouts at Penn State. If Penn State plays on the road Saturday, it travels to its destination after an early Friday workout. The Nittany Lions see and feel the opponent's gridiron for the first time when they step on it just before the Saturday game. This is even true for long trips to the West Coast, in which case Penn State may work out Friday morning before catching the plane.

When playing at home, Paterno takes the team to the Lewistown, Pennsylvania, Holiday Inn on Friday night to sleep away from any campus noise and to keep the players together. Some of the players have eight o'clock classes Saturday morning and they return for them the day of a home game. All members of the team attend one of a number of worship services Saturday before a home game and then the team gathers for the pre-game meal at the Nittany Lion Inn.

After all the week's preparation is done and the team is dressed and sitting in the stadium dressing room, the coaches step out of the room for a couple of minutes. Then the team captains talk with the squad. That's probably more of a pep talk than anything Joe Paterno ever spoke.

Now it's fun time. Game time has arrived and the preparation for Saturday's opponent is concluded. All that's left is the enjoyment of meeting the foe. Football players usually feel it was worth it.

21: Reflections of a Coach

SEVEN YEARS LATER, in 1978, the fun in football was still there for Joe Paterno. Now in his early fifties, at the top of the heap in his chosen profession, more mature and perhaps a little more mellow, his voice has become one that is listened to in the large world of college football. No longer the brash upstart, the precocious kid on the block, Paterno has taught his peers something and he, in turn, has learned a great deal about himself and his life.

Has Paterno's philosophy of football changed? He doesn't think so. In fact, Joe says rather emphatically, "Actually, my philosophy has been reinforced. Oh, I guess a little erosion is bound to set in in some areas, but I am still preaching the same things I was preaching when I first became a head coach. I still feel that football is a game that has to be played with enthusiasm, that there has to be a certain recklessness involved, the players have to take chances and they can't be afraid to lose. They have to enjoy football. And that goes for the coaches, too.

"I am more convinced than ever that it is the greatest game we have. Properly supervised, and I would be the last guy in the world to say that it is perfect, it is a wonderful game to be around.

It is great to be a part of a sport that gives pleasure to so many people. I really don't think my philosophy has changed at all. If anything, I am more firmly committed to the things I believed in back in 1966 and 1967."

Generally speaking, this philosophy has paid handsome dividends for both Joe Paterno and Penn State. It also has, on a few occasions, almost cost the Nittany Lions the services of their prized and successful coach.

The pros have had their eyes on Paterno for some time. The Pittsburgh Steelers almost got him in 1969 and the Boston Patriots came even closer after the 1972 season. So close, in fact, that some folks in State College were wringing their hands and wondering aloud how Penn State football would ever survive.

The Boston Patriots, weary of wallowing in the depths of the National Football League, were in the market for a coach who could pull the downtrodden Pats up by their bootstraps. Billy Sullivan, the president, decided that what his team needed was a shot of fresh blood, that the old game of musical chairs where pro teams simply signed up coaches who had been fired by other clubs would not work. So, he set out to get a top college coach and his first choice was Joe Paterno, the resident genius at Penn State who had been turning out all those great teams and those players who were making it big in the pros.

Sullivan's first approach to Paterno was during the 1972 season after Penn State had played and beaten Boston College. Actually, Ed Kiley, a former teammate of Joe's at Brown who was associated with Sullivan in some business capacity, made the initial contact.

"Kiley called me," recalls Joe, "and said that Billy Sullivan wanted to talk to me about the coaching job with the Patriots. He said he thought I would find Sullivan's offer interesting, that it wasn't just an ordinary offer but involved a great deal of money, stock options, security and a lot of other things and I would be foolish not to talk to Billy. I said I wanted to sleep on it and would get back to him.

"The more I thought about it, the more interested I became with the whole idea. There had been other pro opportunities in the past and I almost took the Pittsburgh job several years earlier. But this was different. I liked the Boston area and I had to think seriously about owning part of a pro team and the kind of money they evidently had in mind. So, I agreed to talk with Sullivan in December after the season ended and before we began to get ready to play Oklahoma in the Sugar Bowl. We met at the Plaza Hotel in New York City and he gave me an idea of what he was talking about. It was quite a package and included a lot of things, like complete control of the team as general manager and coach, stock options, long-term security and an awful lot of money. I'm not quite sure how much but it all added up to something over a million dollars. I was especially intrigued by the money back in 1972. I had had some good teams at Penn State, but I wasn't making much money. In fact, I was making peanuts, and I don't mean the kind Jimmy Carter made. I told Billy I was interested but that I didn't want to talk about it again until after the Sugar Bowl game. I didn't think it was fair to my coaches, the squad or to Penn State."

Paterno then got involved in preparing his team for the Sugar Bowl and he tried to put the whole thing out of his mind until after New Year's Eve. But that didn't stop the rumor mill from working overtime. Newspaper stories speculated on what Joe would do and so did Penn State fans. There was even talk about who would succeed Paterno. Would it be a member of his staff? Would it be George Welsh, his offensive coach who later became the head man at Navy? Meanwhile, the athletic hierarchy at the university kept a low profile and refused to comment. For a few days before the game with Oklahoma the rumors quieted down, and then Billy Sullivan got them stirring again. He showed up in New Orleans and the tongues began wagging.

"Billy is a nice guy and I like him," Joe says, "but he is a real salesman and, when he came to New Orleans, that really made it tough for me and my staff. Up until then, I think the staff really didn't believe I was going to leave Penn State. When they saw Sullivan on the scene, they began to wonder.

"I wanted some time to go back home after the game and think about the whole thing alone. Well, when I got there, after we had lost to Oklahoma, the pressure *really* began to mount. People were sending me cards saying, 'Don't go, Joe,' and I got letters and phone calls from people advising me to stay at Penn State. Frankly, I didn't know what the hell to do.

"Well, one night I sat down with Jim Tarman and we talked for hours about what and where my future was, what I wanted to do with my life. Jim left and then Sue and I talked. We talked about the challenge of pro football, that I was going to run the whole show, that I would be the boss, that I could do things my way. That's what I always wanted, to be the boss. But, now that I think back, I was really kidding myself. It was the money. I was flattered to be able to say that I would be making that kind of money. Finally I said, 'Sue, I'm going to take the job.'

"Sue looked at me and said, 'Joe, whatever you want to do is fine with me. If you want to go, okay, we'll go.' I kind of had the feeling that she didn't want to go, but she never said anything.

"I called Billy Sullivan that night and told him I would take the job, to get his lawyers, I would get mine and we would meet at the Plaza in New York the next morning at nine o'clock to go over the details."

To all intents and purposes, the issue was settled. Joe Paterno was going to become the general manager, coach and majordomo of the Boston Patriots. It was to be the end of an era at Penn State that began a long time ago with Rip Engle and was now ending with Joe Paterno, who had become the winningest college football coach in the country.

"I went to bed and couldn't sleep," Joe remembers. "I thought to myself, 'What the hell am I doing? This isn't right. I don't want this job and I'm only going after it for the money.'"

Paterno got out of bed at 5:30 A.M. and called Sullivan in Boston. He wanted to get him before he left for New York with his satchelful of money, stock options and all the other goodies that went with the job. "I told Billy that I had changed my mind, that I appreciated his interest in me and I was sorry to cause him so much inconvenience. But I didn't think he would want me under these conditions."

Sue woke up as Joe was talking to Sullivan and, when he finished, she asked, "What the devil are you doing?"

"Well," Joe replied, "I just called Sullivan to tell him that I was staying at Penn State."

With that, Sue started to cry. "I knew it was because she was pleased," said Joe.

"I'm sure I made the right decision," Paterno says now. "All I know is that I've done a great job of helping some people get rich and successful. When I turned down the Pittsburgh job, they took Chuck Noll, who got the Steelers to the Super Bowl, and when I turned down the Patriots, they took Chuck Fairbanks, who is doing a super job. So, I guess I haven't hurt anybody."

Paterno even found some humor in his decision. When Joe spoke at banquets, he would parade along the dais, asking, "Can everybody get a good look at me? Yeah? Good. You are now looking at the jerk who turned down a million dollars." He usually received a standing ovation.

There have been other pro offers, too. Leonard Tose of the Philadelphia Eagles talked to Paterno a few years ago and Al Ward, when he was general manager of the New York Jets, went down to State College to chat with Joe before Lou Holtz's ill-fated one-year tenure as coach. Nothing came of either overture and Paterno has tried to discourage other clubs from approaching him.

That doesn't necessarily mean, however, that pro football is out of Paterno's future altogether. Joe, with his usual perceptiveness, leaves himself some elbow room.

"It's possible, I guess, and the money would be a big factor," Joe admits. "A few years from now, I might take a look at myself and say, 'What have I got for my family?' I have five kids and I worry about what is available for Sue and them. When I'm sixty, my youngest child will be fourteen. Circumstances and situations change and none of us can look into the future. So, I wouldn't say never about pro football. But there are only a couple of jobs I think I would be interested in. Maybe some place like the New York Giants, especially after seeing that new Giants Stadium in the New Jersey Meadowlands. And being a New Yorker myself, that is if they still include Brooklyn as part of New York, might make a difference. However, right now, I don't think so. But, when I look ahead to 1981, I'm not so sure that I want to be the coach at Penn State. That's when we have to play Southern Methodist, Nebraska, Missouri, Syracuse, Miami, North Carolina State, Alabama, Notre Dame, Pitt, West Virginia and Boston College!"

Of course, being a big-time college football coach isn't all going to post-season bowls and being courted by the pros with million-dollar offers. The outside demands made on a coach's time are tremendous. Alumni groups all over the country want him to speak at their meetings, charitable organizations want him to head up fund-raising drives, television sportscasters are after him to appear on their shows, sportswriters want interviews and hundreds of fans write letters and expect answers. Actually, a big-time winning coach is as much a celebrity as a Hollywood movie star and he lives in the same kind of goldfish bowl.

Joe Paterno achieved that status soon after he became a head coach and he has paid the price for his success. Aside from coaching his football team from mid-August until January 1 and for six weeks of spring practice, he must spend time recruiting to ensure the constant flow of players who make him a winning coach. This is his job. The rest of his time is spent running for planes to make speeches, hopping in his car to drive to a high school banquet or making television appearances. The hours he spends at home are rare and to be treasured.

"The more you win, the more you have to fight to keep your identity as a working football coach and to be able to just coach football," Joe points out. "And because you win, and because of television, people know who you are. They recognize you. When you go out, you have to be careful about where you go, what you wear and how you look. You're really on stage all the time. You can't sit down and read a newspaper in a hotel lobby, or have a quiet dinner by yourself or with your wife. There are always people who want to chat or to join them for dinner or a drink. I don't mean that I want to be a recluse. I realize that there are certain obligations you have to the public and certain things you have to do. But it would be nice to be able to be alone once in a while. I guess I shouldn't complain, though. Losing coaches have plenty of time to themselves."

More than anything else, perhaps, the 1976 season created changes in Paterno's thinking and the way he did things. That was the year his Nittany Lions got off to one of their worst starts, losing three of their first four games, and finished the regular season with a 7-4 record, pretty fair by most standards but a "bad season" for a Paterno-coached team. The only thing that saved

Penn State was a turnabout after the fourth game when the Lions trounced Army, 38-16, and then went on to win their next five games before losing to Pitt in the finale.

In a way, that mediocre season became a blessing in disguise. It taught Paterno many things and caused him to change both his coaching and administrative style.

"Any time you lose, you learn a lot," Joe explains. "One thing I learned was that you have just so much stamina. I couldn't continue to run around and do things for a lot of people. I was spending too much time off the campus and not enough time with my staff and my squad. In the earlier days, the players used to come in and talk to me, but now I wasn't around as much and I didn't get to see them as often as I liked.

"I still had to spend a great deal of time recruiting and I was off making speeches to alumni groups, appearing at high school banquets, attending testimonial dinners for some of our players and lecturing at clinics. I spent a lot of time making speeches to try to earn extra money. Industrial corporations wanted me to speak on management, organization and motivation and I was doing too much of that. I also was getting involved in too many charitable efforts. I was just spending too much time away from my coaching.

"I really believe that what happened in the 1976 season was my fault. My staff didn't understand what we wanted to do. I hadn't spent enough time with my coaches and hadn't communicated with them well enough. And I didn't have the same relationship with my players. Because of all the demands on my time, and the fact that I was trying to do too much, I probably had 40 percent less time to coach than I used to."

Paterno frankly admits, "I guess the biggest thing I have learned, not only from that season but as I have gotten older, is that I can't do as many things by myself. In my early years as a head coach, I would get up early, stay up late at night and I was on top of every single little detail. I would plot every offensive and defensive move we would use in a ball game and try to devise the game plan by myself. Finally, it reached a point where it got to be a problem for me physically. I felt that I had to have input on everything that went on every minute of the day and every day of the week.

"After that 1976 season, I came to the realization that I had to let my staff, especially my younger coaches, do more. I was hurting them. I would get into meetings and dominate them, letting them run longer than they should, and I wasn't listening enough to my assistant coaches. Without realizing it, I think I gave them the impression that I didn't have confidence in them."

There is nothing like a 7-5 year (Penn State lost to Notre Dame in the Gator Bowl) to make a coach take stock of himself. Paterno spent the next couple of months reviewing what had happened and trying to find reasons. He especially took a long, hard look at himself.

"I began to do things differently," says Joe. "I learned to delegate authority better and let my assistant coaches have more to say. Although I always had encouraged them to have more input, I hadn't always paid enough attention to them or their ideas. I don't think it was complacency, but we used to go into a season thinking, well, we've done it before and we'll do it again. We were in a rut, I guess, and we never stopped to analyze what we had done before.

"We sat back and went over everything we had done and critiqued ourselves. We hadn't done as well as a staff. We realized that we had been too indecisive, we had changed too many things without analyzing why we were changing them. Our game plans weren't solid enough soon enough. Maybe on a Wednesday, when we should have been prepared for Saturday's game, we were still screwing around changing a play or two. We weren't as well organized. I think all of us, and especially myself, had gotten a little slipshod in our coaching because nothing bad had happened to us. We had been successful and I guess we just took too much for granted.

"So, I tried to change things. I let my coaches meet by themselves and then come to me with their ideas and we would discuss them, sometimes argue, and think them through. I also cut down on the number of clinics I do. Instead, I send our assistant coaches whenever I can. This is part of giving them more responsibility."

Paterno's ability to recognize what had gone wrong and his acceptance of his responsibility for those shortcomings are indicative of the kind of man he is. He has never been one to pass the buck, or the blame, for failure. Instead, he goes out of his way to put the burden squarely on his own shoulders, even if it doesn't belong there. Joe also is quick to adjust to change and the success his team had in 1977 is proof of that.

"I enjoyed the 1977 season so much," Joe says. "It took a little doing, but I made the switch from that thirty- and forty-year-old coach who was 'go, go, go' and involved in everything to where I can handle all that is involved in my program now better than before. I'm really pleased with the way we reorganized ourselves and the way the staff handled itself. We've all matured. I think I have made my own personal adjustment and I am trying to get disengaged from some of the distractions. It hasn't been easy, but I think I am doing it."

But maturity and change haven't kept Joe from getting into brouhahas from time to time. He speaks his mind, right or wrong, and probably will continue to do so as long as he can raise his voice above a whisper. For example, there was that time in 1972 when Paterno publicly proclaimed his lack of enthusiasm about Temple coming on to the Penn State schedule in 1975.

"I'm not happy about it," Joe told an alumni group in Philadelphia. "I had nothing to do with scheduling until a year ago and the Temple game was arranged prior to that. I just don't think it is appropriate or in the best interests of Penn State to play Temple."

Back came the expected reaction from Ernie Casale, Temple's athletic director. "I'd like to keep it at an athletic director's level and both athletic directors feel the game is a good thing. I know none of my coaches have anything to do with scheduling.

"Paterno is on top now and I suppose he feels he wants to play the top team in the country. Maybe he doesn't have as much to gain by playing us."

Three years later, Paterno's lack of enthusiasm for playing Temple was proved right—but not for the same reason. Penn State barely beat the aroused Owls, 26-25, after coming from behind in the final minutes. In 1976, Temple again gave the Nittany Lions all they could handle before bowing, 31-30, when the Owls failed to complete a 2-point pass conversion try after time expired.

By that time, Paterno had stopped talking about whether or

not it was "appropriate" for Temple to be on the Penn State schedule.

Then there were a couple of incidents in 1977. Paterno had agreed to come to New York with a group of All-America players from several colleges to take part in a pre-season college football promotional tour sponsored by ABC and the NCAA. When Joe learned that ABC planned to televise the Ohio State-Oklahoma game into New York instead of the Penn State-Maryland regional TV contest on the same day, he made known his displeasure and told ABC he had changed his mind about taking part in the meeting.

A few months later, disappointed over not being invited to the Orange Bowl, Paterno publicly put part of the blame on Herschel Nissenson of the Associated Press because "a lot of people like you are enamored of other parts of the country."

Paterno also continues to put the rap on the AP and UPI polls and has refused UPI's invitation to be one of its voters. "I would vote at the end of the year, but I don't believe in weekly polls," Joe says. "It generates a 'roll-up-the-score-to-improve-our-ranking' mentality. Philosophically, I just can't live with that. We talk about sportsmanship and all the other values that we hope we're teaching while coaching football. How can you relate that to the attitude which the polls foster?"

One thing is sure. When Joe Paterno disagrees with someone or something, he doesn't mutter to himself. He is heard from.

Although Penn State football was a huge success in 1977, the year was marred by a personal tragedy in the life of the Paterno family. In mid-October, the day before the Syracuse game, eleven-year-old David Paterno was critically injured in an accident at Our Lady of Victory School in State College. It seemed that David and a group of his friends had found an unused and unattended trampoline in the school auditorium and they decided to try it out. Shortly thereafter, while Joe was preparing to join his squad for the trip to Syracuse, he got a phone call. David had fallen off the trampoline and off the stage on which it stood and landed on his head. He was unconscious.

Paterno rushed to the school and then rode in the ambulance.

with David to the hospital where x-rays were taken, and the doctors there recognized that the boy was suffering from more than just a concussion. David was still unconscious and it was decided that he should be taken to the Geisinger Medical Center in Danville, Pennsylvania, about fifty miles from State College, where further examination showed that the youngster had suffered a six-inch crack in his skull above his right ear.

Meanwhile, Sue Paterno and several other coaches' wives had left for Syracuse earlier in the day in an automobile van. They had nearly reached the New York State line when Pennsylvania state troopers intercepted them and told Sue what had happened. She was taken back to Danville to join Joe while the doctors tried everything possible to treat David's fractured skull. They gave him medication, they swathed his head in ice, they did a tracheotomy, they put him on a respirator. Nothing seemed to work. The only thing that could save David's life was a miracle.

Joe and Sue remained at David's bedside. Football was forgotten. Just hours before the kickoff, Joe called his coaches in Syracuse to tell them the team would have to play without him. Bob Phillips, the quarterback coach, handled the offense and Assistant Jerry Sandusky coordinated the defense. All Joe could do that day was pray for the miracle that would help save David's life.

Paterno had help. Coach Frank Maloney and his Syracuse team prayed for David's recovery. The Penn State squad also prayed. "The only thing we could do," said Linebacker Ron Hostetler, "was to pray for David and win it for Joe." Defensive Tackle Matt Millen said it was "like going into battle without your general." Penn State won the game, 31-24, but it was a hollow victory and there was no celebrating afterwards. Just sadness—and prayer for David Paterno.

While Sue and Joe kept the vigil at Geisinger, David remained unconscious over the weekend and all through Monday, surviving only on the life-support system. Finally, on Thursday the youngster began to come out of the coma. By the end of the day, the doctors told the Paternos that David would live but it was still too early to determine whether or not there had been brain damage or paralysis. The next day, he had improved and the news was better. David's reactions were good, he would need time to recuperate but he would recover fully. Two months later, he had recovered sufficiently to make the trip to the Fiesta Bowl in Phoenix and he soon was back to the normal life that any eleven-year-old enjoys.

The near-tragedy had a great effect on Joe Paterno's life. It changed his values and priorities. Things which had once been so important became less important. He and Sue were just grateful that their oldest son had survived.

"When I sat in that hospital that Friday night, and I knew David was dying, the last eleven years flashed through my mind," admits Joe. "All the unbeaten seasons, the bowl games, the high rankings, none of it meant a damn. The only thing I could think of was that of all my five children I had spent the least time with David. He had been born just about the same time I became a head coach and, somehow, I never had much time for him. I was so deeply involved in football, so busy trying to make Penn State the best, that I didn't have enough time to spend with my family. And I didn't really know David. Here was my oldest son, and it looked like he wasn't going to make it through the night, and I didn't even know him.

"That first night was a horrible one. I never even thought about the Syracuse game the next day. It didn't matter whether or not I was there, or whether or not we won. The only thing that mattered was David. And, thank God, when things took a turn for the better a few days later, Sue and I were just so grateful. We couldn't get over the way people all over the country had reacted. David and we got over two thousand letters, people sent money, quarters and dollars, mass cards and notes telling us they were praying for him. People like Bert Jones of the Baltimore Colts wrote him letters. I learned later that Frank Maloney, the Syracuse coach, had his entire team say a prayer for David. What a great thing that was! All of a sudden, football wasn't so important any more. I realized that there was a lot more to life than winning football games and going to bowls."

It was a traumatic experience for the Paternos and their family and friends but, fortunately, the ending was a happy one. However, it also gave Joe reason to reassess his life's work and to reevaluate what was important to him.

Many of the ideas—or modifications of them—that Paterno had proposed back in the early 1970's have been adopted by the NCAA, like limits on recruiting visits by both players and coaches, a limit on scholarships, more emphasis on student-athletes graduating, more enforcement and a greater crackdown on recruiting violators, cutting down on excessive entertainment, but Joe believes that there is still room for improvement in many areas and he doesn't hesitate to speak out about them.

For instance, Joe feels there should be more rigid academic standards for high school graduates to qualify for grants-in-aid. "I think a 2.0 average in high school is a joke!" he says. "Because a kid can get a B in typing, C in history and D in English and it all averages out to a 2. There also is pressure in high schools to see that athletes qualify academically for a grant-in-aid. Why, we have had high schools refuse to tell us what a boy's average is. They'll ask, 'What does he need?' That is reprehensible for anyone associated with education and we refuse to talk with them or consider the boy."

Paterno also believes that there ought to be a firmer rule for normal progress toward a degree. Now every school can have its own program. "What we have at Penn State is ideal," Joe points out. "Every student-athlete must be within ten credits of his class or he is ineligible. He may come to the end of his four years and lack ten credits for his degree. He then has to go one additional semester to get it."

Another thing that rankles Paterno is the rule which made freshmen eligible for varsity competition, "I thought we took a big step backward when that happened. Now you have kids playing a varsity football game before they have even attended a class at their schools! It has happened at Penn State, even though I don't like it, because we have to do it to stay competitive with other schools. Then we took a double step backward when the NCAA made it legal to red-shirt freshmen. That, to me, is a horrible thing. When it was made retroactive, it became worse. It opens a real Pandora's box. Goodness knows what will happen now. Some schools are going back through their records to see if there is any way they can get another year of football out of some of their players."

One big bone of contention in college football has been the

numbers game involving scholarships. Not so much with the thirty a year which each school is limited to, but with the total of ninety-five which any school can have at one time. The problem is that four times thirty simply does not equal ninety-five and schools are faced with finding ways to cut their squads while still recruiting thirty players a year.

"I'm happy with the thirty a year," claims Paterno, "but not with the overall total of ninety-five. I could buy twenty-seven and ninety-five, I guess, but a lot of people believe they can't have quality football if they don't recruit at least thirty players each year. We usually take less than that at Penn State, but you have to give those other schools the benefit of the doubt. Maybe the answer is to increase the ninety-five to somewhere between 100 and 105. Or make freshmen ineligible and stay with the present thirty and ninety-five. I'm all for that!"

While Paterno thinks the NCAA has beefed up its enforcement program, even though some folks think that it may not always be handled properly, he and a lot of other coaches around the country deplore the fact that it sometimes takes several years for violators of recruiting regulations to be punished.

"What we want is action now," declares Joe. "The way it is now, a guy can beat your brains out three or four times before he gets socked with probation."

Alabama's Bear Bryant agrees. "You can buy a team, coach it, win a championship and be dead before they [the NCAA] get the results of an investigation," asserts Bryant.

One suggestion that Paterno and others recommend is that coaches police themselves, either through a proposed new Division I-A (which was adopted by the NCAA membership in 1978 but wound up with almost as many schools as the old Division I instead of the seventy-five to eighty universities envisioned by the big-time football powers) or by the American Football Coaches Association.

"We know who is cheating," claims Joe. "I know when we lose a kid because of money or other illegal inducements. Let's call in those coaches, confront them and then eliminate them from coaching. But we would need the backing of all university presidents. We'd have to be sure that if a coach got fired at Penn State for cheating, he wouldn't be hired at Georgia Tech or Notre

Dame. We would have to have this kind of muscle to enforce
what we are trying to accomplish—to drive the cheaters out of
college football. And we could do it quickly, more quickly than
the NCAA does it now."

Indiana's Lee Corso, another outspoken coach, is even more
vehement on the subject. "I'd like to see public censure," Lee says.
"I'd like them run out of the profession. I see coaches cited for
breaking the rules, then winning and given new contracts. We've
got to make it evident that these men aren't to be glorified.

"I can tell you which schools are going to be investigated five
years from now. They're the same ones who were under investigation five years ago, ten years ago and fifteen years ago. I think basically the problem is among the alumni. I don't have any alumni
recruiting for me, and I don't have any trouble sleeping at night."

Paterno and Corso, sometimes called the poor man's Joe Paterno because Indiana doesn't win as often as Penn State, are just
as determined as they are outspoken in their efforts to eliminate
the cheaters from college football. But they can't do it alone. They
need the cooperation of the majority of their colleagues, including
the cheaters.

Long a proponent of a national championship playoff, Paterno
has proposed a new plan for such a playoff, one which conceiv-
ably could win support from the major post-season bowls which
have opposed it. However, there may be an element or two in
Joe's plan which Walter Byers, the NCAA's executive director,
may not be all that crazy about.

Paterno proposes that a playoff for the national championship
take place *after* the bowl games. "Play the bowls," Joe concedes,
"then have a blue ribbon panel made up of sportswriters, sportscasters, coaches and maybe a couple of college presidents and
Walter Byers, or someone else for NCAA, as ex-officio members.
They would pick the top four schools after the bowls and then
pair them off in a playoff to decide the national championship.
Take the 1977 season. Five of us wound up with 11-1 records—
Notre Dame, Texas, Arkansas, Penn State and Alabama. Sure, one
of them would have been left out but that would be up to the
committee to decide and we'd have to live with it.

"There would be more money from television, I'm sure, with a
separate contract. Alternate the semi-finals and final among the

bowls or pick a warm weather site or an indoor stadium. Just pay the schools their expenses. Tie it in with the pros and their play-offs, maybe play the championship game the week before the Super Bowl. The games probably would net four or five million dollars, but the money wouldn't be touched for ten years. Invest it in gilt-edge bonds or securities or just put it in the bank at the highest rate of interest. In ten years, you would have fifty million dollars and form a special committee, not the NCAA, made up of college presidents and maybe coaches to administer the fund. They would lend the money to colleges that need it badly at a low rate of interest, perhaps three percent. Maybe these schools want to expand their stadiums or their intercollegiate athletic programs, or use it to help finance their women's athletic programs.

"We would be accomplishing two things. We would have a true national champion and also a lot of money to help the poorer schools, the ones which don't get bowl bids or lucrative TV shots. I know it sounds radical, and I haven't heard much support for it, but I think it makes sense."

Making sense, that is one of the things Joe Paterno does best.

22: Whither Joe Paterno?

JOE PATERNO'S FIRST FIVE YEARS as the head coach at Penn State have been filled with glory and accomplishments and a minimum of disappointment. The football program, which gained its initial impetus during Rip Engle's successful reign, has matured and prospered under Joe's masterful guidance and with the full cooperation of the Penn State athletic family.

Paterno's influence and leadership have been unmistakable, not only in football, but also in setting the entire athletic tone of the university. His vibrant and progressive ideas, aimed at making Penn State the mecca of Eastern athletics and a name to be reckoned with nationally, are visible in many ways. In addition to upgrading the football program, Paterno has stimulated and inspired the other coaches at Penn State to go at their jobs with a fresh approach.

As Johnny Bach, the former basketball coach, put it, "Joe Paterno's success has rubbed off on every other sport. At some schools the football coach selfishly looks out for football and isn't interested in the other sports. Joe is not only the football coach at Penn

State but he is the leader of our entire athletic program. He is a steadying influence on all the other coaches. It's stimulating to work with him, and you can't be around a man like Joe Paterno without having his class rub off on you."

Joe Paterno's position in the athletic hierarchy at Penn State is unique. At most schools the football coach—unless he is also the athletic director—is heard from only when he wants something to help his program or when his little domain is threatened. His is merely a voice in the crowd and the coaches of other sports usually view him with suspicion. But Paterno, because of his dynamic personality and ability to think clearly and imaginatively, plays a leading role in determining policy at Penn State. His views are sought after and, when he speaks out, he finds attentive ears. It is a tribute to his intellect and qualities of leadership.

Some anonymous sage once said, "Success breeds success," and that is an accurate description of what has happened at Penn State in recent years. But it has not been accidental. It has been the result of cooperation among Joe Paterno, Bob Scannell, the present Dean of Health, Physical Education and Recreation, and Athletic Director Ed Czekaj and, before them, Ernie McCoy, who held both positions. Equally important, Paterno's views were accepted by Dr. Eric A. Walker, until he retired as president of the university in 1970. They also have been acceptable to Dr. Walker's successor, Dr. John W. Oswald. Dr. Oswald comes to his interest in athletics naturally. He captained the football team in his undergraduate days at DePauw University and survived five years of Adolph Rapp, the venerable and contentious basketball coach, when he served as president of the University of Kentucky.

The signals at Penn State are all "go." At Paterno's suggestion, Jim Tarman, for many years regarded as one of the top sports information directors in the business, was moved up to a new post as Associate Athletic Director to bolster that area. John Morris, a Penn State graduate, was named Sports Information Director. Efforts are being made to further Penn State's national image in football and other sports. Plans were quickly put on the drawing board to enlarge the seating capacity of Beaver Stadium.

However, despite the progressive thinking, Penn State is not rushing headlong into uncharted waters. What concerns the athletic administrators—and Joe Paterno—is the financial climate of college football. Like everywhere else, Penn State's overall athletic budget has soared in recent years and the administration is seeking ways to cut the fat from its expenditures, but not at the expense of watering down the football program. They reason, correctly, that it is football that makes the money to support the other sports at the university and good business practices dictate that you don't cut back on a successful enterprise.

The direct result of Joe Paterno's influence, of course, has been the success of the football program. More and more quality athletes, who are also quality students, have been attracted to Penn State. Yet, unlike some of its counterparts in big-time college football, Penn State is not regarded as a "football factory," either by the large, fast and talented young men who migrate there through the persuasion of Joe Paterno and his hard-working staff of assistants or by the university's neighbors in the academic world. It is conclusive proof that winning football can be achieved without compromising moral or academic standards.

"What Joe wants for Penn State football is what we want for the university," says Bob Scannell, "and both are compatible."

Paterno's goals for Penn State football are high and he doesn't think they have yet been achieved. He wants his teams to be the best in the nation and he works tirelessly toward that end. Along with that, Joe wants the Nittany Lions to play the best teams in the country. Notre Dame, Ohio State, Missouri, Southern Methodist, Texas Christian, Texas A & M, Stanford, Nebraska, Tennessee and others will be turning up as annual opponents in the future at the expense of the Ohio U.'s and Kent State's which have been on recent schedules. Paterno is trying to expand that list to include other big-time powers, even though it may hurt the Lions' national ambitions.

What rankles Joe Paterno is that many people were inclined to downgrade Penn State's performance in 1968 and 1969, when his teams were unbeaten but still ranked No. 2 behind Ohio State and Texas, which had similar records. By implication, the pollsters—and President Nixon in 1969—indicated that the Nittany Lions' schedule was less demanding than the ones faced by Ohio State and Texas. Yet Penn State's eleven rivals in '69, the year the Nittany Lions were No. 2 to Texas, had an aggregate record of

58-52-2, while the eleven teams beaten by the Longhorns were a poor 47-64-2. Who, Joe wonders, had the weaker schedule?

"We were snubbed by everyone," Paterno still complains, "from the President of the United States down to the Hall of Fame because we were from the wrong side of the tracks—the East."

Joe Paterno's aim is to move Penn State to the right side of the tracks with the rich kids in college football by continuing to upgrade the program and strengthen the schedule while, at the same time, keeping football in its proper perspective as part of the educational process of the university. He is not satisfied with mediocrity on either the coaching level or in results and he has no patience with those who want to move slowly. Happily, Paterno's associates in the Athletic Department agree with him.

"Some day," Joe predicts, "Penn State is going to have a national championship team. I feel very strongly that we are going to be the best in the nation and, not just occasionally, but frequently. I don't want people to cheer us when we almost 'upset' a team. I want them to expect us to win every game and to be disappointed when we lose."

With such a commitment to excellence, and people who have the foresight and talent to make it happen, the future appears to be bright for Penn State football. But regardless of what the future holds in store for Penn State—and Joe Paterno—this brilliant coach has left his indelible mark on the entire athletic program.

But, whither Joe Paterno?

An interesting question. In fact, Joe Paterno's future poses several interesting questions. Will he remain at Penn State indefinitely? Will he move on to another college, and possibly greener pastures, when the right opportunity presents itself? Or does his coaching future lie in professional football?

The folks at Penn State, naturally, would prefer not even to discuss the possibility of ever losing Joe Paterno. They would prefer to keep him forever and reap the benefits of his thinking and coaching. But they are aware of the many overtures which have already been made to Joe by other colleges, and Bob Scannell is realistic enough to admit that a man of Joe Paterno's many talents is destined for great things.

Joe has already made his mark in college football. While he was still an assistant under Rip Engle, he was recognized as one of the bright young innovators in the game. His phenomenal success in his first five years as a head coach quickly and firmly established him as a leader in his chosen profession. Some people are constantly shocked by his iconoclastic views on college football, but everyone is impressed with his superb coaching ability.

It isn't likely, however, that Joe Paterno will ever leave Penn State to coach football at another college. He has already turned down several more lucrative college coaching positions and undoubtedly will reject even more of them as his Nittany Lions continue to win and achieve the prominence they deserve.

Joe and his family are happy at Penn State. He enjoys the challenge of boosting the Nittany Lions to the top of the national college football heap and he likes the latitude he has in helping to fashion and shape the university's athletic policies. His salary, while not commensurate with the big figures hauled down by many of his contemporaries in college football, manages to sustain his modest way of life. Joe's position as a full professor gives him status in the academic community and he is highly respected on campus by students and faculty alike. He and his wife, Sue, treasure the many friendships they have made at State College. All in all, it is a comfortable existence, the kind most men would be content with for the rest of their working lives.

But Joe Paterno is not most men. He is an unusual man. Joe operates on the theory that life is a gamble and that any man worth his salt has to take chances. He believes in destiny, that people who are destined for great things usually achieve them. Ambitious, restless and extremely perceptive about life, Joe is always looking for new challenges to stimulate him intellectually.

Where will Joe Paterno find these new challenges? The most likely place is in professional football, which has already evinced more than passing interest in him as a head coach. A few years ago the Pittsburgh Steelers were interested enough to offer him the kind of a coaching contract that would have given him more money than he can ever earn in college football, plus financial security for his family and many attractive fringe benefits. Joe was tempted to take it, not so much for the money involved, but for the challenge it presented to him as a coach. He turned it down, though, because he was not quite ready to make the move. Since then, other pro teams have sounded him out and he has listened. In 1972, he turned down the Boston Patriots and what would have been financial security for life for him and his family. He still was not ready.

Pro football has changed in the last decade from a stereotyped game to one which has borrowed liberally from the most innovative minds in college football and this intrigues Joe Paterno. He also recognizes the great impact the game has had on the populace in this country through its exposure on television. More important, Joe is impressed with the challenge which pro football would present to him, mentally and intellectually.

Joe Paterno fits the pro football image. As a coach, he has the mental toughness and exactness of a Vince Lombardi, the imagination of a Hank Stram and the dedication of a Sid Gillman. He would also add another dimension which most pro football coaches sadly lack—charisma.

It is no secret to his associates and friends at Penn State that Paterno has thought about the possibility of pro football being somewhere in his coaching future. When the Patriots' offer came up after the 1972 season, there were a lot of nervous folks in University Park and State College. They didn't relish the idea of losing Paterno but they also appreciated the opportunity it offered him. When Joe finally turned down Boston's Billy Sullivan, the collective sigh of relief could be heard all over the campus and throughout the state of Pennsylvania.

But, if and when Joe Paterno decides to turn to professional football, it will have to be on his terms, and he has definite ideas on what they should be. He believes very strongly that he would have to have full control of his team. He doesn't particularly care whether or not he also will be the general manager, although that would be preferable, but he wants to have the final word on trades and the choices in the annual college draft. He would also want to have the privilege of surrounding himself with his own people so that he could do things his way. Take it or leave it, that is Joe Paterno's style.

"I don't think any coach can do the job expected of him if he can't have control," says Joe.

There is still another possibility in Joe Paterno's future. Politics. He already has been approached on several levels but has resisted. However, the ingredients are all there and his friends would not be at all surprised if one day Joe tossed his hat into a Pennsylvania political ring. It would make opposing football coaches happy, too.

Joe admits that the thought has entered his mind. "My wife, Sue, and I have talked about it a lot lately," he says, "but right now I don't think so."

There is another factor which could persuade Joe Paterno to turn his talents to the political arena. He has so little time with his family that Sue sometimes refers to him as "Joe who?" when he shows up at home after one of his frequent long recruiting trips.

"I think I would leave coaching when I no longer wanted to push myself sixteen or seventeen hours a day," Joe says. "If there's one disadvantage to coaching, it's not having any time to myself. I'd like to spend more time with my family."

Paterno has all the qualifications for politics. A deft conversationalist, he is equally at home in mixed company in someone's living room or on a clinic platform lecturing to coaches. Joe has an acute awareness of what is going on about him in the world and he takes a positive attitude toward the problems and ills of our society. Honest and sincere, he isn't afraid to speak out on subjects of substance, even if his views are unpopular. Of course, that much frankness might not get him elected, but the voters would know where he stands, which isn't always the case with politicians these days.

"The trouble in this country now," says Paterno, with his typical candidness, "is too many politicians making too many promises, especially to the people in the ghettos. Any candidate who can't back up his promises should get out!"

Mickey Bergstein, the general manager of radio station WMAJ in State College, who has been broadcasting Penn State sports for more than two decades and is an old Paternophile, thinks Joe would be a natural for politics. Mickey has shared many a speaker's platform with Paterno and never ceases to marvel at the way he captures an audience.

"I can see Joe sitting in the Governor's chair in Harrisburg," says Mickey with a chuckle, "telling everybody that Pennsylvania is No. 1, no matter what the President says."

What does Sue Paterno think about her husband's future?

"Joe would succeed at whatever he did," Sue says flatly. "And whatever he wants to do is all right with me."

Who knows, maybe one day Sue's confidence in her husband will be rewarded. She could be the first former football coach's wife to make it to First Lady of the sovereign State of Pennsylvania.

Joe Paterno's Coaching Record at Penn State

1966

PENN STATE		OPP.
15	Maryland	7
8	Michigan State	42
0	Army	11
30	Boston College	21
11	UCLA	49
38	West Virginia	6
33	California	15
10	Syracuse	12
0	Georgia Tech	2
48	Pittsburgh	24

Won 5, Lost 5

1968*

PENN STATE		OPP.
31	Navy	6
25	Kansas State	9
31	West Virginia	20
21	UCLA	6
29	Boston College	0
28	Army	24
22	Miami (Fla.)	7
57	Maryland	13
65	Pittsburgh	9
30	Syracuse	12
	Orange Bowl	
15	Kansas	14

Won 11, Lost 0

*Paterno named Coach of the Year by American Football Coaches Association, Eastern Coach of the Year by New York Football Writers Association.

1967

PENN STATE		OPP.
22	Navy	23
17	Miami (Fla.)	8
15	UCLA	17
50	Boston College	28
21	West Virginia	14
29	Syracuse	20
38	Maryland	3
13	N. Carolina State	8
35	Ohio U.	14
42	Pittsburgh	6
	Gator Bowl	
17	Florida State	17

Won 8, Lost 2, Tied 1

1969†

PENN STATE		OPP.
45	Navy	22
27	Colorado	3
17	Kansas State	14
20	West Virginia	0
15	Syracuse	14
42	Ohio U.	3
38	Boston College	16
48	Maryland	0
27	Pittsburgh	7
33	N. Carolina State	8
	Orange Bowl	
10	Missouri	3

Won 11, Lost 0

†Paterno named Eastern Coach of the Year by New York Football Writers Association

1970

PENN STATE		OPP.
55	Navy	7
13	Colorado	41
16	Wisconsin	29
28	Boston College	3
7	Syracuse	24
38	Army	14
42	West Virginia	8
34	Maryland	0
32	Ohio U.	22
35	Pittsburgh	15

Won 7, Lost 3

1971

PENN STATE		OPP.
56	Navy	3
44	Iowa	14
16	Air Force	14
42	Army	0
31	Syracuse	0
66	Texas Christian	14
35	West Virginia	7
63	Maryland	27
35	N. Carolina State	3
55	Pittsburgh	18
11	Tennessee	31
	Cotton Bowl	
30	Texas	6

Won 11, Lost 1

1972

PENN STATE		OPP.
21	Tennessee	28
21	Navy	10
14	Iowa	10
35	Illinois	17
45	Army	0
17	Syracuse	0
28	West Virginia	19
46	Maryland	16
37	N. Carolina State	22
45	Boston College	26
49	Pittsburgh	27
	Sugar Bowl	
0	Oklahoma	14

Won 10, Lost 2

1973

PENN STATE		OPP.
20	Stanford	6
39	Navy	0
27	Iowa	8
19	Air Force	9
54	Army	3
49	Syracuse	6
62	West Virginia	14
42	Maryland	22
35	N. Carolina State	29
49	Ohio U.	10
35	Pittsburgh	13
	Orange Bowl	
16	Louisiana State U.	9

Won 12, Lost 0

1974

PENN STATE		OPP.
24	Stanford	20
6	Navy	7
27	Iowa	0
21	Army	14
55	Wake Forest	0
30	Syracuse	14
21	West Virginia	12
24	Maryland	17
7	N. Carolina State	12
35	Ohio U.	16
31	Pittsburgh	10
	Cotton Bowl	
41	Baylor	20
	Won 10, Lost 2	

1975

PENN STATE		OPP.
26	Temple	25
34	Stanford	14
9	Ohio State	17
30	Iowa	10
10	Kentucky	3
39	West Virginia	0
19	Syracuse	7
31	Army	0
15	Maryland	13
14	N. Carolina State	15
7	Pittsburgh	6
	Sugar Bowl	
6	Alabama	13
	Won 9, Lost 3	

1976

PENN STATE		OPP.
15	Stanford	12
7	Ohio State	12
6	Iowa	7
6	Kentucky	22
38	Army	16
27	Syracuse	3
33	West Virginia	0
31	Temple	30
41	N. Carolina State	20
21	Miami	7
7	Pittsburgh	24
	Gator Bowl	
9	Notre Dame	20
	Won 7, Lost 5	

1977

PENN STATE		OPP.
45	Rutgers	7
31	Houston	14
27	Maryland	9
20	Kentucky	24
16	Utah State	7
31	Syracuse	24
49	West Virginia	28
49	Miami (Fla.)	7
21	N. Carolina State	17
44	Temple	7
15	Pittsburgh	13
	Fiesta Bowl	
42	Arizona State	30
	Won 11, Lost 1	

RECAPITULATION
Won 112, Lost 24, Tied 1
Percentage—.824

The Nation's Winningest Coaches*

COACH AND SCHOOL	YRS.	WON	LOST	TIED	PCT.
1. JOE PATERNO, PENN STATE	12	112	24	1	.821
2. BO SCHEMBECHLER, MICHIGAN	15	126	30	6	.796
3. PAUL (BEAR) BRYANT, ALABAMA	33	273	76	16	.770
4. FRANK KUSH, ARIZONA STATE	20	164	49	1	.769
5. WOODY HAYES, OHIO STATE	32	231	68	9	.765
6. DAN DEVINE, NOTRE DAME	19	147	48	8	.744
7. CARMEN COZZA, YALE	13	84	32	1	.722
8. CHARLES McLENDON, LOUISIANA STATE U.	16	120	52	7	.690
9. BOBBY BOWDEN, FLORIDA STATE	12	88	40	0	.688
10. VINCE DOOLEY, GEORGIA	14	103	49	5	.672

*According to official records of coaches with at least ten years as a major college head coach at a four-year college, as released by the National Collegiate Sports Service after the 1977 season.

Penn State's Top 10 Rankings Under Joe Paterno

1967—10, Associated Press
1968— 2, United Press
International
3, Associated Press
1969— 2, United Press
International
2, Associated Press
1971— 5, Associated Press
1972—10, Associated Press
8, United Press
International

1973—5, United Press
International
5, Associated Press
1974—7, United Press
International
7, Associated Press
1975—8, United Press
International
8, Associated Press
1977—4, United Press
International
5, Associated Press

Index

Index